Branded

Branded

Branding in Sport Business

Edited by

Jason W. Lee

CAROLINA ACADEMIC PRESS

Durham, North Carolina

Library of Congress Cataloging-in-Publication Data

Branded : branding in sport business / [edited by] Jason W. Lee.
    p. cm.
Includes bibliographical references and index.
ISBN 978-1-59460-506-2 (alk. paper)
1. Sports--United States--Marketing. 2. Sports--Economic aspects--United
States. 3. Branding (Marketing)--United States. 4. Advertising--Social as-
pects--United States. I. Lee, Jason W. II. Title.

GV716.B75 2010
796.0068'8--dc22

                                            2009040507

CAROLINA ACADEMIC PRESS
700 Kent Street
Durham, North Carolina 27701
Telephone (919) 489-7486
Fax (919) 493-5668
www.cap-press.com

Printed in the United States of America

Contents

Part IV • Media, Memorabilia, People, and Places

Part V • Controversies and Failure

Preface: Product Branding in Sport Business

Jason W. Lee,
University of North Florida

The concept behind this book is to provide a primary resource examining brands that have impacted sport business and used sport business to cultivate brand equity. The book includes 34 chapters written by a variety of authors who provide an insightful analysis of the issues associated with branding.

Effective branding efforts can serve as tremendous assets for companies, and its implementation in sport is prevalent. Brands range from a collection of images that represent products to a variety symbols associated with products and their producers. Consumers build associations and affinities to these brands based on their collected experiences with goods, services, people, and places.

Brands are the embodiment of the accumulation all the information connected to companies, people, places, goods, and services. Brand images can include an assortment of aspects, including any range of symbols, color schemes, fonts, logos, and other such imagery. Brand affiliation is also found through the association with catchy slogans, ad campaigns, and other tangible and intangible characteristics. Consider the following examples:

- McDonald's—I'm lovin' it!
- Kellogg's Tony the Tiger
- The image of KFC's Colonel Sanders
- The red and white script text of Coca-Cola
- Names and images of products like Quaker Oats or Apple computers

The images that fill one's mind when reading these examples are brand associations. Further examples highlight the impact of effective branding, such as when a brand name is so closely associated with a product that it largely becomes a de facto name for the goods or services that are provided in that industry. Visible examples of such are Kleenex (facial tissues), Xerox (photocopying), and Q-tips (cotton swabs). These are just a small sampling of the value and potential impact of branding.

This text identifies both simplicities and complexities in pinpointing the value of branding in the sport industry. The world of sport provides fertile ground for the development and growth of branding opportunities. For example, brands such as Nike and Adidas are industry giants with global appeal. Furthermore, the Nike swoosh is one of the most recognizable symbols in the world.

This text is designed to serve as a stand-alone read or as a supplemental text in the following academic areas:

- Sport business
- Sport marketing
- Sport promotion
- Marketing
- Branding
- Sport finance
- Other peripheral areas

In addition to its academic value, this book may be of potential interest for sport industry professionals or those who read about such matters for enjoyment.

This work, whether read for academic purposes as a collegiate text, as industry reference, or for other interest, is designed to be informative and entertaining while providing a high-quality resource unveiling pertinent issues involved in branding. All of the included profiles identify and examine aspects that offer insight and relevance to branding with sport and in other areas of industry. The profiles provide details about primary issues by exploring general background information, an assortment of particular areas and issues of interest, and a strong analysis of why such subjects provide a valuable learning model. Such analysis enhances this book's value by probing the nuances of the profiled brands.

This text serves as a guide for a journey that explores aspects, opportunities, and associated characteristics of brands impacting the sport industry. It covers industry giants, up-and-coming companies, and more by providing a diverse compilation of brand profiles. The brands have been segmented into categories based on similar attributes and purposes including:

- Apparel and equipment companies;
- Sport properties, leagues, and events;

- Primarily nonsport entities who using sport to enhance brands (such as Home Depot or FedEx);
- Food and beverage providers; and
- Various brands provided in a potpourri assortment, included in Part III.

Additionally, this text will offer insight into questionable and controversial brand associations in the world of sport. A sampling of thought-provoking, real-life situations involving questionable (if not completely inappropriate) associations is profiled as well.

Each chapter is developed to include (1) a *The Line-Up* section, including an overview of the company and the cases being addressed; (2) a basic *Time-line* identifying relevant historical events and providing points of reference regarding significant points of history for the brands; (3) a *The Final Score* component at the conclusion of the profile, which critically examines industry perspectives and implications regarding the profiled brands; (4) the identification of key concepts in the *Post-Game Comments* section; and (5) the opportunity for further practical and theoretical explorations through answering the issues addressed in the *Discussion Questions* (useful for facilitating class discussions). Additionally, *Web Resources** are provided to offer further background information on the brands profiled. Furthermore, a variety of exhibits and appendicies are included to add detail to issues of great importance.

Lastly, Carolina Academic Press and I would like to thank Mossy Oak for their subvention toward the printing of the color photos.

*Note in regards to the provided Web Resources:

Please note that while Web Resources are provided throughout this work, with the ever-changing nature of the Web, site URLs may change or be removed at any time. Efforts have been made to be up-to-date, but inevitably changes may occur and it is important that readers and educators be mindful of this. Efforts should be made, when deemed relevant, to check and see if the sites are active and up-to-date. Additionally, readers and educators are also encouraged to explore any relevant areas of update that may pertain to the profiled brands (i.e., industry changes, companies merging, technological innovations) as this will allow the content to discussion to be more thorough and contemporary.

Branded

Chapter 1

Introduction to Branding

Kimberly S. Miloch,
Texas Woman's University

Sport brand management, or branding, is of great significance for the sport enterprise. The unique and ever-changing environment of sport often presents sport entities with distinct opportunities to cultivate and reinforce a specific brand identity, while also presenting unique barriers in brand cultivation. The manner in which a sport entity crafts and disseminates its message, combined with its ability to capitalize on opportunities for branding and respond to challenges, has a dramatic impact on the public's perception of the brand. In today's marketplace, brand perception plays a key role in the financial vitality and long-term success of sport companies.

Establishing a favorable brand image is essential in today's cluttered marketplace. A favorable brand image often influences consumers' purchase decisions, particularly with premium brands. Consumers purchase products that are most familiar to them and will often pay a premium for well-established brands that have achieved a high-quality image. Thus, brand management should be a central focus of any enterprise.

Effective and appropriate brand management cultivates loyalty among consumers. Brand loyalty is a key focus of marketers because it places the respective brand at an advantage over competing brands. As marketing scholars and business professionals note, loyal consumer bases are likely to spend more money on the brand's products and provide a consistent and predictable revenue stream (Berry, 1999; Gladden & Funk, 2001; Miloch, 2005; Shocker, Srivastava, & Ruekert, 1994). Brand-loyal consumers are far less likely than other consumers to purchase the products of competing brands. In fact, loyal consumer bases assist in product marketing because they are more likely to recommend the brand's products to other consumers. Marketers save both time and money when disseminating their core brand messages because loyal consumers are already educated on the specifics of the products (Bedbury, 2002;

Boone, Kochunny, & Wilkins; Gladden & Funk, 2001; Godin, 2002; Kuo, Chang, & Chen, 2004; Madrigal, 1995; Shocker, Srivastava, & Ruekert, 1994). In sport, consumer loyalty often leads to and may create more favorable relations with corporate entities in regard to sport sponsorship. These types of relations are advantageous because they allow sport entities to create additional revenue sources (Miloch, 2005).

In understanding the branding process, one must first distinguish a brand from a product. A *product* is a good or service that is purchased by a consumer, often used to satisfy a particular need (Aaker, 1991; Keller, 1998). A brand invokes meaning for a product, and is linked to the consumers' associations. "A brand is a product, then, but one that adds other dimensions to differentiate it in some way from other products designed to satisfy the same need" (Keller, 1998, p. 4). Aaker (1991) defines a *brand* as "a distinguishing name and/or symbol intended to identify the goods or services of either one seller or a group of sellers, and to differentiate those goods or services from those of competitors" (p. 7).

As the marketplace has changed and advanced, so have brand management strategies. Bedbury (2002) argues that the traditional definition and model of branding must be modified to consider today's current marketplace and suggests that a brand is more than a name or symbol. Instead, "a brand is the sum of the good, the bad, the ugly, and the off-strategy. It is defined by your best product as well as your worst product" (p. 15). Bedbury (2002) continues with this modern characterization of branding, suggesting that "branding is about taking something common and improving upon it in ways that make it more valuable and meaningful" (p. 14). As illustrated by Bedbury (2002), brand managers must implement and develop brand management strategies with the consumer as a central focus. To achieve brand loyalty, marketers must build brands that satisfy both the functional and emotional needs of today's consumer.

The Brand Building Process

Brand Awareness

Brand building begins with establishing a baseline awareness of the brand in consumers' minds. Consumers will not purchase a brand they do not know exists. Thus, brand awareness is the first step in building a strong brand image and establishing brand equity. Brand awareness is defined by Aaker (1991) as "the ability of a potential buyer to recognize or recall that a brand is a member of a certain product category" (p. 61). This is reinforced by Keller (1998), who notes that "brand awareness involves giving the product an identity by linking brand elements to a product category ... it is important to have high levels of brand awareness under a variety of conditions and circumstances" (p. 87). Brand awareness serves as the foundation for developing strong brand equity. It assists in generating associations for the brand and in creating a sense of familiarity between the consumer and that brand. Cultivating brand awareness also aids in enhancing brand recall and brand recognition and thus may influence consumers' purchase decisions (Aaker, 1991).

Brand Associations/Brand Image

Once consumers become brand-aware, they begin to form brand associations. Marketers must possess an understanding of an entity's brand and the messages and perceptions surrounding that brand. To appropriately manage a brand's identity, marketers must identify the brand's position in the marketplace and determine how consumers perceive it. Consumers' perceptions of a brand are rooted in their associations with a specific brand. Keller (1998) identified and explained three types of brand associations and provides the framework for this discussion on brand associations. These include brand attributes, benefits, and attitudes. It is important to note that both favorable and unfavorable perceptions influence brand equity (Keller, 1998).

Keller (1998) indicates that brand attributes are characterized both by product-related attributes and non-product-related attributes. Product-related attributes are the physical features of a product that make it capable of performing a specific function. In contrast, non-product-related attributes indirectly impact consumers' purchase decisions by associating elements such as price, logos, and consumers' prior experience with the product.

Brand benefits denote the psychological meaning or value that consumers attribute to a specific brand. Brand benefits are both functional and symbolic, and can also be experiential. Similar to brand attributes, functional benefits are linked to product-specific attributes, whereas symbolic benefits are linked to extrinsic non-product-related attributes. For example, a consumer may purchase a Volkswagen instead of a Chevrolet because he or she better identifies and relates to the image of what a Volkswagen driver should be, as portrayed by Volkswagen. In other words, the consumer gains a greater intrinsic reward by purchasing and driving the Volkswagen. Experiential benefits are linked to both product-related and non-product-related attributes. Experiential benefits characterize the sensory feeling that a consumer gains when using a specific product.

Brand attributes and benefits shape consumers' brand attitudes, and brand attitudes are the most influential brand association. Although abstract and difficult to measure, brand attitudes are grounded in the consumers' overall evaluation and perception of the brand. These attitudes form the basis for brand equity. As Bedbury (2002) notes, "the most successful brands consistently evoke positive feelings over time. With each new product, service, or marketing campaign, the brand is refreshed and recharged" (p. 15).

Brand Equity

Brand equity refers to the added value a product gains based on its brand name (Boone, Kochunny, & Wilkins, 1995). Brand equity "measures the added value of established brands over their generic equivalents" (Boone, Kochunny, & Wilkins, 1995, p. 33). Typically, consumers pay more for products with well-established brand names and products that have favorable brand images because the perception of the product is favorable. "A brand's equity is the premium a purchaser would pay for a branded good or service compared to the amount that would be paid for an identical unbranded version of the same item" (Boone, Kochunny, & Wilkins, 1995, p. 33). Brand equity is typically assessed by examining key factors associated with brand strength, including consumer loyalty, brand awareness, perceived quality of the specific brand, brand associations, and any other proprietary assets related to the brand (Aaker, 1991). Each of these factors must be addressed and evaluated when building and managing brand equity.

Sport entities are unique because they must create and reinforce their respective brand images, but are also often used to assist in the cultivation and management of nonsport entities' brands. Sport brand management and brand management through sport highlight the central focus of this book.

Branding in Sport

The unique and ever-changing nature of sport has always presented marketers with distinct challenges. The mass emotional appeal of sport combined with its simultaneous and heterogeneous nature can be both appealing and deterring to consumers. The sport product is most often produced at the same time it is consumed. Thus, it is considered to be simultaneous. Consumers must consume the product at the same time it is produced, or the product is lost forever. This means the product is also perishable, having no shelf life, a key element that makes the sport product unique when compared with traditional products. Because the sport product is constantly changing, it is considered to be heterogeneous. Sport fans may attend several minor league baseball games each season, and the product will perform differently each time. This nature is both advantageous and disadvantageous when marketing the sport product. The heterogeneous nature of the sport product is directly linked to the unpredictability of product performance. The sport product can also be highly unpredictable, and although this unpredictability can sometimes be an advantage in marketing the product, it is often a hindrance when the product performs inconsistently or poorly. This unpredictability combined with a decline in traditional revenue sources has forced sport entities to place a greater emphasis on attracting and retaining loyal consumers. Many sport entities have now recognized the importance of brand management and are implementing strategies to enhance their brand equity in an effort to meet marketplace challenges. This was discussed by Gladden and Milne (1999):

> by expanding the focus of strategic marketing to include efforts to increase brand awareness, brand associations, and brand loyalty, the sport manager can improve the frequency and degree to which positive marketplace consequences are realized (p. 28).

Sport entities often have a key advantage over nonsport entities in regard to brand management. The vast majority of sport entities garner significant coverage in the media. This is true even at the grassroots and amateur levels of sport, where the local and regional media may be the only source of exposure. Certainly, major sport entities garner significant coverage on the national and even international level. Regardless of the size and scope of the sport entity, media coverage usually generates exposure—positive or negative—and acts as a means to reach the masses (or at least the targeted audiences). Sport entities that capitalize on this exposure and appropriately enhance their media relations and management efforts will see a greater return on investment when compared to industry competitors and nonsport counterparts. Boone, Kochunny, and Wilkins (1998) suggest that the extensive media coverage received by sport should serve as a chief benefit when cultivating brand perceptions.

Additionally, many sport entities also have a geographic monopoly, meaning they are the only sport entity of the type in the geographic region (Boone, Kochunny, & Wilkins, 1998). This eliminates the majority of competition with similar products and limits the consumer's ability to select a similar sport product. For example, a Major League Baseball fan in Dallas would need to travel to Houston to access a Major League Baseball event other than the Texas Rangers. Similarly, a U.S. Tennis Association member may access professional tennis in a respective region, but to see tennis at the Grand Slam level, he or she would need to travel to New York City for the U.S. Open. Because competition is limited within the respective geographic region, sport entities can cultivate a brand image without the worry of responding to competitors.

Branding through Sport

As traditional advertising methods became more cluttered, nonsport entities began to explore advertising opportunities within the sport industry. Typically, this has taken the form of sponsorship; initially, it provided companies with a form of uncluttered advertising. As the popularity and effectiveness of sport sponsorship has grown, advertisers have sought opportunities for uncluttered space and activation. Sport entities have been responsive to these needs, and as a result, sport sponsorship remains an appropriate and effective strategy for nonsport entities to use in reinforcing and managing their respective brand images. Companies such as Coca-Cola, Home Depot, Budweiser, and Federal Express have all used sport to enhance their overall strategic brand efforts.

The mass appeal of sport lends itself well to nonsport entity partnerships. Additionally, niche sports and single sport events provide additional avenues for nonsport entities in reinforcing and enhancing their overall strategic branding initiatives. With well-designed partnerships and a key focus on meeting the nonsport entities' objectives, sponsorship can be lucrative for both the sport entity and the sponsoring agency. Sport sponsorship can often lead to significant revenue generation opportunities for both parties and have a lasting impact on consumers' brand perceptions.

In the coming chapters, you will gain a greater understanding of best practices in sport brand management. The chapters exemplify the advantages and challenges faced by sport marketers in day-to-day operations. Some examples embody best practices in brand management, and other examples illustrate the negative impact associated with brand mismanagement. Regardless of the example, readers will gain a much greater insight into the importance of sport brand management.

References

Aaker, D. (1991). *Managing brand equity. Capitalizing on the value of a brand name.* New York: Free Press.

Bedbury, S. (2002). *A new brand world.* New York: Free Press.

Berry, L. L. (1999). *Discovering the soul of service: The nine drivers of sustainable business success.* New York: Free Press.

Boone, L. E., Kochunny, C. M., & Wilkins, D. (1995). Applying the brand equity concept in Major League Baseball. *Sport Marketing Quarterly, 4*(3), 33–42.

Gladden, J. M., & Funk, D. C. (2001, March/April). Understanding brand loyalty in professional sport: Examining the link between brand associations and brand loyalty. *International Journal of Sports Marketing & Sponsorship, 3*(1), 67–86.

Godin, S. (2002). *Purple cow: Transform your business by being remarkable.* New York: Penguin Group.

Keller, K. (1998). Strategic brand management: *Building, measuring, and managing brand equity.* Upper Saddle River, NJ: Prentice Hall.

Kuo, T., Chang, C., & Cheng, K. (2004). Exploration of consumer loyalty in recreational sport/fitness programs. *Sport Journal, 7*(1), 1–8.

Madrigal, R. (1995). Cognitive and affective determinants of fan satisfaction with sporting event attendance. *Journal of Leisure Research, 27*(3), 205–227.

Miloch, K. (2005). Making it in the minors: Seven simple steps to achieving sustained financial health. *SMART Online Journal, 2*(1), 58–62. Retrieved May 21, 2008, from http://www.thesmartjournal.com/minors.pdf.

Shocker, T., Srivastava, S., & Ruekert, P. (1994). Challenges and opportunities facing brand management. *Journal of Marketing Research, 31*(2), 149–158.

Part I

Apparel and Equipment

Chapter 2

Akadema:
Innovation on the Diamond

Jason W. Lee,
University of North Florida

Company: Akadema
Location: Hawthorne, NJ
Internet Address: www.akademapro.com

Discussion Questions

- What were the origins of Akadema?
- What is the primary focus of this company?
- Why would Akadema make efforts to be associated with legends like Ozzie Smith, Carl Yastrzemski, and Gary Carter?
- Why does Akadema seek associations with Minor Leaguers?
- What future challenges and opportunities await a company like Akadema?

The Line-Up

Based in Hawthorne, New Jersey, Akadema is a company that has earned a reputation for being an innovative and quality-oriented company that is making a strong impression on the baseball equipment industry. Akadema stresses quality and uniqueness. Among the unique features that Akadema offers its consumers are a custom glove-building program and a line of gloves called the Hoboken Collection. By tapping into technological advancements that supersede those of their competitors, the company has been able to play the role of David to industry Goliaths like Rawlings, Spalding, and the like. Though their efforts are not aimed at squashing the competition, the innovations and the insight of its founders have allowed Akadema the ability to take away from their competitor's market share and position themselves as a player in the world of baseball equipment producers.

Timeline of Events

1994
- Brothers Joe and Lawrence Gilligan start a baseball training facility named the Academy of Proplayers.

1997
- Joe and Lawrence Gilligan begin selling baseballs and equipment for major brands, such as Rawlings, at their training facility. This venture was known as Academy Equipment.

1998
- Drawings in which Lawrence had conceptualized sketched designs during his Minor League playing days of baseball gloves are discovered and Joe suggests that they start their own equipment company—and Academy Professional Gloves is born.

1999
- Company moves to Garfield, NJ in old Yoo-hoo plant.

2000
- Academy Professional becomes Akadema Inc.
- First gloves show up in Major Leagues (used by Clay Bellinger and Anthony Telford).
- Batting glove line is introduced.

2001
- Akadema releases its first patented glove, the Reptilian.
- Ozzie Smith becomes spokesperson.
- Kris Totten, former Minor League player becomes Vice President of Sales.
- Wood Bat line is introduced.

2002
- Xtension Metal bats are introduced.
- Patented Praying Mantis catcher's mitt (Akadema's best selling glove) is introduced.
- Crystl Bustos, USA Softball star is signed to a ten-year deal.

2003
- Akadema completes its advisory board, including Hall of Fame stars Carl Yastrzemski and Gary Carter.
- The Claw, an outfield patent glove is introduced.

2004
- The Funnel patent glove is introduced.

2005
- Akadema's wood bat custom production is moved in house.
- Ken-Wel and Reach brand trademarks are purchased. Former Ken-Wel and Reach endorsements are licensed with estates which include: Babe Ruth, Lou Gehrig, Yogi Berra, Mickey Cochrane, and Dazzy Vance.
- Akadema is featured in the Billy Bob Thornton film *Bad News Bears*.

2006
- Akadema's custom gloves program is established.
- Footwear (spikes, cleats, and turf shoes) are introduced.
- Company enters a four-year sponsorship agreement with the Northeast Conference.
- Akadema products featured in the Adam Sandler movie *Click* and the David Spade movie *Benchwarmers*.
- Akadema becomes an Official Supplier to USA Softball and the American Softball Association.
- Manny Ramirez is signed to a four-year deal.

2007
- Akadema's apparel line is introduced.

2008
- Company purchases $2.1 million building in Hawthorne, NJ. Company moves its entire operation to Hawthorne. The baseball glove shop is also brought to Hawthorne to make USA Patriot Series glove.
- Shane Victorino becomes first gold glove awarded to an Akadema endorser.
- Akadema becomes official supplier to National Pro Fastpitch League.

2009
- Nearly 30 Major League Players are under contract for product endorsements for the current year.
- Catcher's gear line is introduced.

An Upstart Company

The origins of Akadema can actually be traced back to 1994, when brothers Joe and Lawrence Gilligan (See figures 2.1 and 2.2 in image insert; Joe on the left and Joe and Lawrence on the right) started a baseball training facility named the Academy of Proplayers. In 1997, they began selling baseballs and equipment from major brands at their training facility, and this venture proved to be so successful that the brothers decided to branch out into what became Academy Equipment (due to a trademark restriction, the name was eventually changed to Akadema).

Currently, Akadema one of the top ten baseball manufacturing companies in the United States, although they will admit there is a significant gap between them and industry giants like Nike, Rawlings, and Wilson. With this in mind, the founders know that their company may not be as large as the aforementioned competitors. Suffice it to say that although these companies are major players in the sport equipment world, baseball may not necessarily be a very large part of their company portfolios. Unlike these larger corporations, Akadema sees itself as being one of the top three or four family-owned baseball equipment companies.

Akadema's basic corporate philosophy is that they strive to beat the competition with innovation, quality, and service. These measures are the only way a smaller company like Akadema can distinguish themselves and survive. By identifying their keys to success and following up on them, Akadema has been able to experience growth. The company sees primary areas as being key to success. The keys are innovation, quality, and micro or counter brand power (see Exhibit 2.1).

Exhibit 2.1 Akadema's Keys to Corporate Success

1. **Innovation:** Akadema are innovators in the baseball glove market. They have focused their corporate efforts on the market that they see as being unchanged in a generation—the baseball glove market. With six patents for gloves and one for a wooden bat, they are leaders in the industry for creating functional products made to improve play, rather than design gimmicks.

2. **Quality:** Akadema recognizes that people are looking for quality and love it when their expectations are met or exceeded. Akadema genuinely feels that they have succeeded in providing superior products in each market segment they represent. The company makes an effort to do this by studying their competitor's products and trying to make improvements, rather than figuring ways to make a better profit margin. An example of this is found in the girls' fast-pitch line, where competitors may implement cheap lace to cut costs. Akadema uses the same quality of lace as that used for their pro baseball players. Though they realize that such attention to detail costs more, they also appreciate that girls' softball gloves are some of the best-selling gloves, and they want to provide high-quality equipment to consumers.

3. **(Micro or) Counter Brand Power:** Believing that people are looking for companies and products that are original or innovative, Akadema takes pride in being a small brand that is worn by pros, not because Akadema has the most money to spend on pros, but because the pros believe in the product and want to be different. They also point out that a thirteen-year-old boy or girl may share the same feelings. They see it as though consumers are not looking for "grandpa's glove" or a glove made by a "sneaker company," but rather are looking for their own brand that can set them apart.

Through implementing such components, Akadema feels that it can take on billion-dollar companies in the marketplace, or at least carve its niche.

Products

In Akadema's short history, the company has been able to make their mark against stiff competition. By being one of the nation's hottest baseball equipment companies, Akadema has been able to offer a line of innovative, high-quality products for baseball and softball players on all levels. Akadema's presence was introduced with the Professional Glove Series, and the company has not stopped there. They have continued to be an innovator in the industry by unveiling glove models such as the Reptilian, Praying Mantis, Prodigy, and ProSoft Glove Series (half of Akadema's gloves carry their own patents) (see Exhibit 2.2 for information on the Hoboken Collection). Additionally, bat lines such as Amish Wood, Tacktion, and Xtension Aluminum are making waves. Akadema also offers a variety of other game-related products and accessories, including bat bags, eyewear, and game spikes/turf shoes.

Exhibit 2.2 The Hoboken Collection

The Hoboken Collection is a vintage line of baseball gloves. The idea for the glove formed when examining old designs during the patent process. The gloves were fascinating to the Gilligans, and they decided to reproduce them. They have been used in some interesting ways. Glove collectors who don't want to pay $1,000 for the real item buy these gloves. Executives buy them to place their favorite autographed balls in. The National Baseball Hall of Fame and the Yogi Berra Museum use them in their hands-on education exhibits. Professional teams use them as a drill for "better hands." They are also used by old-fashioned baseball teams who play by 1880 rules.

Marketing Strategies

Akadema's attention to detail through marketing efforts demonstrates the company's vision to distinguish its brand over its competition through attention to quality and detail. One prominent example of such initiatives is their product endorsement program. Akadema's product endorsers include a variety of individuals ranging from legends of baseball to stars of tomorrow. They have a three-prong pro marketing approach. The three prongs include Major League Baseball players, Cooperstown legends, and minor league players.

Major League Players

This approach engages between fifteen and twenty Major Leaguers and is highlighted by Manny Ramirez, one of the most popular and recognizable players in Major League Baseball. In addition to Ramirez, Akadema has endorsement deals with a variety of players who they hope will be future superstars. Association with such athletes who wear their gloves allows for the Akadema logo to be displayed throughout the United States and the world, introducing the brand to millions of young players and fans.

Cooperstown Legends

The Cooperstown legends approach includes seven Hall of Fame players, with four living legends and three deceased. At the forefront of this approach are Ozzie Smith, Gary Carter, and Carl "Yaz" Yastrzemski. Each of these individuals has helped design Akadema products. They also serve another purpose: these players are well known to parents ages thirty to fifty who are buying their child his or her first glove. Legends Bob Feller (living) and Lou Gehrig, Mickey Cochrane, and Dazzy Vance (deceased) are involved in endorsements or estate licensing deals for Akadema's old-fashioned vintage line. Additionally, Akadema now owns trademarks of some of the oldest brand names, such as Reach (1880) and Ken-Wel (1916), which leads them to lightheartedly state that they can now boast that their brands are as old as some of their competitors.

Minor Leagues

The third prong involves the endorsement of between 200 and 300 Minor League players. The motivation to use minor league players is sparked by the magnitude of players coming out of high school and college who now use

Akadema. These athletes' appeal is enhanced because they are often seen as being local heroes. Akadema hopes that praises of their products will be told at baseball camps and other venues where those players may work out during the off season, and this will provide positive word-of-mouth advertisement.

In addition to the aforementioned marketing endeavors, Akadema has a strong presence in collegiate athletics. Aside from prominent sponsorship considerations with the Northeast Conference, Akadema has had relationships with universities such as Brigham Young University, University of California-Riverside, Liberty University, East Tennessee State University, Hofstra, and many more Division I schools. They also have a presence in smaller collegiate environments. Such sponsorship arrangements primarily provide a showcase for Akadema's aluminum bats (CEO, Joe Gilligan points out that schools such as the University of California-Riverside and Liberty had very successful offensive numbers using their Xtension Metal bat).

The Final Score

In attempting to persuade for those who are not users of Akadema products, CEO Joe Gilligan claims that his company offers "a simple pitch." If one tries their products, one will see why Akadema has been able "to convert hundreds of thousands of players." So far, this strategy has worked well. Their affiliation with notable superstars from the past, as well as a contemporary superstar like Manny Ramirez, allows Akadema to gain association with notable individuals while still making room for further affiliation with what they hope to be stars of tomorrow. The future of Akadema looks bright.

Though Akadema has been built into an impressive enterprise, there is still much room for advancement. The company hopes to be able to continue bridging gaps in the baseball equipment market between themselves and competing companies. A continued emphasis on technological innovation and stressing quality will sharpen this focus. The company also hopes to penetrate areas of the baseball market that they are not currently servicing, including catcher's equipment, balls, more accessories, and more options for footwear. Beyond that, the company hopes to expand other team sports equipment or soft goods, like footwear and apparel for the mass market.

An additional area that Akadema will need to focus on to fill the gap between them and their competition is expanding its global presence. To date, Akadema's marketing efforts have been based predominantly in North America, with the vast majority of efforts occurring in the United States and with Canada serving as their biggest export country.

   Realizing the importance of expanding its presence in the global market, Akadema has made some efforts outside of North America. The company feels that their efforts thus far have been successful in Europe, considering the small size of the baseball market there. They also feel that they have made significant strides in baseball hotbeds, such as South America and Central America, regarding involvement with professional players. Though the company has had some business in Asia and Australia, it has a long way to go in those regions. As Joe Gilligan sates regarding these geographic areas, Akadema has only had "small sales, with no major avenues opening up as of yet." As far as future global aspirations go, it will be extremely important for Akadema to be able to tap into Pacific Rim countries like Japan and Korea, where there are large market areas in which the company has not had any meaningful dealings so far. The company notes that this is disappointing because they know of some Japanese players who buy their gloves from Akadema and ship them to Japan. They plan to continue exploring ways to access these and other foreign markets.

   Though product line expansion and global expansion are not the only paths to continue success, it does provide a mechanism for a small company to expand its horizons and reach new plateaus. Attention to detail mixed with innovation will continue to carve a niche for Akadema. Following such initiatives will allow the company to close the gap between them and other industry behemoths.

Post-Game Comments

- Akadema is an example of an upstart company that has had to be innovative and resourceful to survive.
- Akadema has been able to establishing its place in a difficult market, although the founders recognize that they are in a completely different league than some of the industry giants like Nike and Rawlings.
- Akadema seeks to differentiate themselves from the competition through innovation and attention to quality and detail.
- Akadema realizes that there is much room for expansion in global markets and seeks to do this by eyeing many opportunities for future growth and global expansion.

Web Resources

http://www.akademapro.com
http://www.akademapro.com/articles.html
http://www.akademapro.com/endorsement.html
http://www.northeastconference.org/news/baseball/2006/4/7/necakademarel.asp?
    path=baseball
http://www.sportsbusinessjournal.com/article/28249

Additional Resources

Lee, J. W. (2006). Insider's perspective: Joe Gilligan. *SMART Journal*, 3(1),
    75–80. Available at http://www.thesmartjournal.com/ip-akadema.pdf.

Chapter 3

Heelys:
These Shoes Are on a Roll

Jason W. Lee,
University of North Florida

Company: Heeling Sports Limited (HSL)
Location: Carrollton, TX
Internet Address: www.heelys.com

Discussion Questions

- What leads to the appeal of products like Heelys to children in the target age group of eight to fourteen?
- What are some of the special features of Heelys?
- How was the concept of the product developed?
- What benefits can the company get from Team Heelys?
- How is Heelys combating competition in the form of counterfeit and knock-off product producers?
- How does the company address concerns over potential safety issues associated with Heelys use?

The Line-Up

Though some may not yet know them by name, most readers have most likely encountered products known as Heelys. Heelys are an American-born concept that has turned into a global phenomenon in which individuals (primarily children) are seen on sidewalks and in stores skating around. In many locations, all one has to do is enter a retail store or a grocery chain and see youngsters skating alongside their parents, *in their shoes.* These individuals are riding their Heelys in an activity that is referred to as "heeling." Though the act of heeling may resemble what previous generations might identify as skating or rollerblading, Heelys are a twenty-first-century adaptation of those earlier pursuits. They are fashionable footwear that allows users to glide along surfaces while being the envy of those who have not had the fortune to get their own pair. When this unique product emerged, it turned into the dream of many children and the exercise in futility of many parents who have had to scurry about town looking for retailers who still have some product on the shelves because they were selling like the proverbial hotcakes. In some cases, the mania around Heelys stirred up a frenzy akin to earlier highly sought-after treasures like Tickle Me Elmo, Furby, and so on.

Timeline of Events

1998
  • The prototype for Heelys is conceptualized.
2000
  • Heelys are officially introduced.
2001
  • Heelys are made widely available, eventually being distributed to more than sixty countries.
2002
  • HSL purchases the Soap Shoe brand and their "grind plate" technology.
2003
  • Team Heelys signs their first professional skater, Ryan Dawes.
2006
  • HSL becomes a publicly traded company.
2007
  • Heelys unveils the "Gamer" (a video game themed shoe), a non-wheeled shoe.
2008
  • Heelys names Don Carroll President and CEO.
2009
  • Heelys announces Tom Hanson as new President and CEO.

What Are Heelys?

Heelys are a hybrid product, combining shoes and skates to form shoes that roll. Heelys are durable, lightweight athletic shoes featuring a stealth wheel in the heel. This combination of function and design allows for those wearing them to be able to transition their movement from walking or running to skating at any time. Heelys also provide a feature in which wearers can remove the wheel in their footwear to transform them to a regular pair of street shoes. Though Heelys footwear comes in a variety of styles, most are akin to what many would call a skate-themed shoe, something that skateboarders and those who identify with that lifestyle would wear.

Where Did They Come From?

Heelys were invented by founder and current company president Roger Adams. The concept was born in 1998, when Adams observed that children in California were whizzing by him on various modes of wheeled personal transportation, such as inline skates and skateboards. At this point, he realized that he stumbled on to something that could be an innovative concept appealing to people wanting something new and unique. After much tinkering and conceptualization, Adams was able to secure $2.4 million from the Dallas-based venture capital firm Capital Southwest and the company was on its way.

Exhibit 3.1 Founder, Inventor, Businessman: Roger Adams

Roger Adams is a self-proclaimed "skate brat" who was listed in the *Guinness Book of Records* at nine months of age for being the youngest person to ever skate. Though he grew up as part of his family's skate business in Tacoma, Washington, he had gotten away from his skating roots and did not return until he was inspired to create Heelys.

Heelys were introduced in late 2000 and were widely available by 2001. Since hitting the shelves, Heelys eventually produced great sales, moving from limited domestic sales at its inception to becoming a pop culture item in the United States and abroad, distributed to more than sixty countries throughout the world. In most recent times, the success of Heelys has waned and the company has endured multiple top-management changes.

Heeling All Over the World

Heelys have impacted popular culture. They have been featured on popular TV programs such as *CSI: Miami* and in popular media, such as CNN, *Sports Illustrated*, and the *Wall Street Journal*. Certain celebrities have an affinity for the shoes with wheels as well: some of the notable fans of Heelys include Shaquille O'Neal (who happens to wear a size 22) and R&B sensation Usher.

Heelys have introduced a new sport activity. They are the primary equipment for the sport called heeling, which has drawn skateboarders, skaters, and others to take part.

There is a squad of Heelys aficionados called Team Heelys. Team Heelys is composed of Heelys riders ranging from age eight to twenty-two. The team trains and travels together to perform impromptu public demonstrations, retail exhibitions, and promotional product giveaways. They signed their first professional skater, Ryan Dawes, in January 2003.

Heelys: Present and Future

Heelys, Inc., is a subsidiary of Heeling Sports Limited (HSL). HSL is a publicly traded company. HSL felt that going public was a natural step because they have experienced rapid growth and needed to raise additional working capital. The initial public offering was used as a way to secure the necessary resources required to meet organizational growth objectives.

The basic philosophy behind the company's promotional campaigns has been built around brand recognition. Commercials seek to highlight the features and benefits of their shoes. As they see it, Heelys products are all about having fun. There are concentrated efforts aimed at getting this concept across, especially to their target audience of boys and girls ages eight to fourteen (as well as Mom, Dad, and whoever else will be purchasing the products for this age group).

Believing that wheeled footwear is not simply a fad, Heelys plans to enact methods that will use developing technological advances and product initiatives that are relevant to their consumers. An example of such initiatives was seen when Heelys acquired the Soap Shoe Company. HSL purchased the Soap brand in September 2002 and has benefited from being able to offer a variety of products featuring a grind plate in the arch of the shoe that made Soap shoes popular among children, who used these shoes to "grind" on curbs and railing (see Exhibit 3.2). The acquired grind plate technology allows users to integrate more tricks into their arsenal. Heelys sales are diminishing as the decade comes to an end.

Exhibit 3.2 Grinding

"Grinding" is derived from a skateboarding term used to describe tricks in which skateboarders can slide along edges of rails, steps, and curbs. Grind plate technology allows for individuals to grind with their shoes, rather than a skateboard.

The Final Score

Heelys are remarkable products that have been met with mass appeal. The company has also felt the impact of declining demand and sales. The company has continually evaluating new avenues for growth and enhancement. Whether it involves other wheeled activities or branching out into other shoe categories, Heelys will continue evaluating the market to determine the best methods for developing a branding strategy. Heelys seeks to parlay such strategies into a movement in which heeling can be developed into more of an active lifestyle sport, adding to the popularity of the brand.

Heelys has proven to be an innovative company. It currently holds numerous utility and design patents and trademarks in the United States and also globally. Heelys recognizes that securing proper patents is perhaps the most significant key to the company's success and growth. This significance is heightened due to the presence of numerous companies that are producing and selling knock-offs and counterfeit products. HSL will continue its efforts to identify such companies while working within the framework of local patent law to stop trademark and patent infringement.

Innovation have driven the company since its inception.

Though Heelys have experienced great success, the company is not without its detractors. Besides declining sales, news outlets such as CBS News have aired reports documenting the potential for injury associated with Heelys use. Understandably, users assume a certain amount of risk when using these products, which feature a wheel mechanism that allows for skating. Just like a long list of other fun means of personal transportation like inline skates, roller skates, skateboards, bicycles, and scooters, Heelys encourages caution. Concern over the potential for injury has been proactively and reactively addressed by HSL. HSL seeks to find ways to encourage their products users to use good judgment and wear proper safety gear.

As the old adage states, an ounce of prevention is worth a pound of cure. In this case, prevention can come in the form of wearing appropriate safety gear (such as knee pads, helmets, etc.) and good decision making. The promotion of the goals and the related concern over the potential for injury is demonstrated in company's Web-based materials and on the products themselves. For example, expressed warnings are provided on purchasing a pair of Heelys. Information and warnings are inside the packaging of the shoes. Among the most visible warnings include an advisory decal that the company provides stating that through removal, users are recognizing the risks associated with heeling (see Exhibit 3.3). Though "Heelymania" has appeared to wane, the presence of these skate-shoes is still prevalent, and it will be interesting to see what direction this company's popularity will take.

Exhibit 3.3 Heelys Product Warning

Heelys shoes come with a product warning sticker that states:
Warning! Read Full Warnings on Box & Tag
Before Peeling Off Sticker!
By peeling off this sticker, you agree to waive the right to sue Heeling Sports Limited and their owners, directors, employees and/or representatives for any injury, death, property damage, or incidental or consequential damages arising from the use of this product. You also agree to assume and accept all risks of seriously bodily injury arising from the use of this product. The agreement is intended to provide a comprehensive release of liability, but it is not intended to assert any claims or defenses prohibited by law.

Post-Game Comments

- Heelys are a phenomenon that has swept through the U.S.
- The concept for Heelys was developed in 1998 by company president Roger Adams.
- Heelys are a hybrid product combining shoes and skates to form shoes that roll.
- Heelys were introduced in late 2000 and were widely available by 2001. They are now available in more than sixty countries worldwide.
- To date, there have been over 4.5 million pairs of Heelys sold worldwide, equating to over $130 million in sales.
- Heelys, Inc., is a subsidiary of Heeling Sports Limited (HSL) and is a publicly traded company.
- Heelys' future is bright; the only obvious drawback to products offered by HSL has been concern expressed over safety considerations involving

shoes that roll. The company has been proactive in combating these concerns by providing warning and education regarding safety measures.

Web Resources

http://www.allbusiness.com/banking-finance/financial-markets-investing/
    12051710-1.html
http://www.cbsnews.com/stories/2006/03/03/earlyshow/living/parenting/main1365
    761.shtml
http://www.heelys.com/aboutus/Pages/FAQ.aspx
http://www.heelys.com/aboutus/Pages/International.aspx
http://www.heelys.com/aboutus/Pages/News.aspx
http://www.heelys.com/learntoskate/Pages/Basics.aspx
http://investors.heelys.com/index.cfm
http://www.marketwatch.com/story/heelys-names-tom-hansen-president-ceo-
    2009714189480
http://www.time.com/time/globalbusiness/printout/0,8816,1174698,00
http://www.wwd.com/footwear-news/heelys-ceo-resigns-1980528

Additional Resources

Lefton, T. (2006, December 4). … 2 DVDs, and a purse with an NFL teeeeeam. *SportsBusiness Journal*, 8. Available at http://www.sportsbusinessjournal.com/article/53087.
Staffaroni, M. (2006, personal communication). CEO Heeling Sports Limited.

Chapter 4

Life is good: It's All about Living the Good Life

Jason W. Lee,
University of North Florida

Company: Life is good
Location: Boston, MA (with other offices throughout
New England)
Internet Address: www.lifeisgood.com

Discussion Questions

- What were the origins of Life is good?
- What is the message behind Life is good?
- Why do you think the company lists its name with a lowercase *g*?
- What logos or symbols are associated with the Life is good brand?
- How is the company connected to its home base in New England?
- What does Life is good hope to gain from expanding their festivals throughout the United States?
- What types of products are available in the different collections offered by Life is good?

The Line-Up

The Life is good story is very much one of the little company that could. From the humble beginning of two brothers peddling their wares on the streets of Boston and on college campuses, the Jacobses have become unlikely business successes who believe that life is good. Along with the presence of their cartoon mascot, Jake, Life is good is a simple brand that stresses fun, comfort, individuality, and positivity. To date, more than in 25 million T-shirts have been sold, and product and distribution expansion suggests that the company will be sharing the good life for quite a while.

Timeline of Events

1989
- Brothers Bert and John Jacobs design their first T-shirt.

1994
- The inception of Life is good.

2001
- Life is good's first fund-raising venture occurs as the company sells U.S. flag-themed T-shirts to raise funds for victims and family members of victims following the terrorist attacks of September 11.

2003
- First Life is good Festival is held. Since 2003, Life is good Festivals have been enjoyed by 300,000 people and have raised over $3 million for charities serving children in need.

2005
- Life is good Kids Foundation is established.
- Life is good purchases The Shirt Factory as distribution center in United States.
- Life is good experiences T-shirt sales of 4 million units.

2006
- Life is good sees an $80 million year for the brand.

2007
- Hosts Life is good at Fenway (Park) and in the process raises a total of $824,524 for children's charities.

2008
- Life is good Festivals branch out to eighteen festivals in fourteen states aimed at bringing communities together for a great cause.
- To date, Life is good has sold approximately 25 million shirts worldwide.

How Life Became So Good

The origin of the Life is good brand dates back to 1989, when brothers Bert and John Jacobs designed their first T-shirt. The green entrepreneurs started out with a simple plan to peddle their tee shirts in the streets of Boston and on college campuses throughout the East Coast.

Though initial efforts proved unsuccessful, the Jacobs brothers stuck with it and eventually found inspiration in the form of an image hanging on their apartment wall. That image was to be the "face" of Life is good—Jake. Jake is a hat-wearing stick figure with a huge smile. Using Jake as the graphic for a new shirt, the brothers were able to sell out of the initial printing of Jake shirts at a street fair in Cambridge, Massachusetts. Soon, Jake's image was branching out to local retailers, and the rest is history.

Jake

Life is good is a unique and eye-catching brand. The company's logos and other symbols help to build a strong brand image and consumer recall. Perhaps the most notable image associated with Life is good is Jake. According to Jim Laughlin, director of Life is good Festivals, "Jake is the face of Life is good. He is the Ambassador of Optimism, a cultural hero, an original, a leader, a free spirit, and above all—an optimist. His power comes from his disposition. He has life figured out because he is happy today. He's confident, witty, charismatic, energetic, independent, adventurous, cool, and irrepressible" (see Figure 4.1 in the image insert).

Whether he is hiking, running, playing guitar, or hanging out with his sidekick Rocket (his dog; see Figures 4.2 and 4.3), Jake is the embodiment of Life is good's brand appeal. He proclaims the Life is good motto of "Do what you like. Like what you do." As such, Jake has continued to be the symbol of optimism and growth for all things pertaining to Life is good.

In addition to Jake and Rocket, the prominent themes and visuals associated with Life is good include basic logos displaying the company's name, various methods for displaying the company motto, as well as other relevant sayings and captions.

Exhibit 4.1

When referencing the company and its registered brand, always make sure it appears with a lowercase g, as in Life is good, Life is good, Inc., or Life is good Festivals.

A Truly [Wicked] Awesome Company

Life is good is a product of New England. Life is good prides itself in being a Boston-based company that strives to maintain a strong presence and connection with its home region. Efforts to preserve a strong and visible presence throughout New England include maintaining their Boston design center as their urban hub, which serves as the site where the festivals and marketing and design teams reside. Hudson, New Hampshire, also in New England, serves as home to the customer service, finance, human resource, and shipping departments. There are also three retail locations that are owned and operated by Life is good in Boston, and Newburyport, Massachusetts, and Portland, Maine. The company wants to make sure to always keep the home site of Boston as a location for holding major events.

A Festive Company

If asked to explain the philosophy behind the advertisement campaigns for Life is good, readers may be surprised to find out that the company claims that they do not "advertise," but choose to focus marketing efforts through venues such as their homegrown Life is good Festivals.

In a precursor to the Life is good Festivals, the company's first fund-raising venture occurred when they sold U.S. flag-themed T-shirts, raising over $200,000 for victims and family members of victims following the terrorist attacks of September 11, 2001. This endeavor was a forerunner to the charity festivals, which are now a major component of the company.

Why festivals? Well, who doesn't like a good party? Life is good certainly embraces the notion of enjoying a get together. The company uses the festivals as a means to make a strong and unique expression about the brand, as well as a statement about organizational values and mission focus. Seeking to make a positive impact on consumers while projecting a positive corporate brand image, Life is good provides family-focused festivals that are noteworthy seasonal events in the Northeast. These events are quickly spreading nationwide as Life is good takes their festivals across the country from Lake Placid, New York, to Tampa, Florida, to San Diego, California.

The Festivals are intended to provide two services: (1) spread "good vibes" through bringing communities together and (2) generate consciousness and funds for children's charities (these are funded through the Life is good Kids Foundation). Life is good believes in giving back, and a notable way that the company does this is through the expansion of their festivals. These festivals allow the company to give back, have fun, and allow for brand differentiation through emphasizing a positive social mission while raising brand awareness.

In the most successful festival fund-raiser to date, Life is good took the festival concept to Boston's hallowed baseball grounds at the famed Fenway Park, where a crowd of 15,000 took part in the event in the summer of 2007. This event generated an impressive $824,524.

Life is good has also built partnerships with several other organizations that are glad to associate with the company and their fun, worthwhile endeavors. The Life is good Festival partners are Dick's Sporting Goods, UPS, Verizon Wireless, Four Points by Sheraton, and Citizens Bank, among others.

What Will Make Life is good Even Better

Life is good is a company that describes itself as having a "strong, unique brand with broad appeal, emphasizing optimism, simplicity, and good, clean fun." The company has been successful and has stayed focused on seeing the good in life and accentuating optimism, fun, and doing what the founders feel is right for their specific brand. This self-proclaimed design-driven company seeks innovative and eye-catching methods (see Figure 4.4 in image insert) to be seen in whichever setting Life is good may be found (including retail sites such as sporting goods stores, outdoor retailers, golf shops and gift shops, as well as running, lifestyle, health and fitness, and spa venues).

Life is good has established a presence in a broad and diverse selection of re-tail channels. Their most notable retail partners include Dick's Sporting Goods, REI, Bob's Stores, and Hudson News outlets, which are found in major airports. Additionally, products are available in Genuine Neighborhood Shoppes (GNS). The GNS program is unique to the Life is good brand, as it is composed of in-dependently owned and operated shops that sell exclusively their company products.

In addition to the more traditional retail settings, the Life is good Web site provides a means to exhibit the breadth of their product offerings. These services seek to offer online availability to individuals who may have limited access to Life is good products. Life is good also uses their corporate Web site as a means to educate consumers about activities and events like their char-itable festivals and the Life is good Kids Foundation. As the company ex-plains, the Life is good Kids Foundation supports charities that provide assistance and leave lasting impressions, such as Project Joy, is an initiative aimed at providing education, training, and resources for effective early child-hood education.

The aforementioned online and retail ventures are important because they serve as showcases for Life is good's growing product lines. There are various new product lines on the horizon that will target various aspects of sport and leisure for Life is good. Life is good recently unveiled a new line of organic products, referred to as the Good Karma line. These products are aimed at being in the forefront of responsible and sustainable practices in apparel production and manufacturing. Additionally, the company seeks to make further movement into areas such as home goods, pet, and sporting goods segments. Furthermore, there are also plans to expand the brand into children, toddler, and baby labels called Good Kids, as well as performance-oriented and athletic-inspired warm-up and workout gear called Good Move. Further details associated with Life is good product offerings are available in Exhibit 4.2.

Exhibit 4.2 Life is good Product Collections

LIG Core: Life is good's line of classic T-shirts, tanks, button-ups, hoodies, and so on.

Good Moves: Athletic apparel that is "powered by optimism."

Good Karma: Environmentally friendly apparel for those who want to "live in harmony" with their surroundings.

Good Home: Home accessories such as mugs, calendars, picture frames, and the *Life is good* book.

Good Times: Items for fun times like beach outings, backyard gatherings, or adorning one's favorite ride.

Beyond the regular product offerings, Life is good also gets in the holiday spirit by providing holiday-themed or seasonal items. Whether it is a flag-adorned coffee mug for July 4 (see Figure 4.5 in image insert, additional Life is good images are shown in Figure 4.6), a jack-o'-lantern T-shirt for Halloween, gear featuring a snowman or other winter icons, or a multitude of items that lets people know that spring has sprung, Life is good has something that encapsulates the given time of the year.

The Final Score

Whether through Life is good Festivals or their multitude of products, Jake and the Jacobs brothers can attest that life is good. The company's mission is to have the "greatest positive impact on any consumer brand in history." This is a noble goal statement, and certainly the company works toward building a positive image.

The popularity of Life is good is evident in its sales volume. The company has sold approximately 25 million T-shirts since its inception in 1994. Life is good products are available in all fifty states and in thirty countries worldwide.

In 2006, Life is good saw an $80 million year for the brand, with growth projected to exceeding $100 million in subsequent years. Life is good International is expanding its distribution networks and licensing agreements. By 2010, the company forecasts having 6,000 retailers and 200 GNS locations.

Through the Life is good Festivals, the brand is able to reap the benefits of a dual-natured focus: spreading their characteristic good vibes and being a philanthropical resource force that embodies corporate social responsibility.

The popularity and infectious nature of the Life is good brand are hard to deny. Just taking a look at the clothing line sends a clear message of fun, colorfulness, simplicity, and positivity. As long as the company puts focuses on quality, comfort, and the pursuit of happiness, Jake and the boys should be able to keep on smiling from ear to ear.

Post-Game Comments

- Life is good is a Boston-based company that strives to maintain a strong presence in their home turf of New England.
- The company's logos and other symbols help build a strong brand image and consumer recall, and Jake is the most notable face associated with the brand.
- To increase brand identity, the company and its registered brand always appears as a lowercase g.
- The Life is good brand is categorized by their "Do what you like. Like what you do" tagline.
- The Life is good Festivals are intended to provide two purposes: (1) spread "good vibes" through bringing communities together and (2) generate consciousness and funds for children's charities.
- Life is good offers various facets of life—aimed at meeting the wants of those wanting to experience to good life.

Web Resources

http://www.lifeisgood.com
http://www.lifeisgood.com/about
http://www.lifeisgood.com/about/genuine-neighborhood-shoppes.aspx
http://www.lifeisgood.com/category/core-collection
http://www.lifeisgood.com/category/good-home
http://www.lifeisgood.com/category/good-karma

http://www.lifeisgood.com/category/good-move
http://www.lifeisgood.com/category/good-times
http://www.lifeisgood.com/festivals
http://www.lifeisgood.com/festivals/LIG-kids-foundation.aspx

Additional Resources

Buchanan, L. (October, 2006). Life lessons. *Inc.* Retrieved March 4, 2009, from
    http://www.inc.com/magazine/20061001/life-lessons.html.
Laughlin, J. (2007; 2008, personal communication). Director of Life is good
    Festivals Division.

Chapter 5

Mossy Oak: It's Not a Passion, It's an Obsession

Eric Forsyth,
Bemidji State University

Company: Mossy Oak
Location: West Point, MS
Internet Address: www.mossyoak.com

Discussion Questions

- What is the defining success behind Mossy Oak brand camouflage?
- What other camouflage pattern(s) would you suggest as a good fit for the Mossy Oak brand?
- What suggestions would you make for Mossy Oak to grow its brand globally?
- What marketing strategies would you develop for the Mossy Oak brand?
- What products would you suggest be inlaid with Mossy Oak camouflage patterns?

The Line-Up

Mossy Oak has grown into a multifaceted outdoors icon through its popular camouflage patterns. With its own retail stores, top-rated outdoor shows, wild game products, and rural land real estate business, Mossy Oak has become the most diverse company in the outdoors industry.

Mossy Oak is first and foremost a camouflage brand. Their passion is hunting, yet their obsession is to conceal hunters in all terrains (woods, fields, waterfowl flyways, and open country). Mossy Oak's achievement in concealing hunters in the outdoors through its camouflage patterns is second to none.

39

They have won the *Bowhunting World* Readers' Choice Award for best camouflage pattern eleven times.

Mossy Oak loves the outdoors. In sustaining its outdoor heritage, Mossy Oak surrounds itself with partners that share in their core values: spending time with family and friends, land stewardship, and conservation.

Timeline of Events

1986
- Mossy Oak is created as a hunting apparel manufacturer.
- Mossy Oak introduces first camouflage pattern, Bottomland, which becomes the background pattern for many future camouflage patterns.

1987
- Mossy Oak introduces second camouflage pattern, Greenleaf, developed for spring turkey and early bow-hunting seasons.

1989
- Mossy Oak introduces third camouflage pattern, Treestand, developed to replicate limbs and branches where treestands are situated in the treetops.
- Mossy Oak starts to license its camouflage patterns through sporting goods stores.

1990
- Mossy Oak introduces fourth camouflage pattern, Full Foliage, developed to become the standard for green patterns.

1993
- Mossy Oak introduces fifth camouflage pattern, Fall Foliage, developed to replicate fall autumn colors.

1995
- Mossy Oak introduces sixth camouflage pattern, Break-Up, developed using digital images to replicate realistic surroundings of the woods.
- Mossy Oak introduces seventh camouflage pattern, Shadow Grass, developed to replicate marsh grass surroundings.
- Mossy Oak Productions launches with its first TV show on TNN.
- Mossy Oak expands a new licensing model with its partners.

1997
- Mossy Oak introduces eighth camouflage pattern, Shadow Leaf, developed to replicate spring and early fall environment surroundings.
- Mossy Oak introduces ninth camouflage pattern, Shadow Branch, developed to replicate the surroundings of trees—limbs, branches, and leaves—while sitting in a treestand.

1998
- Mossy Oak opens its own retail store, Mossy Oak Outdoors Outlet.

1999
- International Paper partnership launched with Biologic Wild Game Products.
- Mossy Oak opens its first Mossy Oak Properties office in Livingston, Alabama.

2000
- Mossy Oak introduces tenth camouflage pattern, Forest Floor, developed to replicate the surroundings of late fall and early spring woods.
- Russell Athletics buys Mossy Oak's hunting apparel manufacturing division.

2002
- Mossy Oak improves its sixth camouflage pattern, New Break-Up, developed using higher resolution images of leaves, branches and limbs.
- Mossy Oak improves its seventh camouflage pattern, New Shadow Grass, developed to create a 3D visual effect of marsh grass surroundings.
- Mossy Oak Properties, Inc., established.

2003
- Mossy Oak Properties franchise launched.

2004
- Mossy Oak introduces eleventh camouflage pattern, Obsession, developed to replicate early fall and late spring foliage environment surroundings.
- Mossy Oak Land Enhancement Services launched.

2005
- Mossy Oak introduces its twelfth camouflage pattern, Brush, developed to replicate open range environments.
- Biologic, a division of Mossy Oak, is merged with Alabama Farmers CO-OP.

2006
- Mossy Oak Properties reaches record franchise revenue.

2007
- Mossy Oak introduces thirteenth camouflage pattern, Duck Blind, developed to be effective in all waterfowl environment surroundings.
- Mossy Oak launches Web-based TV network.
- Mossy Oak streamlines hard goods decoration process with launch of Mossy Oak 3D graphics.
- Mossy Oak Nativ Nurseries founded.

2008
- Seventeen years after the initial launch, Mossy Oak reintroduces a modified version of its third (and best pattern launch) camouflage pattern, Treestand, developed for late fall seasons while sitting from an elevated position.

- Mossy Oak Properties reaches record network growth with more than fifty offices established throughout the United States.

2009
- MOOSE Media is launched; formed to support a partnership with the Pursuit Channel. MOOSE is the acronym for "Mossy Oak Outdoor Sport and Entertainment."

2010
- Mossy Oak introduces its newest dimension in camouflage, Break-Up Infinity; featuring unprecedented depth, unequalled detail, and elements with remarkable contrast.

"It's Not a Passion. It's an Obsession."

Imagine being in the woods on opening day of the hunting season. You plan, strategize, and take all the necessary steps to become one with nature in a chase to fulfill your hunting dream. The moment comes when it is just you and your chosen wildlife. All of a sudden, the animal or bird detects you, and your dream vanishes as it sprints or flies away. In frustration, you contemplate what has just happened and ask yourself, "What can I do to blend in with the surroundings of nature?"

Hunters are a unique breed. One of the things that make them unique is their obsession for their favorite pastime: the hunt of a lifetime. Mossy Oak's slogan fits hunters' favorite pastime perfectly: "It's not a passion. It's an obsession." Mossy Oak's obsession is in their camouflage brand patterns. Their obsession helps hunters blend in with the natural surroundings of their environment to get as close to wildlife as possible without being detected.

The Visionary Behind Mossy Oak

Through his obsession with wild turkeys and getting as close to these birds as possible without being detected, one man thought of a way to blend in with nature. Mossy Oak's founder and CEO, Toxey Haas (see Figure 5.1 in the image insert) gathered up leaves, branches, sticks, bark, dirt and grass, and took his bags of nature into a local textile manufacturer. Camouflage hunting apparel—putting realistic images and patterns of the woods on fabric—was born in spring of 1986.

Fulfillment of Mossy Oak's Obsession: Blending in with Nature

Figures 5.2 and 5.3 in the image insert are photos taken by a hunter's trail camera during a bear hunt. In the first photo, take note of the surroundings in this particular outdoor scenery; dirt, grass, brush, trees, bark, branches, leaves, twigs, and logs. The hunter's stand is only ten yards away from this bear. The second photo is of a hunter covered from head to toe in camouflage. The hunter's apparel is inlaid with the Mossy Oak camouflage pattern Break-Up. Elevated and against the backdrop of trees, branches, and leaves, this hunter is undetectable to the black bear's eyes. Mossy Oak's obsession has allowed this hunter to get within ten yards of the bear without being detected.

Up Close in the Field

Since designing their first camouflage pattern in 1986, Mossy Oak has improved their patterns over time by embedding digital images for a more realistic look. Before any camouflage pattern is offered to the public, it is first field-tested by Mossy Oak's outdoor professional staff. The company is obsessed with creating the best camouflage patterns possible so outdoorsmen and -women will have an enjoyable and successful experience in the field. Figures 5.4–5.9 (see image insert) take a closer look at Mossy Oak's camouflage patterns that are currently being use in the market today; Break-Up, Obsession, Duck Blind, Brush, Treestand, and Break-Up Infinity.

More than Camouflage

Though first and foremost a camouflage brand, Mossy Oak has incorporated the outdoor lifestyle with apparel, licensees, Biologic Wild Game Products, media productions, rural land real estate, land enhancement services, Nativ Nurseries (no e on Nativ), and an online store. These are addressed in Exhibit 5.1.

Exhibit 5.1 Mossy Oak Is More Than Camouflage

MOOSE Media: Mossy Oak Outdoor Sport and Entertainment was recently formed to support the partnership between Mossy Oak and the Pursuit Channel, which will serve as the sales and marketing arm for both Mossy Oak Productions and the Pursuit Channel network.

Mossy Oak Biologic Wild Game Products: After working closely with New Zealand farmers to grasp their techniques, wild game forage seeds are now being used here in the United States for luring deer, turkey, fish, and waterfowl. Today, Mossy Oak offers their wild game products through retailers around the country.

Mossy Oak Productions: Mossy Oak's broadcasts offers weekly series of outdoor entertainment that carries a message of family fun, fellowship, and natural resource stewardship. Production titles include *Hunting the Country*, *Mossy Oak Classics*, *Whistling Wings*, *Wildlife Obsession*, and *Obsession Revealed*. Mossy Oak Productions also offers series of DVDs that appeals to every outdoors enthusiast—from deer to birds to predators.

Hunting the Country Magazine: Mossy Oak's magazine, *Hunting the Country*, is published four times a year with feature articles and stories from some of the best known outdoor writers in reference to the woods, hunting heritage, field points, destinations, rifles and loads, land management, off-roading, and many other topics. Currently, the magazine is on hiatus until a new publisher is found.

Mossy Oak Properties: Mossy Oak selected a professional real estate staff who understand and appreciate rural land and are dedicated to its stewardship. Currently, Mossy Oak offers a network of land brokers across the Southern United States and intends to expand into all continental forty-eight states.

Mossy Oak Land Enhancement Services: Mossy Oak has developed a team of land management professionals to serve clients in their habitat management goals.

Mossy Oak Nativ Nurseries: Mossy Oak Nativ Nurseries was founded to provide landowners and managers a grove of trees that would provide nature food for wildlife without having to plant annually.

Mossy Oak Online Store: Mossy Oak's online store offers a wide spectrum of products: hunting apparel, men's/women's/children casual apparel, hunting accessories, automotive, home furnishings, merchandise, DVD/video, and other products for the outdoor enthusiast.

Mossy Oak My Outdoors: Mossy Oak My Outdoors is a part of the interactive Web community (available at www.mossyoak.com) that allows sportsmen and -women to share stories, pictures, journals, and make new friends. Users can read a variety of perspectives and professional blogs and make comments to the issues of today's outdoor activities.

Marketing Strategies

Mossy Oak spends approximately $2 million annually on marketing alone. The company has become a household name among hunters. Mossy Oak exposes their brand through a continued public relations push using press releases, media CDs, outdoor writer hunts, newsletters, pro staff utilization, sponsorships with conservation organizations, and a presence at national outdoors trade shows. Their marketing strategies have resulted in consumers knowing what Mossy Oak stands for and creating consumer loyalty.

Brand Growth

Mossy Oak has exposed its brand globally through a licensing royalty model and aggressive partner marketing. With approximately 800 license partners, Mossy Oak creates over a billion and a half camouflage pattern impressions each year. A sampling of some of notable licensing partners is listed in Exhibit 5.2. Their equation is simple: partners' quality product(s) + Mossy Oak's camouflage patterns = partners for success.

Exhibit 5.2 Sample Mossy Oak Licensing Partners Listed According to Associated Categories

Firearms: Browning, Remington
Footwear: Danner, La Crosse, Rocky
Apparel: Under Amour
Archery: Easton Arrows, Parker, PSE
Automotive: Toyota Tundra trucks
Power Sports: Polaris
Optics: Bushnell, Leupold, Nikon

Exhibit 5.3 Mossy Oak and Boo Weekley

Mossy Oak's main consumers are hunters, and one them is professional golfer Boo Weekley (see Figure 5.10 in the image insert). Not only has Weekley made quite a splash on the PGA Tour, he is very outspoken about his passion for hunting and fishing. While traveling on tour throughout the country, Mossy Oak representatives met many professional athletes who enjoyed hunting and fishing during their off-season. These conversations with professional athletes that sparked the idea of a new TV show titled

Second Season, which aired on the Golf Channel in 2004. Boo Weekley is now a member of Mossy Oak's Prostaff, and continues to make celebrity appearances at various golf tournaments sporting the Mossy Oak logo. It is no wonder that Weekley has become a remarkable representative for the Mossy Oak brand.

The Final Score

It may have begun with a bag full of the outdoor elements, but not even Mossy Oak really knows where it will end. The company is driven by their passion for hunting and their obsession to develop the best camouflage patterns possible.

With the longest-running advertising campaign in outdoor market history, Mossy Oak has placed its reputation and credibility on the line by personally guaranteeing the quality of their products. As a result, consumers trust Mossy Oak.

Post-Game Comments

- Mossy Oak was the first company to offer realistic images and patterns of the woods on hunting apparel.
- Mossy Oak camouflage patterns allow hunters to get as close to wildlife as possible without being detected.
- Mossy Oak camouflage patterns can be found on more than a billion products each year.
- The essence of Mossy Oak is summed up in their slogan: "It's not a passion. It's an obsession."

Web Resources

http://www.mossyoak.com
http://www.mossyoak.com/content/articlezonelist.aspx?z=1
http://www.mossyoak.com/content/CamoPatternsSlideshow.aspx
http://www.mossyoak.com/content/PastAndPresent.aspx
http://www.mossyoak.com/content/tmpltBios.aspx?articleid=820
http://www2.nemcc.edu/mspeople/toxey_haas.htm

Additional Resources

Biologic: Scientifically Proven Wild Game Products (2008). [Brochure].

Gavin, E. (2008, personal communication). Graphic design manager, Haas Outdoors, Inc./Mossy Oak.

Kinton, T. (2008). Mossy Oak's Nativ Nursery. *Gear Showcase* [Special Edition], Mossy Oak Publications.

Mossy Oak (2007). Base Camp for Partners Toolkit.

Mossy Oak (2008). Media CD.

Robinson, J. (2008; 2009, personal communication). Assistant manager, Public Relations, Mossy Oak.

Robinson, T. (2008; 2009, personal communication). Public relations manager, Mossy Oak Brand Camo.

Chapter 6

Roots: Branding to the World, One Beret at Time

Patrick Kraft,
Indiana University

Company: Roots
Location: Toronto, Canada
Internet Address: www.roots.com

Discussion Questions

- What has Roots done to capitalize on the success of the 2002 Winter Olympic Games?
- Roots continued to develop Olympic berets for the 2006 Winter Olympic Games in Torino. Because they used the berets again, did it diminish the popularity of the product? Should roots have focused its efforts on creating another unique product to enhance its exposure at the 2006 Winter Olympics? If so, what should they have done?
- Could Roots have done anything more to enhance their brand image at the 2002 Olympic Games?
- Would the Roots 2002 Team USA Olympic line have been as successful had the games been somewhere other than the United States?
- Is it in Roots's best interest to attempt to partner with as many countries in the Olympic Games as they can?
- Has Roots become a fad or is it a sustainable brand?

The Line-Up

Michael Budman and Don Green were two boys from Michigan who took their enjoyment of the outdoors and turned it into a $100 million fashion enterprise. Roots Inc. was built from a friendship formed by Budman and Green at Camp Tamakwa in Ontario. These two Americans took their love of all things outdoors and established themselves as Canadian entrepreneurs, founding their very successful and ever growing Roots apparel line. The influence of the outdoors on their product line and image is demonstrated simply by looking at the company logo, a beaver.

Budman and Green were inspired by their passion for an active lifestyle and created a line of casual sporting gear based on quality, creativity, and integrity. This enthusiasm for sport has parlayed itself into a wonderful branding partnership. Athletics has provided many opportunities for the company to gain national and global recognition. Roots prides itself on the fact that some of the greatest athletes in the world wear their brand, including Olympians to hockey players. The company understands that comfort, durability, and style are elements that are important in an individual's active lifestyle.

Timeline of Roots Olympic Involvement

1976 (Olympic Winter Games, Innsbruck)
- Roots outfits the Canadian Olympics team with their negative heel shoe, the Puffboot, worn during the Opening Ceremonies Parade.

1988 (Olympic Winter Games, Calgary)
- Roots designs and makes jackets for the first ever Jamaican bobsled team, which had been training in Canada with no winter gear prior to the games (The story of the Jamaican bobsled was the focus of the 1993 film *Cool Runnings*, which also featured the Roots jacket.).

1994 (Olympic Winter Games, Lillehammer)
- Roots honors the 1994 Canadian Olympics Team with a special edition line: "Roots salutes the Canadian Olympic Team."

1998 (Olympic Winter Games, Nagano)
- Roots signs on as the official outfitter for the Canadian Olympics team for the categories of opening parade wear, podium wear, village wear, and closing ceremony wear. The outfits are such a big hit that they become the most traded uniform among the athletes and visitors in Nagano.
- The red "Canada Poorboy" hat becomes an instant success. Celebrities around the globe are seen wearing the hat and the consumer demand is so high that stores sell out as soon as shipments arrive (over 500,000 of these hats are sold).

- Canadian snowboarding gold medalist Ross Rebagliati becomes a Roots Spokesman and Canadian ice skating gold medalist Elvis Stojko becomes an endorser for Roots, appearing in posters and at special events for the company.

2000 (Olympic Summer Games, Sydney)
- Roots is the exclusive outfitter for the Canadian Olympic Committee and the Canadian Paralympics Team in the categories of parade wear, podium wear, and village wear.
- For the first time, Roots outfits a team at the Summer Olympics, demonstrating that they can be successful in producing uniforms for both summer and winter games.

2002 (Olympic Winter Games, Salt Lake City)
- Roots continues to be the official outfitter for the Canadian Olympics and Paralympics Teams as well as the U.S. Olympics and Paralympics teams for parade wear, podium wear, and village wear.
- Team USA's outfits brings Roots into mainstream Americana. Their beret once again becomes a craze as people line up for hours to get the Roots Team USA Beret; over a million of these are sold.
- President George W. Bush wears a Roots Team USA leather jacket when making his welcoming speech in this event televised to a world audience.
- U.S. athletes outfitted in Roots clothing are escorted during the opening ceremonies by six New York City firefighters and police officers in a solemn procession in honor of those who had fallen in the terrorists' attack of September 11, 2001.
- Roots becomes the official outfitter for the Great Britain Olympics Team, providing them with parade duffle coats.

2003
- As a continued supporter of the Olympics movement, especially the Canadian Olympic Committee, Roots provides financial sponsorship and products to support the activities of the official committee bidding for Vancouver to host 2010 Winter Olympics. Roots provides the Vancouver Bid Committee with uniforms for the final bid presentations.

2004 (Olympic Summer Games, Athens, Greece)
- Roots continues as the official outfitter for the Olympics teams of Canada, the United States, Great Britain, and adds Barbados.
- Roots creates merchandise for the Olympic Spirit Store, the world's first permanent Olympics-themed attraction, located in their backyard of Toronto.

2006 (Olympic Winter Games, Torino)
- Roots is no longer the official Olympic outfitter for Canada (Hudson's Bay Company becomes the new official outfitter).
- Roots is the official sponsor of the Canadian speed skating team and the Jamaican bobsledding team.
- Roots continues its partnership as the official outfitter for the U.S. Olympics and Paralympics Teams. The company also signs U.S. Olympic gold medal speed skater Apolo Ohno to represent Roots, including making appearances and being featured in advertisements.

2008 (Olympic Summer Games, Beijing)
- Roots is no longer official outfitter for U.S. Olympic teams as Ralph Lauren Polo becomes the designer for the Beijing Games.

[Note: Timeline is based primarily from Roots Olympic Timeline; Available at http://about.roots.com/on/demandware.store/Sites-RootsCorporate-Site/default/Page-Show?cid=MEDIA_INFO_OlympicTimeline]

What Is Roots?

Roots, established in 1973 as a natural footwear company, has become Canada's leading lifestyle brand, known around the world for its wide range of quality leather goods, clothing, and accessories (see Exhibit 6.1). Roots has evolved into a multifaceted merchandise company that far exceeds their early beginnings. Starting as a tiny store in Toronto selling its first product, the Roots Negative Heel Shoe, the company has grown to more than 125 locations in Canada and the United States as well as 20 locations in Asia. Their line of products aims to maintain the feeling of the great outdoors.

Exhibit 6.1 The Roots Product Line

The Roots Baby Collection provides extra-soft fabrics, large neck openings, and snap closures. The collection makes sure that the clothes are as comfortable as possible.

The Roots Kids collection provides the latest trends for kids to wear both at school and at play while maintaining comfort and durability for every season.

Roots Leather includes luggage, shoes, handbags, and jackets that are handmade in the company's leather factory in Toronto.

Roots Home provides consumers an opportunity to decorate their homes in Roots style. Roots Home includes wood, stainless steel, and chrome furniture, bedroom sets, soft leather furniture, accent pieces, and plush towels and linens.

Roots Men and Women is an urban athletic, retro-inspired design collection constructed from lamb's wool tweed, antique wash denim, and cotton pique. The Men's and Women's product lines include graphic T-shirts, hoodie sweatshirts, the Roots fragrance for both men and women, and a watch line.

Building a Brand on the World Stage

Sport and an active lifestyle have been integral aspects of the Roots brand from the very beginning. Green and Budman believe that having a casual but durable product for their customers' active lifestyle; this has helped develop a bond between the brand and the consumer. Since 1998, when Roots began its formal Olympics involvement by outfitting the Canadian Olympics team, the company has experienced unprecedented success with its official Olympics merchandise.

Developing a brand takes more than just a quality product—it takes foresight, creativity, and the right connection with your consumer. For Roots, this connection developed because of creative partnerships with both the Canadian and U.S. Olympics teams. The key element was to develop a strong sense of awareness for their products. It is widely acknowledged that without brand awareness, brand attitude and brand image cannot be formed. Roots had a strong brand image in their home country of Canada, especially after the success experienced during their 1998 partnership with the Canadian Olympics team. Green and Budman knew they had a high-quality product that could be successful anywhere, but the awareness of their brand image was low outside of Canada. Brand attitude cannot be formed, and the intention to buy cannot occur unless brand awareness is in place.

This awareness of the Roots brand reached the stratosphere on February 8, 2002, the opening ceremonies at the XIX Olympic Winter Games in Salt Lake City. Knowing that the opening ceremonies of any Olympic Games is one of the most watched TV programs of the whole year, Roots used this world stage as a gigantic fashion show. From the minute the U.S. athletes stepped out during the opening ceremonies parade, the country took notice. The 2002 Team USA gear became the talk of the games.

"The Olympics were incredible," recalls Roots CFO Alan Goldberg. "Literally, the day after the opening ceremonies, Roots garments were on TV everywhere, and we were in magazines and newspapers. The products just started to fly out of the stores.... We had waiting lists of tens of thousands of people who signed up just to get a hat" (Rabon, 1998, p. 1).

Roots gear was everywhere, but one singular item had a lasting effect on the games. There are few products that make a splash like that of the 2002 beret worn by the U.S. Olympic Team. This style of beret experienced similar success in Canada during the 1998 games, but went to the next level when Team USA wore the red, white, and blue beret during the opening ceremonies. The hat became synonymous with the games itself. The Roots beret was everywhere: it had gone from a simple accessory to a pop culture phenomenon in the blink of an eye. The beret and other Roots gear were featured on news broadcasts, talk shows, fans, celebrities, music stars, politicians, and athletes and their families. The company sold over a million berets. The berets and the Roots gear lead to $40 million in sales of the 2002 Olympics merchandise.

The Genius Behind the 2002 Olympic Team USA Partnership

The initial deal in 1998 to become the official outfitter for the Canadian Olympics Team took Green and Budman over two years to finish. This partnership was well worth the time and investment. Besides the fact that it was a goodwill gesture in support of Canadian amateur athletics, it was the beginning of a successful branding program.

This initial contract, which created a partnership that guaranteed Roots exposure via the opening and closing ceremonies and podium wear, was genius. Green and Budman understood that these events would create a platform for billions of eyes to see one thing: the greatest athletes in the world wearing Roots gear. When athletes endorse a product, especially in a "feel good" atmosphere like the Olympic games, it is much easier for the consumer to develop a positive emotional tie to the product. When companies seek to invest in athletes as endorsers, it is imperative that they make sure the athletes are attractive to the company's target audience embody the values associated with the brand identity. Roots covered both of these aspects in a single marketing platform.

The 2002 partnership with the United States once again demonstrated the foresight and confidence that Roots had in its product line. The first element of success was that the athletes enjoyed the product line. The athletes would be on TV wearing their fashionable and trendy clothes with no visual obstruction during the most visible moments of the games. The opening and closing ceremonies and award stand moments were glorified fashion shows for the Roots brand. Roots's Olympics team designs captured the world's attention and developed a trendy fashion aspect to Olympics gear that had not been seen before.

The Final Score

The reason for the success of this partnership has to do with the brilliance of the deal, which lay in its simplicity. Roots did not have to create a marketing platform with many different elements to it because of the confidence in their product. The company simply needed to provide a quality product that would be enjoyed by both the athletes and the consumer and then let the exposure take care of itself. Some key elements that helped take the 2002 Roots partnership with Team USA to the next level are as follows.

Added Value of the Partnership: The added value that was created from the partnership between Team USA and Roots was enormous. Added value is difficult to gauge from a financial perspective, and in this case it is almost impossible. Added value is created from the exposure that is generated above and beyond the price of the sponsorship. In the case of Roots, it would be argued that the opening and closing ceremonies and the award stand exposure would not fall under added value, because it was exposure that Roots paid for in either cash or product (value in kind). However, the exposure that followed these events can be looked on as added value. The media coverage alone from an American perspective is priceless. It is almost impossible to add up the entirety of the exposure. One would have to collect every photo in every paper that ran a picture of anyone with Roots gear, along with every TV feature or highlight that showed Roots gear.

Guerilla Marketing: Guerilla marketing is defined by marketingterms.com as unconventional marketing intended to get maximum results from minimal resources. In Salt Lake City, Roots probably did not intend to have a guerilla affect on the marketplace, but it happened anyway. The company had millions of walking billboards because Americans had the opportunity to travel to the games. Consumers saw the gear that was being worn by not just celebrities but also by their neighbor who just returned from Salt Lake City, and this helped build the brand as a must-have product. As more fans purchased gear, the more the brand image spread across the country and became more popular. The consumers were building the Roots brand unknowingly.

Emotional Branding: Roots had an instant consumer base in the millions of Americans who traveled to Salt Lake City to watch the Games. Sports and sporting events are very emotional, and unlike other events, individuals instantly feel a sense of pride and will purchase those products that represent their country in the Olympics. The number of people that traveled to Salt Lake City and the Winter Olympic games was huge. Even without a solid product, Roots would have had consumers who would purchase their products, simply on the pride and emotion of representing their country. However, because of word of mouth and exposure, the sales numbers skyrocketed. This speaks volumes to the quality and design of the 2002 gear.

Pop Culture Effect: Few things affect style and fashion like pop culture. The beret and the 2002 Roots gear surged into pop culture. The beret itself became the hot item for celebrities and athletes. It wasn't just that celebrities were sporting the beret or other Roots gear—pop culture was also influenced by the amount of popular media coverage that featured the beret. The coverage that Roots was experiencing via several popular media outlets played a significant role in increasing the company's brand image. Stories of athletes offered hundreds of dollars for their beret or the six-hour-long lines at Roots stores all added to the lure and pop culture success. The more exclusive an item is, the more popular it becomes.

Celebrity Endorsers: Any outfitter that partners with a sport team will instantly have athlete endorsers. This is especially true for the Olympic games, because the team is large. However, in 2002 Roots developed a product that was well liked by the athletes, who wore the issued Roots gear even when not required to do so. This helped endorse the product to the consumers. As athletes were seen in the stands, in interviews, going to practice, or eating dinner around town, they were all celebrity endorsers of Roots gear. Other prominent figures were seen wearing Team USA Roots outfitting, including P. Diddy, Jay Leno, Katie Couric, and even President George W. Bush.

Post-Game Comments

- Roots continues to stay true to their motto of creating clothes for the active lifestyle that are comfortable, durable, and stylish.
- Roots has used their Olympics partnerships to help develop their brand to a global audience.
- The 2002 partnership with the U.S. Olympics team became a marketing platform that took the brand to new heights.
- The influence of media and pop culture helped drive awareness to the Roots brand.
- Understanding your product and how you can communicate your brand image to your consumer in the best way can be more successful than any marketing deal.

Web Resources

http://www.marketingterms.com/dictionary/g/
http://www.roots.com/new_canada/html/pc_company_profile.shtml
http://www.roots.com/new_canada/html/pc_OlyTimeLine.shtml
http://www.roots.com/new_canada/html/prod_collections.shtml

Additional Resources

Bennett, D. D. (1994). Shopping for sponsorships? Integration is paramount. *Brandweek, 35*(7), 18.

Drane, D., Phillips, D., Williams, A., & Crow, B. (2005). Sport celebrities as endorsers: An analysis of Tiger Woods. In B. G. Pitts (Ed.), *Where sport marketing theory meets practice: Selected papers from the Second Annual Conference of the Sport Marketing Association* (pp. 179–187). Morgantown, WV: Fitness Information Technology.

Kamins, M. A. (1990). An investigation into the "match-up" hypothesis in celebrity advertising; when beauty may be only skin deep. *Journal of Advertising, 19*(1) 4–13.

Macdonald, E., & Sharp, B. (2003). Management perceptions of the importance of brand awareness as an indication of advertising effectiveness. *Marketing Bulletin, 14*, article 2.

McCracken, G. (1989). Who is the celebrity endorser? Cultural foundations of the endorsement process. *Journal of Consumer Research, 16*(3), 310–321.

Rabon, L. (1998). *Roots behind the brand.* Retrieved April 7, 2009, from http://www.findarticles.com/p/articles/mi_m3638/is_n13_v39/ai_2111-1946/pg_2.

Rossiter J. R., & Percy L (1987). *Advertising and promotion management.* Singapore: McGraw-Hill.

Rossiter J. R., Percy, L., & Donovan, R. J. (1991). A better advertising planning grid. *Journal of Advertising Research, 31*(5), 11–21.

Stone, G., Joseph, M., & Jones, M. (2003). An exploratory study on the use of sports celebrities in advertising: A content analysis. *Sport Marketing Quarterly, 12*(2), 94–102.

Chapter 7

Under Armour: Protect This Brand!

Patrick Kraft,
Indiana University

Jason W. Lee,
University of North Florida

Fritz G. Polite,
University of Tennessee

Company: Under Armour
Location: Baltimore, MD
Internet Address: www.underarmour.com

Discussion Questions

- How will the creation of new product extensions impact the brand image of Under Armour?
- Now that Under Armour has become a power brand, what other large marketing initiatives (entering into large presenting sponsorships of events, spending more on TV advertising, or using elite athletes as endorsers) should be considered? Why?
- What effect will international expansion have on the brand in the United States?
- How will the Team Girl marketing campaign help develop or hinder the brand?
- How can Under Armour continue to lead and compete against its larger competitors in the industry like Nike, Adidas, and Reebok?
- What other creative initiatives could be on the horizon for Under Armour, like the impact of YouTube, text messaging, smart phones, TiVo, gaming advertisements, and so on?

The Line-Up

Brand marketing of sport products and apparel is an extremely competitive business. The company Under Armour has made a significant mark by developing and marketing its unique products. Their mission is: "To make all athletes better through passion, science and the relentless pursuit of innovation."

Under Armour (UA) strives to be a leader in development, marketing, and distributorship of branded apparel and accessories. UA has domestic offices in Baltimore and Denver, as well as international offices in Amsterdam, Toronto, Hong Kong, and Guangzhou, China. Their products are sold worldwide. The spectrum of use ranges from amateur to world-class elite athletes. UA is also experiencing positive profitability: in its 2008 first quarter report, net revenues increased 26.6 percent to $157.3 million, and apparel net revenues increased 24.6 percent to $129.2 million. This financial information indicates a positive performance, which can be associated with positive brand building as well as vertical brand extension.

Under Armour is no longer the new kid on the block and is building its market share, expanding its presence, and establishing its brand as a strong stimulus in the minds of consumers.

Timeline of Events

1996
- Kevin Plank develops his first microfiber T-shirt, designed to keep athletes dry during workouts and games.
- Plank founds Under Armour Athletic Apparel.
- College football powerhouses Georgia Tech and Arizona State purchase the gear, followed by NFL team the Atlanta Falcons.

1997
- Twelve NCAA Division I-A teams and ten NFL teams wear the gear.
- Under Armour makes its first appearance in the Super Bowl as the Green Bay Packers defeat the New England Patriots.

1998
- Under Armour strikes a deal with Sports Robe, the wardrobe and uniform provider for the Warner Bros. film *Any Given Sunday.*
- Under Armour signs a licensing deal with the NFL Europe League to become its official supplier of performance apparel.

1999

- Under Armour signs on with Eastbay catalog (circulation 7 million) and becomes the fastest-selling soft-good product in Eastbay history.
- Under Armour strikes a deal with Warner Bros. to supply gear for upcoming football movies.

2000

- Under Armour helps launch the XFL football league with a product contribution.
- Becomes official supplier to Major League Baseball, the National Hockey League, and USA Baseball.
- Under Armour wins *Business Week*'s "Small Business Under 30" Award, presented to the top business leaders nationwide under the age of thirty.
- The company wins the Sporting Goods Business Apparel Supplier of the Year, for an unprecedented fourth consecutive year.
- Under Armour also receives the Victor Award for the Best New Product Launch of the Year from The Sports Authority.

2002

- Under Armour wins The Sports Authority "Supplier of the Year."

2003

- The Women's Performance Gear product line is officially launched in retail outlets and on the company Web site.
- Under Armour begins running ads with a football "warrior" theme and the tag line, "We must protect this house!" (The company continues to use this tag line to this day.)

2005

- Under Armour releases its initial public offering. The stock had the second highest increase in share price ever for the first day of trading, debuting at $13 and doubling to close at just over $26 per share.
- *Business Journal*'s "40 under 40" Award is presented to Kevin Plank in 2005 (as well as 2006 and 2007).

2007

- Kevin Plank announces a new marketing strategy called "Team Girl," which will focus its efforts on female athletes.
- European headquarters in Amsterdam are up and running and creating an impact on the international market place. Internationally, Under Armour also has a strong market presence in the United Kingdom, Canada, Europe, Japan, Australia, New Zealand, and South Africa.

Building the House

Under Armour was created by Kevin Plank, a former collegiate athlete, who felt his needs and those of his teammates were not being met when it came to performance wear. Since the initial conceptualization, Plank has built a T-shirt company into a market share leader and in the process brought a fledgling and obscure market category into the forefront of consumer minds.

Plank was a University of Maryland football player who began as a walk-on fullback and, through hard work and determination, left as a full-scholarship athlete and captain of special teams. This same will, determination, and work ethic has been the backbone of one of the most successful apparel companies of all time. Under Armour's mission is to provide the world with technically advanced products engineered with superior fabric construction, exclusive moisture management, and proven innovation. In essence, every Under Armour product is meant to make life better for its users.

The Uncomfortable Cotton

While Plank was playing football, he felt that the workout gear the team was wearing could be enhanced. The cotton products that were being worn in all sports, not just football, were heavy when saturated in sweat and were not properly wicking perspiration away from the body. Plank felt this feeling of heaviness was having a significant negative mental affect on the athletes. He believed that if athletes could feel lighter, they would be more comfortable and would perform better. Understanding the importance of the mental aspect of competition, he believed a dry and light product would enhance the psyche of the athlete.

Plank's initial plan was to create a T-shirt that would work with each individual athlete's body type and training environment. He wanted a product that would help enhance performance by regulating body temperature, while keeping an athlete cool, dry, and light. He found it interesting that the tight-fitting compression shorts that the players wore kept them dry and comfortable, unlike the heavy cotton shirts. His search for similar material to that of the compression shorts lead him to the popular fabric polyester.

Letting the Product Develop the Brand

In the beginning, Under Armour faced the same challenges that any new company faces: how to develop their brand and generate awareness. The difference between Under Armour and most other new companies was that the marketplace was dominated by some of the most popular brands in the world. It was essential to create a unique marketing strategy because its budget was much smaller than that of its competitors. Under Armour used several marketing initiatives to develop their corporate brand image and target consumers. These marketing initiatives were strategically aligned with their overall corporate strategy. The primary methods used to rise above the clutter of an already crowded marketplace were:

- Athlete endorsement and product seeding
- Word of mouth
- Popular culture
- Product placement

It was essential to find a way to leverage the increased exposure that sport was garnering in the marketplace to Under Armour's advantage. It was essential that the company become creative marketing agents and find unique ways to break through the chaos to reach their target consumers.

Athlete Endorsement through Product Seeding

Plank knew that if he could get his new style of performance T-shirts in the hands of athletes, they could be used as marketing agents. Using athlete endorsers as marketing tools for brand development proved successful. Plank recruited several of his friends in college football and the NFL to use his product free of cost. He continued to use athletes as walking billboards by seeding the product to all who requested it.

Word of Mouth

Under Armour's method of seeding the product to the athletes helped increase word-of-mouth marketing. As more athletes wore product, a buzz of positive energy for the product surfaced in locker rooms across the country. Soon product requests were not just coming from Plank's initial marketing agents but from teammates of these agents.

Infusion of Pop Culture and Buzz Marketing

Under Armour had a hip, fresh look to it that was exactly what the consumer desired. There were similar products in the marketplace, but nothing carried with it the feeling and attitude of Under Armour. The popularity and uniqueness of the look and feel of the product became an attractive element in the brand development process and made Under Armour a "buzzworthy" commodity.

Product Placement

With a marketing budget that would not come close to denting that of their competitors, it became essential that Under Armour leverage any opportunities they could to attract their target market. The technique of product (or brand) placement has grown significantly over the past decade, especially due to the increased success of nontraditional media outlets like video games and YouTube. This can be seen by the rapid growth of the product placement industry, which according to Soar (2007), was worth $3.6 billion in 2006 and should reach $9 billion by the end of the decade. Marketers now frequently use product placement as a vehicle for organic brand growth. Creative advertising campaigns include multiple marketing methods aimed at reaching the consumers who do not sit through commercials. Involvement around the action of the game, infield signage, or computer-enhanced signage has become very valuable.

Under Armour started to infuse their products in popular TV shows and movies. This placement helped feature the product in the mainstream and allowed the brand to reach out to a larger market. Prominent examples of Under Armour's visibility in movies and television are provided in Exhibits 7.1 and 7.2.

Exhibit 7.1 Movies in Which Under Armour Is Featured
- *Bad News Bears*
- *Dodgeball*
- *Grid Iron Gang*
- *Fantastic Four*
- *Friday Night Lights*
- *Game Plan*
- *I Now Pronounce You Chuck and Larry*
- *Million Dollar Baby*
- *Mr. 3000*

Exhibit 7.2 Television Programs in Which Under Armour Is Featured

- *The Amazing Race*
- *The Apprentice*
- *Clubhouse*
- *Friday Night Lights*
- *MTV's The Inferno*
- *Playmakers*
- *Real World/Road Rules Challenge*
- *Two-A-Days*
- *The Today Show* (Matt Lauer segment in Antarctica)

The Final Score

Founder Kevin Plank's early strategy of letting the product develop itself through marketing initiatives like athlete endorsement, product seeding, word-of-mouth marketing, popular culture, and product placement successfully developed the Under Armour brand image in the eyes of the consumers. As the company has continued to grow in market share, stature, and revenue, the use of more traditional marketing methods like TV advertisement, team sponsorship deals (in-field signage, promotional elements), in-game TV sponsorships, and title sponsorships for events (i.e., High School All-American football game) or entire sport organizations (B.A.S.S. fishing) have become supplementary marketing platforms. Under Armour has branched out into the world of outdoor and hunting apparel. Through all of this, Plank has not deviated from his original concept of developing a product that would help make all athletes, amateur to professional, feel good about themselves when being active.

Under Armour has created waves within the marketplace by exploring nontraditional methods of marketing and branding techniques. Focusing on corporate responsibility, values, and superior technology, the company has entrenched its products as viable competitors among the sport apparel giants. The company's long-term growth predictions indicate high expectations.

Exhibit 7.3

"At Under Armour, we have a culture of growth balanced with a culture of profitability. As we map out the future growth of this brand, we will continue to make the appropriate level of investment in our team and our infrastructure while continuously striving towards greater operational execution."

—Wayne Marino, COO of Under Armour

Under Armour is forcing the competition to rethink their traditional marketing and branding plans. Time will tell whether it is fully able to capture a significant portion of the market and maintain it within an extremely competitive industry.

Post-Game Comments

- Under Armour has maintained its brand image from its inception. The target consumer is the athlete that desires a product that is lighter, faster, stronger, and better.
- Kevin Plank took a niche product and developed it into a market share leader.
- Under Armour believed their product was exactly what the athlete wants, so they let the product speak for itself.
- Under Armour used creative marketing methods to develop the brand, including athlete endorsement by product seeding, word-of-mouth marketing, leveraging pop culture, and product placement.
- The use of Plank's athlete endorsers as marketing agents for the brand helped build credibility in the locker room, which led to an increase in exposure.
- Under Armour became increasingly mainstream using product in movies and TV programs.
- The influence of media and pop culture helped drive awareness of the Under Armour brand.
- The company is a testament that it doesn't take the most intricate marketing strategies or huge budgets to be successful; it is understanding your product and how to communicate the company's brand image to the consumer.

Web Resources

http://investor.underarmour.com/investors.cfm
http://sports.espn.go.com/espn/print?id=1831396&type=story#
http://www.bizjournals.com/baltimore/stories/2003/11/03/newscolumn1.html

http://www.bizjournals.com/baltimore/stories/2005/08/22/daily4.html
http://www.brandchannel.com/brandcameo_films.asp
http://www.fibersource.com/f-info/More_News/nyt-032104.htm
http://www.fundinguniverse.com/company-histories/Under-Armour-Performance-Apparel-Company-History.html
http://www.gobros.com/under-armour/under-armour-history.php
http://www.uabiz.com/releasedetail.cfm?RelcaseID=227809
http://www.underarmour.com

Additional Resources

Salter, C. (2005, August). Protect this house. *Fast Company, 97,* 70.

Soar, M. (2007, April 23). The mysterious relationship between advertisers and movies. West End Chronical (Montreal, Quebec, Canada). Retrieved April 3, 2009, from http://www.westendchronicle.com/article-97559-The-mysterious-relationship-between-advertisers-and-movies.html.

Part II

Sport Properties, Leagues, and Events

Chapter 8

The Harlem Globetrotters: A Truly Global Brand

Steven N. Waller,
University of Tennessee

Fritz G. Polite,
University of Tennessee

Company: The Harlem Globetrotters International
Location: Phoenix, AZ
Internet Address: www.harlemglobetrotters.com

Discussion Questions

- How did the Harlem Globetrotters originate?
- What is the primary focus of the HGI company?
- What characteristics are associated with the brand?
- What are the unique distinctions of HGI?

The Line-Up

Branding is considered one of the most critical elements in influencing whether a product will fail or flourish. Brand reflects an image or personality that helps distinguish and define a product that constitutes value and solicits a stimulus in the mind of the consumer. The Harlem Globetrotters International (HGI) has maximized their brand value and identity on an international scope. Because of its strong global brand presence, companies have realized the positive attributes being associated with events featuring HGI.

The Harlem Globetrotters are recognized as one of the most popular teams in the history of sports. With their unique brand of basketball and entertainment, the Globetrotters have been referred to as America's Ambassadors of Goodwill. They are one of only six teams to have been inducted into the Naismith Memorial Basketball Hall of Fame in Springfield, Massachusetts. This groundbreaking team has played in over 120 countries, en route to being the most traveled sports team in the world. Having recorded over 22,000 wins since their inception as the Savoy Five in Chicago, Illinois, in 1920, the Globetrotters brand has continued to flourish through the team's style of play and family entertainment for over seventy-five years. This case study examines the historical significance of HGI, the methods that have been incorporated toward its longevity, and the framework of the establishment of the brand.

Timeline of Events

1927
  • The Globetrotters play their first game in Hinckley, Illinois.
1937
  • Participate in the World Professional Basketball Tournament.
1939
  • The Globetrotters begin to develop routines to highlight the players' skills.
1948
  • Defeat the NBA World Champion Minneapolis Lakers.
1950
  • Chuck Cooper (Globetrotter) becomes the first black player drafted by the NBA.
  • The Globetrotters embark on their first European tour.
1951
  • Twenty-fifth anniversary includes game in Brazil (50,000 spectators).
  • Return to Europe and drew 75,000 (Berlin, Germany).
1952
  • First around-the-world tour, 108 games.
1966
  • Abe Saperstein (founder) dies.
1969
  • Team plays 9,500 career games.
1976
  • Macromedia acquires the Globetrotters.

1986
- International Broadcasting Corporation acquires the Globetrotters.

1993
- Mannie Jackson acquires the Globetrotters for $6 million.

2003
- The Globetrotters win their 21,000th game.

2007
- Last living original Globetrotter (Tony Peyton) dies.

Building the History and the Brand

The Harlem Globetrotters history is one of a rich legacy of changes, adaptations, and resurgence. The beginnings of the organization started on the South Side of Chicago. In the 1920s, many Midwestern cities held basketball games prior to large dances. The players who performed before such dances at the Savoy Ballroom in Chicago became known as the Savoy Big Five. Several of the players left the team due to a dispute and formed the Globe Trotters. Ultimately, the name was consolidated to *Globetrotters*. The team's founder, Abe Saperstein, decided to choose Harlem as the team's namesake because of its strong presence as a mecca for sports, music, and culture.

Several players were instrumental in laying the foundation for the longevity of the organization, as well as many of the current practices. Albert "Runt" Pullins was an excellent shooter as well as dribbler, and Inman Jackson was a superb athlete who had a unique charisma. Such individuals were at the center of the intricate weaves and formations that the world has become familiar with today and laid the groundwork for what is now known as the showman.

The original Globetrotters were definitely about fun and games. They were extremely competitive, and only when leading would they begin to improvise. The Globetrotters participated in the World Professional Basketball Tournament in 1937 against their eventual archrivals, the New York Rens. During this time, both teams were considered powerhouses stocked with talented players. The Globetrotters defeated the Rens the following year and eventually were crowned champions. They also beat the Minneapolis Lakers two years in a row. This was a monumental win for the Globetrotters and proved to the world that they were a legitimate elite competitive team. This game was also significant because the all-black Globetrotters defeated the all-white Lakers and began the transition toward breaking the color barrier in the National Basketball League (prior to the formation of the NBA). Chuck Cooper became the first black player drafted by an NBA team, and many credit the Globetrotters with assisting in this process.

The Globetrotters eventually expanded the entertainment aspects of their business by infusing comic routines into the game and incorporating high levels of passing, shots, and dribbling exhibitions. Skillful ball handling, juggling, and intricate trick shots were also a signature of the new Globetrotters.

Saperstein began to develop the notion of two teams of Globetrotters: one competitive and the other entertainment. Not only would it allow him to corner two methods of delivering the product, it was also a great way to double profits. Many of the players would alternate between the competition team and the show team. Some of these players went on to NBA Hall of Fame-level careers, including Connie "The Hawk" Hawkins, Nat "Sweetwater" Clifton, Wilt "The Stilt" Chamberlin, and Marques Haynes. Interestingly, Baseball Hall of Famers Bob Gibson, Ferguson Jenkins, and Lou Brock were all Globetrotters as well.

Transforming and Marketing the Brand

During World War II, several players were drafted, which greatly depleted the talent level of the team. Another factor was the lack of resources available to them. Gas rationing created challenges for the team because they traveled by bus or car. Saperstein was resourceful enough to begin touring military bases and donating proceeds to the war effort. This was a brilliant way to continue to tour while establishing a positive connection to the community and service members. As the team was more positively received, Saperstein began to elevate the amount of travel, along with extending the reach. Most of the military bases would provide complimentary food and sometimes assist with travel and lodging arrangements.

In 1950, the Globetrotters began to entrench themselves as international sport spectacles and introduced a unique form of basketball to the world. The Globetrotters embarked on their first European tour in 1950, playing in Portugal, Switzerland, Germany, France, Belgium, England, and Italy. The organization celebrated its twenty-fifth anniversary in 1951 and embarked on a South American tour. The Globetrotters played in front of more than 50,000 in Rio de Janeiro, Brazil. They also played in front of 75,000 in Berlin's Olympic Stadium. In 1952, they took their first world tour, consisting of 108 games in a multitude of countries.

In 1966, the Trotters were extremely active in numerous media outlets. They appeared on several TV talk shows, including the *Steve Allen Show*, the *ABC*

Hollywood Palace, CBS's *Omnibus*, and the *Late Late Show*. They were regulars on the popular *Ed Sullivan Show*, appearing six times, and were contracted by CBS to telecast a premier production of one game per year.

The Globetrotters drew high TV ratings and were a popular choice for TV executives. They played before two popes and at military posts, including Alaska, North Africa, India, Pakistan, and Tasmania. They also ventured into Bulgaria, Romania, Hungary, Yugoslavia, Czechoslovakia, Poland, Germany, France, Sweden, Portugal, and Austria. The Globetrotters were the first sports organization to play at the New York World's Fair.

Saperstein was the central figure in booking and reconciling contracts for many years. He also made several poor decisions that greatly impacted the Globetrotters. He invested heavily in the short-lived American Basketball League. The league folded, and he took a heavy financial loss. He invested in several musicals and vaudeville acts. He lost focus on the Globetrotters and concentrated on expanding show business ventures. He financed an overseas tour of the Ice Capades that failed miserably. At the same time these financial woes were occurring, the Globetrotters were also having other setbacks. Their talent had been depleted by professional leagues, European leagues, and aging veterans. The financial health of the Globetrotters was weakening. Saperstein died in March 1966. On June 8, 1967, the Trotters were sold for $3.71 million to a trio of businessmen.

The Globetrotters entered the early 1970s with a renewed purpose. They were attracting record crowds and recorded over 2 million in attendance for the first time. They also became the first sports team to have its own network TV series. *The Harlem Globetrotters Show* drew impressive ratings and reached audiences in over thirty countries. The Globetrotters played a single game that was broadcast via satellite and viewed by 900 million people in China. The owners obtained the team when it was at a low point and saw a great opportunity to sell while the product was hot. In 1976 they were sold to Macromedia, Inc.

During the 1980s, the Globetrotters were the first sports team to be honored with a square on the Hollywood Walk of Fame. The Smithsonian Institute recognized the Globetrotters as an important part of American social history. In 1986, the team was sold again to International Broadcasting Corporation. The sale of the Globetrotters to IBC proved to be detrimental to the organization. IBC was unfamiliar with the brand and was not in tune with the booking aspects of the Globetrotters. The team was poorly marketed, player talent levels diminished, and the organization declined. IBC was large and not focused on the day-to-day operations of the team. Furthermore, they were experiencing financial difficulties and filed for bankruptcy in 1993.

Mannie Jackson, a former Globetrotter and corporate executive with Honeywell, eventually bought the Globetrotters for $6 million. Jackson was determined to bring the magic back to the storied franchise. His strategic plan centered around history, brand, and excellence. The team was to be rebranded based on the original product and marketed to its fullest potential. The Globetrotters flourished under his direction and began to partner with major global sponsors, including Disney and Walt Disney's Wide World of Sports, Reebok International, FUBU, Denny's, Western Union, Burger King, and several other major corporate giants. Jackson further extended the brand by creating Globetrotters Properties, the parent company's personal licensing and merchandising firm responsible for designing, managing, and marketing the production of Globetrotters branded merchandise. These changes galvanized the franchise and brought the team to new heights.

The Final Score

The Globetrotters were formed and centered on branding, marketing, and showmanship from the team's initial inception. Historically, this has been the foundation of their success. There are few sport organizations that can boast of the history, accomplishments, travels, and social impact that the Globetrotters have had on our society. The challenge remains as to how the company will meet the changing scope of media format within a changing global environment. The challenge of maintaining brand market presence will be the next frontier.

The Harlem Globetrotters have a rich and storied tradition. From humble beginnings to its current status, the organization has maintained a unique brand presence on a global platform. By using a combination of showmanship and elite athleticism, the Globetrotters have enlightened the world to the game of basketball. They continue to be the global leader in entertainment and competitive play. They were instrumental in many of the styles of basketball played around the world. Their appeal reaches multiple spans of the globe and crosses multicultural boundaries. They bridge and connect people, societies, cultures, and countries. The Harlem Globetrotters are truly remarkable phenomena in sports entertainment and the world.

Post-Game Comments

- HGI is an example of sport organization that has evolved and maintains its global brand presence.
- HGI has been able to maintain and expand its product lines even in difficult times.

- HGI is posed to meet the challenges of the new millennium by continuing to build on over seventy-five years of success by focusing on new markets while continuing to perform in existing markets.

Web Resources

http://www.fundinguniverse.com/company-histories/Harlem-Globetrotters-
    International-Inc-Company-History.html
http://www.harlemglobetrotters.com/history/globetrotters
http://www.internationalhero.co.uk/s/supglobe.htm
http://www.pbs.org/pov/pov2005/hardwood/special_overview.html

Additional Resources

Eitzen, D. S., & Sage, H. H. (2003). *Sociology of North American Sport* (7th ed.). New York: McGraw-Hill.

Chapter 9

Montgomery Biscuits: Rising to the Top of Minor League Brands

Jason W. Lee,
University of North Florida

Team: Montgomery Biscuits (AA Tampa Bay Rays Affiliate)
Location: Montgomery, AL
Internet Address: www.biscuitsbaseball.com

Discussion Questions

- What were your initial thoughts on hearing of a team named the "Biscuits?" Did you initially think it was a good choice? After reading the chapter, what are your thoughts?
- What are the advantages/disadvantages to picking such a unique and quirky name?
- What are some other similar sport examples of teams with quirky names? Which of these do you consider to be successful, and which are failures? Why?

The Line-Up

The Montgomery Biscuits are not a typical sport franchise. Though this team's branding is similar to that of any other successful business, the organization has taken concentrated branding efforts and mixed them with the fun and appeal of being involved with sport. This AA Southern League affiliate of the Tampa Bay Rays has thrived by launching a campaign aimed at building a unique image and a strong visual identity. The team's unique name and images, aligned with the organization's focus to provide a quality product, has allowed the Biscuits to be a model minor league sports organization. The attention to branding detail and a mission to offer a fun product have helped spark consumer affinity for this team with a funny name.

Timeline of Events

2003
- The Southern League unanimously approves relocating the Orlando Rays to Montgomery.
- The organization reveals their team name through a contest at Montgomery's annual Jubilee Cityfest.
- Construction begins on Riverwalk Stadium.
- The Biscuits unveil their uniforms.

2004
- The Biscuits play their first game.

2006
- The Biscuits play the MAX Southern League All-Star Game before 7,454 fans at Riverwalk Stadium.
- The Biscuits clinch their first postseason berth in franchise history.
- Biscuits win Southern League championship.
- Selected as MiLB's AA Team of Year.

2007
- Biscuits win Southern League championship for second straight year.
- Once again selected as MiLB's AA Team of Year.

Origins of the Biscuits

The husband-and-wife duo of Tom Dickson and Sherrie Myers have built a reputation for being two of the most successful owners in minor league baseball through ownership ventures including the Lansing Lugnuts and the Charleston Alley Cats. In 2003, they purchased the AA Orlando Rays franchise through their holding company, the Professional Sports Marketing. After purchasing the Rays, the team moved to Montgomery, which was the largest city in the United States without any type of professional sports team.

How Did They Get that Name?

In early 2003, the franchise decided to hold a "name the team" contest and local citizens were encouraged to submit their ideas. Eager to repeat the success of their sister team in Michigan, the Lansing Lugnuts, the ownership was looking for a distinctively unique and fun team name. The culmination of the naming contest resulted in three names being selected as finalists from a pool of over 3,500 entries. The three contest finalists were:

• Mockingbirds
• Yellowhammers (the state bird of Alabama)
• Biscuit Eaters

Looking for something fun, the decision makers were drawn to the "Biscuit Eaters" option. The name was shortened to "Biscuits," and the rest is history.

When the team name was initially announced, their introduction was met with absolute silence. Fortunately for them, the organization was prepared for such a reaction and was geared up to face their critics.

Having gone through a similar situation in Lansing, the ownership knew that the name was going to catch people by surprise, and the team was prepared to answer some questions. Some people initially did not like the name because they were used to the more traditional options, including names that were submitted as potential choices like the Senators (Montgomery is the capital of Alabama) or something more run-of-the-mill like the Tigers. Many people felt that the quirky name was making fun of the South, although the actual concept was to celebrate the South. Nonetheless, the organization initially received substantial negative reactions (roughly 200 per day), but once people saw the logo and the retail merchandise, there was a shift toward understanding how much fun the new team name and image could be. This allowed for image concerns to change rather quickly.

The name Biscuits was selected for a multitude of reasons. Obviously, it is unique and attention-grabbing. It was also seen as an item that is representative of the Deep South. The organization viewed the name as being campy, quirky, and playful and realized that it could be used in a variety of ways. After having some preliminary logos drawn up, they knew it could work.

Making It Happen at the Ballpark:
Keys to Continued Success

The Biscuits organization as a whole understands that all the terrific branding efforts are nice, but they will not work if there are not able to deliver the goods. They want the fan experience to be great, regardless of the point of contact, whether it is calling for tickets, visiting the Biscuit Basket (the team's retail store), or coming to a game.

The organizational philosophy that drives the Biscuits is basic but effective. Serving as the backbone of the organization, the mission is "to provide affordable, innovative entertainment and positively outrageous service while building a lasting relationship with [their] community" (see Figure 9.1 in the image insert).

The Biscuits want their customers to feel that they are getting a product. This is evident in the team's approach to ticket sales. They do not want to take part in activities and gimmicks that see as discounting their brand. As stated in their mission, they seek to provide "inexpensive family entertainment." The team started out pricing tickets from $6 to $10 and remained firm on what they set out as a fair price. They never discount those prices, as is often the case for sport tickets. They see such practices as something that is problematic, citing that it has been the downfall of not only sports teams but businesses all over. They feel that this teaches customers that their product is not worth the asking price and it is better to wait until they are put "on sale."

Exhibit 9.1

Family, Entertainment, Community, Value, and Professional—these are the five words that Marla Terranova, Director of Sponsorships and Marketing of Montgomery Biscuits feels best describes the image of the Biscuits (Lee, 2007, p. 52).

The Biscuits have had a variety of positive impacts on the city of Montgomery. Riverwalk Stadium provides a venue where families, church groups, businesses, and other groups can come for a fun-filled experience.

The presence of the Biscuits was also an integral part of the Montgomery downtown revitalization. Among the developments are the construction of a river walk, new condominiums, and a new hotel. The Biscuits like to point out that ballpark was the first project to bring people downtown and it has shown people that the area is safe and on the rise.

The Biscuits seek to have a visible image in the community through various community relations initiatives. These activities are highlighted by the philanthropic arm of the organization, Biscuit Charities. Through Biscuit Charities, the team partners with five nonprofit organizations each season. Among the activities in this initiative are community events such as the March of Dimes Walk-a-thon, the Lions Club, and certified speakers on domestic violence awareness to assist the Family Sunshine Center.

The Final Score

Recognizing that branding involves the sum of all feelings and emotions that consumers have regarding a sport product, the Montgomery Biscuits have taken efforts to establish strong brand identify in virtually all facets of the organization. They see these efforts as something that needs to go beyond just a name or a logo.

The Biscuits see branding as one of the most important elements in the development and ongoing operation of a business. Benefiting from the fact that baseball franchises provide fertile ground where numerous brand extensions can exist, they have tapped into the notion that branding is influential in determining outcomes—for instance, is someone willing to try a product; how much is someone willing to pay for a product; why will someone remain loyal to a product; or why one product is chosen over another? This organization sees branding as a determining factors in the ultimate success or failure their business or any business for that matter.

The Biscuits' focus has been based on the company's mission. The mission and the associated mission statement should convey organizational strategies and objectives. This is extremely important for new organizations. The team felt they could have a major impact through the selection of the brand name. Before picking the name, the organization looked at various criteria that they wanted to address regarding what image to convey. In selecting the name, they choices were primarily focused on key elements including:

- Wanting to be completely unique
- Seeking to represent the campy, quirky nature of minor league baseball
- Wishing to be representative of Montgomery and the South
- Desiring to appeal to broad spectrum of customers (from kids to senior citizens)

Selecting the name *Biscuits* has worked masterfully for the organization. One advantage of having such a unique name is the ease of recognition for the team and its associated images, for example, situations where people have seen (or may see) imagery of the Montgomery Biscuits and want to know more about them.

Viewers who look at Riverwalk Stadium, the Biscuits Web site, or any of the promotional material produced by the team should realize the forethought that has been put into branding efforts. The imagery and marks of the Biscuits are omnipresent in such venues. For example, the logos and other imagery that are found at Riverfront stadium include:

- The name Biscuits on seemingly anything that is large enough to fit the word on it
- The Biscuits logo is even on the drain covers on the ground
- The script B logo
- Monte (the biscuit character on print and video media)
- Biscuits to eat provided by sponsor Mary B's Biscuits
- ALAGA Syrup (another sponsor) to go on the biscuits.

The distinctive name has also allowed for a variety of unique marketing endeavors. The Biscuits have benefited from eye-catching and amusing advertising and promotional campaigns. As Terranova puts it, the "puns are never ending" (Lee, 2007, p. 51), and these allow for association in the creative process that have led to campaigns such as:

- History in the Baking (inaugural season theme)
- Biscuits Ala Carte (single game ticket campaign)
- Whole Lotta Biscuits—Very Little Dough (season ticket campaign)
- The Biscuit Basket (the team retail store)

A further benefit associated with the name and images has been phenomenal merchandise sales. The Biscuits are one of the highest-selling brands in the minor leagues. Because of the uniqueness of the name, people get excited about the merchandise, and this interest has allowed the Biscuits to be firmly placed in the top ten in retail sales among all minor league baseball teams. To date, the Biscuits have filled Internet orders for merchandise in all fifty states and eleven different countries.

As Marla Terranova explained: "It has been exciting to see people embrace the Biscuits ... The Biscuit Basket is about more than just T-shirts and hats— they really do have something for everybody there, and they get new merchandise constantly, keeping fans coming back" (Lee, 2007, p. 51).

Post-Game Comments

- The Montgomery Biscuits have been extremely successful in establishing a unique image and strong visual identity.
- The organization has benefited from having a unique name and image.
- The Biscuits organization appreciates and enacts strong branding practices while realizing the importance of offering a good product.
- The Biscuits are focused on providing quality and fun and see themselves as being more in the world of entertainment than in sport business.
- Initially, the reaction to the new name was not good. The organization was prepared for such a reaction and enacted a proactive plan to deal with potential concerns.
- Seeking to provide "inexpensive family entertainment," the Biscuits offer affordable ticket prices, but do not discount their set prices; they do not want customers to feel that their product is not worth the asking price.
- The distinctive name has also allowed for a variety of unique marketing endeavors, including eye-catching and humorous advertising and promotional campaigns.
- The Biscuits are one of the highest selling brands in the minor leagues, placing in the top ten in retail sales among all teams.

Web Resources

http://www.biscuitsbaseball.com/bischist.html
http://www.biscuitsbaseball.com/stadium.html
http://www.biscuitsbaseball.com/store.html

Additional Resources

Frazier, M. (2004, May 13). *Branding the Biscuits.* Montgomery Ad Federation, Montgomery, AL.

Lee, J. W. (2007). Insider's perspective: Marla Terranova, director of sponsorships and marketing—Montgomery Biscuits, Tampa Bay Devil Ray AA affiliate. The *SMART Journal*, 3(2), 50–53. Available at http://www.thesmartjournal.com/IP-Biscuits.pdf.

Chapter 10

The National Hot Rod Association: A Brand on the Fast Track to Success

Andrea N. Eagleman,
Indiana University

Organization: The National Hot Rod Association (NHRA)
Location: Glendora, CA
Internet Address: www.nhra.com

Discussion Questions

- In what ways has the NHRA grown since its inception in 1951?
- What growth challenges might the NHRA face in the coming years?
- How has the NHRA built its brand image?
- How can the NHRA sustain this brand image in the future?
- What other sponsors might the NHRA target to continue increasing its range of fans?
- What can the NHRA do to respond to its critics and move closer to NASCAR in terms of popularity?

The Line-Up

The National Hot Rod Association (NHRA) began in southern California in 1951 with the purpose of moving drag racing from the streets to safer race tracks. It has grown into a nationally recognized brand through securing highly recognizable sponsors, TV contracts, a capable and experienced staff, a diverse stable of drivers, and a sense of history and culture.

The NHRA has grown from an organization that hosted one national event in 1955 to one that now hosts twenty-four national events in twenty-two cities across the United States every year and is the largest auto racing organization in the world, with 80,000 members and over 35,000 licensed competitors. How has this organization grown so much in its fifty-five years of existence?

Timeline of Events

1951
- Wally Parks forms the National Hot Rod Association to help legitimate the sport of drag racing and implement safety rules and performance standards. Parks becomes the organization's first president.

1953
- The first official NHRA race is held in the parking lot of the Los Angeles County Fairgrounds in Pomona, CA. Today, this racetrack continues to host annual national events.

1960
- NHRA begins publishing a weekly magazine titled *National Dragster*.

1963
- The U.S. Nationals is covered on ABC's *Wide World of Sports*, making it the first NHRA event to be shown on national television.

1974
- R.J. Reynolds Tobacco announces its sponsorship of the NHRA national drag racing series, set to begin in 1975.

1993
- NHRA is officially recognized by the FIA World Motorsports Council, and the FIA Drag Racing Commission is developed.

1995
- NHRA becomes the first major auto racing sanctioning body to develop a Web site.

1998
- The NHRA Motorsports Museum is opened in Pomona, CA.

2000
- NHRA and ESPN reach five-year multimedia agreement, which is the largest in drag racing history.

2001
- The NHRA Championship Drag Racing Series gets a new title sponsor in Coca-Cola's POWERade brand.

2003
- NHRA is named the best value for the money in an independent survey conducted by *Street & Smith's Sports Business Journal*, ranking higher than fifteen other sports franchises, including the NFL, MLB, NBA, and NASCAR.

2004
- Men's cologne manufacturer Brut signs on as an official sponsor of the NHRA.

2005
- Motel 6 becomes the official motel of the NHRA, a deal that extends through the 2007 season.
- NHRA signs a five-year deal with ESPN2 to broadcast all of its national events.

2006
- Harley-Davidson enters its first major sports sponsorship, becoming the official motorcycle of the NHRA.

2007
- NHRA unveils the "Countdown to the Championship" playoff format points system, similar to NASCAR's "Chase for the Nextel Cup."

What Is the National Hot Rod Association?

Formed in 1951 in southern California with the intent of getting drag racing off the streets and onto safer race tracks, the National Hot Rod Association (NHRA) is the largest motorsports organization in the world. It has over 80,000 members and 35,000 licensed competitors. Though the most visible NHRA drag racing involves the four professional classes of Top Fuel, Funny Car, Pro Stock, and Pro Stock Motorcycle, there are many other categories of racing in which licensed competitors may compete. For example, the NHRA Jr. Drag Racing League allows children between the ages of eight and seventeen to race at tracks across the country.

This chapter focuses on the NHRA in terms of its professional categories of drag racing, specifically the NHRA POWERade Drag Racing Series. The series has been in existence since 1975, when Winston was the first title sponsor of the (then) eight-race series. In 2001, Coca-Cola's POWERade brand took over as the official sponsor of the NHRA Drag Racing Series. There are now twenty-four national events held annually in twenty-two cities around the United States from February to November. Drivers earn points at the first eighteen events based on their finishing place, and the top ten drivers in each category advance to the next level of the "Countdown to the Championship." The top ten drivers compete in the final six events for the POWERade Championship. At the end of the season, four NHRA POWERade Drag Racing Series champions are crowned. The national events draw over 2 million fans to racetracks each year.

Building the Brand through National Exposure

Through its ever-increasing sponsorships and TV contracts, the NHRA continues to build its brand. Before POWERade, the title sponsor of the NHRA Drag Racing Series was Winston cigarettes, which aligned the NHRA brand with unhealthiness, a lower- to middle-class audience, and a very masculine "gearhead" image. With the replacement of Winston with Coca Cola's POWERade brand as the title sponsor in 2001, the brand image has shifted to one of a fun and family-friendly organization and has helped the NHRA reach a broader audience than traditional motorsports fans. In a 2004 interview published in *Street & Smith's Sports Business Journal*, NHRA President Tom Compton was quoted as saying, "We're working on awareness. One of the biggest things we did to try to attack that is to land the Coca-Cola and POWERade brands."

Since the addition of Coca-Cola and POWERade, the NHRA has signed many other nontraditional motorsports sponsors. Whereas in the early days most sponsors were automotive aftermarket businesses, the NHRA has now broadened its stable of sponsors with names such as the U.S. Army, Motel 6, Budweiser, UPS, and Harley-Davidson. All of these sponsorships have helped the NHRA gain exposure with audiences that had no previous awareness of the league.

An independent survey conducted by *Street & Smith's Sports Business Journal* in 2003 showed that the NHRA is not only signing more high-profile sponsors but also satisfying them. The NHRA ranked first in the category of best value for the money in terms of sponsorship, beating out high-profile leagues such as Major League Baseball, the National Football League, the National Basketball Association, and NHRA's chief rival, NASCAR.

In addition to the exposure the league has gained through its high-profile sponsors, it has also gained national recognition for its events, which take place in twenty-two different U.S. cities each year. From the West Coast to the East Coast and several cities in between, there is a national event held within driving distance of many families' homes in the United States (see Figure 10.1 in the image insert).

For those fans that cannot travel to the track but enjoy watching drag racing on television, the league entered into a TV broadcast deal with ESPN and

ESPN2 in 2000. In 2005, this deal was extended with ESPN2 for an additional five years, and all national events receive same-day televised coverage, though it is rarely live coverage. Additionally, a high-definition telecast on ESPN2 HD was offered for the first time with this new deal.

In the Pits: A Unique Fan Experience

A major building block of the NHRA's brand is a unique aspect that no other motorsport or professional sporting league offers: access to a behind-the-scenes look at the event for every fan. Every ticket that is purchased for an NHRA national event also serves as a pit pass. Fans are able to walk through the pits and watch all of the professional teams' crews and drivers work on the cars, and many drivers hand out free "hero cards" featuring a picture of the driver and the race car, which they will autograph for the fans. This experience allows children and adults to meet their heroes. The pits also provide access to sponsor promotions, merchandise tents, and food and drink vendors. In a sport where there can sometimes be long delays between races because of inclement weather or car malfunctions, the all-access pit pass can keep fans at the track and engaged until the racing resumes.

The NHRA's Diverse Group of Drivers

The NHRA professional drivers are an increasingly diverse group, providing the league with a greater opportunity to attract a broader fan base than the traditional core group of motorsports fans. Among the drivers attracting this broader fan base are women, minorities, and younger drivers. In 1977, Shirley Muldowney paved the way for women drivers to be taken seriously in the league when she became the first woman to win the Top Fuel Championship. Now drivers like Melanie Troxel, Ashley Force, Angelle Sampey, and Erica Enders are helping increase female interest in the sport.

In terms of minorities, African American drivers J. R. Todd and Antron Brown are impacting the league. In 2006, his rookie season, twenty-four-year-old Todd won three national events and finished eighth in the Top Fuel points standings, followed by two wins in 2007. Brown, a nine-year veteran Pro Stock Motorcycle driver, has a high-profile sponsorship with the U.S. Army and finished second in the 2006 standings. The NHRA's diverse group of drivers helps the league target a wider variety of fans instead of limiting itself to the everyday car enthusiast.

Remembering its Roots

Along with the league's diverse group of drivers, the NHRA also has strong ties to its roots. Several past stars of the league are now team owners or make frequent appearances at the national events, like "Big Daddy" Don Garlits, Shirley Muldowney, Don "The Snake" Prudhomme, and Joe Amato. By staying actively involved in the league, these drag racing legends help strengthen the NHRA brand and give it a sense of historical pride.

Along with the rich history of past drivers still involved with the league, the one symbol of the NHRA's roots that is present at every race is "The Wally" trophy, which is given to the winner of each event. The trophy is referred to by this name in commemoration of the league's founder, Wally Parks, who now serves as the chairman of the Wally Parks NHRA Motorsports Museum. Additionally, the national headquarters has remained in Southern California, where the league was founded.

A Vision for the Future

While the NHRA has built a strong brand, the league continues to make changes to ensure its future growth. In 2007, the NHRA unveiled a new play-off-style points system similar to NASCAR's Chase for the Nextel Cup. By implementing the Countdown to the Championship, the NHRA hopes to target more casual fans and an even broader base of sponsors. Although NHRA officials do not enjoy the comparisons to NASCAR's playoff system, it is a difficult comparison to avoid, especially since NASCAR is the most popular motorsport among fans in the United States and NHRA's biggest rival in the sport industry.

With its new format for the 2007 season, the NHRA faced some of its critics who felt that changes were necessary for the league to move to the next level and reach the popularity of NASCAR. Some critics have suggested that the league move its national offices to a large city like New York and broadcast all races live rather than on tape delay.

The Final Score

The NHRA organization has experienced a significant amount of growth in its existence. The NHRA has built a nationally recognized brand that is known for its fan-friendliness, easy fan access to drivers, and a strong sense of history and culture through securing well-known sponsors and TV contracts, as well as holding national events across the nation.

The NHRA has worked hard to secure sponsorships with companies who provide a broader range of appeal than the automotive aftermarket. In aligning itself with well-known brands such as Coca-Cola, POWERade, Motel 6, Harley-Davidson, Budweiser, and UPS, the NHRA has made itself more visible for a wider range of fans. Additionally, the league's TV contract with ESPN2 has brought the sport to millions of households that might not have an opportunity to attend a national event.

The marketability of the NHRA drivers is a great force in building the league's brand image. Women, minorities, and young drivers are experiencing increased success in the league, and nontraditional drag racing media outlets, such as the A&E Channel and the Disney Channel, are giving attention to the sport. Increased visibility is helping the league attract more casual fans. Along with the marketability of the drivers, NHRA race attendees experience something unique only to the NHRA: behind-the-scenes access to the drivers and teams. Because each event ticket doubles as a pit pass, every fan has an equal opportunity to meet their favorite drivers and rub elbows with the drivers and crew members of the professional racing classes. This is one of the greatest strengths of the NHRA, as fans view most professional athletes as off-limits and inaccessible.

Finally, the NHRA organization has a strong sense of culture and history that have assisted it in building a strong brand image. Its former drivers are loyal to the league and remain involved, and Wally Parks's original vision of providing a safe place for drag racers has not been forgotten.

Despite its brand success, many critics feel that changes are necessary to move the league into a higher realm of competitiveness in the sport industry. With its move to a new playoff format, it appears that the NHRA is listening to the critics and responding appropriately to ensure its future success. Whether it can move to the next level and challenge its biggest competitor, NASCAR, remains to be seen.

Post-Game Comments

- The NHRA has grown from a grassroots organization to a nationally recognized motorsports brand.
- The brand has been built through strong sponsorships, marketable drivers, and widespread access to NHRA races through both the race locations and TV contracts.

- The NHRA is increasingly targeting a broader base of fans outside of the traditional car enthusiast arena.
- The NHRA offers a fan experience like no other professional sport through its event tickets doubling as a pit pass for every fan.
- The league's strong brand image is rooted in its strong sense of organizational history and culture.

Web Resources

http://www.nhra.com
http://www.nhra.com/apcm/templates/about.asp?articleid=3263&zoneid=101
http://www.nhra.com/content/about.asp?articleid=6566&zoneid=101
http://www.nhra.com/sponsors/index.htm

Additional Resources

NHRA Communications Department. *2004 NHRA POWERade Drag Racing Series Media Guide.* Rancho Cucamonga, CA: Faust Printing.

One-on-one with Tom Compton, National Hot Rod Association. (2004, July 26). *Street & Smith's Sports Business Journal,* 30.

Poole, M. (2005, May 2). Decision time for the NHRA: Go big, or go on as it always has. *Street & Smith's Sports Business Journal,* 11.

Smith, M. (2006, September 4). NHRA targets casual fans with playoff system. *Street & Smith's Sports Business Journal,* 9.

Warfield, S. (2004, December 27). Brut smells opportunity in NHRA. *Street & Smith's Sports Business Journal,* 4.

Warfield, S. (2005, October 31). Five-year deal will keep NHRA on ESPN2. *Street & Smith's Sports Business Journal,* 8.

Warfield, S. (2005, October 31). Leaving the green light on: Circuit makes Motel 6 its official motel. *Street & Smith's Sports Business Journal,* 8.

Warfield, S. (2006, January 23). Hogging it: Harley inks NHRA sponsorship. *Street & Smith's Sports Business Journal,* 5.

Chapter 11

Professional Bowlers Association: Revamped and Ready to Go

Dan Drane,
University of Southern Mississippi

Group: Professional Bowlers Association
Location: Seattle, WA
Internet Address: www.pba.com

Discussion Questions

- What is the relationship between the PBA and broadcast media?
- What impact have the new owners had on the PBA?
- What is the primary focus of the new owners for the PBA?
- What future challenges and obstacles must the PBA overcome to be successful?
- Who is the PBA's primary target market?
- What can the PBA do to attract more sponsors?
- How can the PBA attract corporate clientele?

The Line-Up

Promoter Eddie Elias founded the Professional Bowlers Association (PBA) in 1958. Elias persuaded thirty-three of the country's top bowlers to each donate $50 to start the tour. The PBA's first season began in 1959 with three sanctioned tournaments. In 1961, the PBA got the exposure it desired by securing a contract with ABC that made professional bowling a Saturday afternoon staple for thirty-six years. However, bowling's popularity dwindled in the 1990s,

95

and the relationship with ABC ended in 1997. At that time, prize money and membership in the PBA also decreased dramatically.

In 2000, the PBA received a breath of fresh air when three former Microsoft executives—Chris Peters, Rob Glaser, and Mike Slade—bought the league with hopes of turning it into the next emerging global sport. The new owners purchased the league for $5 million. They immediately switched the nonprofit association to a for-profit organization and moved the headquarters from Akron, Ohio, to Seattle, Washington. The PBA now has 4,300 members and twelve sponsors.

Timeline of Events

1958
- Eddie Elias, a promoter and attorney, starts the PBA with thirty-three founding members.

1959
- The PBA Tour starts with three tournaments worth $49,500.
- The first of many television shows is inaugurated with "Jackpot Bowling."

1961
- The first televised PBA finals are held in the National PBA Invitational.

1970
- Bellows-Valvair co-sponsors four tournaments, while Firestone, Miller High Life, Lincoln-Mercury, Ebonite and American Airlines continue to sponsor major events.

1975
- Earl Anthony becomes the first man in PBA history to break the $100,000 mark in earnings, finishing the season with a record-tying seven national titles and winning $107,585.

1977
- Burger King, Consolidated Cigar, and Quaker State joins the list of major sponsors.

1980
- Willie Willis becomes the first African-American to qualify for the Firestone Tournament of Champions by virtue of his victory in the 1979 Brunswick National Resident Pro Championship.

1982
- PBA Tour goes to Europe for the first time, and Tom Baker returns with the title in the AMF Grand Prix in Paris, France.

1990
- The PBA welcomes Choice Hotels, Chevy Trucks and the American Bowling Congress as new sponsors. Membership topped 3,500 by year's end.

1991
- ABC-TV televises their 30th year of the Pro Bowlers Tour.

1993
- The Children's Miracle Network becomes the official charity of the PBA Tour.

1994
- The PBA introduces "arena finals" at three separate tournament sites. Telecast of the championship round moves from the bowling center to an arena setting where the finalists bowl on four specially installed lanes.

1996
- The PBA signs an exclusive three-year agreement with the Marquee Group, a sports marketing, television production and entertainment company in New York City, to serve as PBA's television representation and marketing partner.

1998
- PBA Founder Eddie Elias passes away.

2000
- Former Microsoft executives Chris Peters, Mike Slade and Rob Glaser purchase in April. The new owners turn the PBA into a for-profit business.

2001–02
- Several changes take place to bring the PBA back to life: the PBA announces a set season (September–March) with a prize fund for 20 tournaments just over $4 million, signs a three-year (with a three-year option) exclusive deal with ESPN and establishes a more consistent programming schedule. After years of decline, the PBA sees a strong increase in membership (+25%) and tournament entries (+35%), as well as an 18% increase in television ratings.

2002–03
- ESPN TV ratings increase for the second consecutive season (+6%) and the 18–34 male demographic increases by 43%. Tournament entries also increased by 14%.

2004–05
- The PBA Tour enters its first season with the brand new exempt format which features a 64-bowler field for each standard event, including 58 full-time exempt bowlers.

2008
- The PBA celebrates its 50th anniversary with a new title sponsor, Lumber Liquidators, and an array of new formats designed to attract more fans. In order to emphasize that being a PBA fan is "cool," the season kicks off with the Chris Paul PBA Celebrity Invitational with sports stars such as LeBron James and Dewayne Wade competing.

Background

The PBA was established in 1958 when thirty-three charter members joined forces to form the Professional Bowlers Association. Today, with nearly 4,300 members, it continues to be acknowledged as the "major league" of bowling in the world. In March 2000, a trio of high-tech entrepreneurs purchased the league in hopes of mirroring the fortunes of NASCAR and creating additional opportunities for its members. The new owners bought the rights to the PBA for $5 million and assumed $2 million in debt. In 2006, the PBA got its first title sponsorship, with what became the Denny's PBA Tour. Although Denny's still is a major sponsor of the league, Lumber Liquidators signed on to become the PBA title sponsor in 2008. The multimillion-dollar deal with Lumber Liquidators is in effect through the 2011 season. In addition to Lumber Liquidators and Denny's, the league has sponsorship agreements with the U.S. Bowling Congress, GEICO, Pepsi-Cola, Brunswick, Bayer, Motel 6, Ace Hardware, Etonic, Columbia 300, H&R Block, and Discover Card. The revamped league has still not turned a profit and prize money was lowered 20 percent in 2006. The new owners are committed to the PBA and say the cuts will help it keep going. It is estimated they have invested $30 million in past six years. Membership is at an all-time high (4,300), the list of sponsors continues to grow, and the TV contract with ESPN is expected to be renewed.

Marketing Strategies

Sports today is about entertainment and competition—people want a reason to have an emotional connection to the athletes they are watching. The old PBA never changed the presentation or the marketing approach. In essence, they never changed with the times. The revamped PBA is attempting to build their brand by forging an attachment with fans and the players. The idea is to turn the players into stars that the fans want to watch.

To accomplish their objectives, the new ownership identified four areas in which they needed to improve.

- First, they needed to create a bowling season. Historically, the PBA made it very difficult to follow the sport. Nobody knew when the bowling season was because it never really started or stopped. The established bowling season now starts in September and ends in March.
- Second, they needed to establish a TV presence. The PBA developed a relationship with ESPN, and now bowling is seen each Sunday afternoon during the season.
- Third, they needed to develop an online presence. The new owners purchased the Web address www.pba.com and redesigned the site. The new site is very interactive, and fans can view Webcasts from each tournament.
- Fourth, they needed to figure out how to draw attention to the sport. The PBA's relationship with ESPN has been instrumental in helping get back in the public consciousness. In 2005, the PBA ran a series of comedic commercials on ESPN with the catchphrase "Sundays are for bowling." The commercials featured a bowling bowl that sabotaged a person's routine Sunday activities. The PBA has also encouraged bowlers to show emotion and personality on and off the lanes. ESPN has run many highlights of the bowlers' antics on their *SportsCenter* segment.

The revamped PBA also established short-term and long-term goals to ensure prosperity of the league. The main short-term goal was to regain some credibility. The PBA could show that their competitions can be exciting, that the bowlers are athletes, and that there is athletic competition to the activity. Development of the PBA Experience was seen as one means of accomplishing this goal. The league's long-term goals include profitability, higher visibility, and attracting a wider audience. The new owners have yet to turn a profit, but they are coming closer each year. Cost-cutting measures were implemented in 2006 to help the league become self-sufficient. The PBA has experienced higher visibility as evidenced by increased ratings on ESPN each year. They are also persistently seeking new sponsors to help grow the brand.

A major obstacle the PBA must overcome is attracting a younger and wider audience to satisfy advertisers and sponsors. The traditional fan base for the PBA is older with a small disposable income. The PBA has made great strides in this effort. From 2001 to 2003, the eighteen- to thirty-four-year-old male demographic increased 83 percent.

Other strategies the PBA has instituted to assist in growing the brand include thinking globally, adding excitement to the competitions, and focusing on alliances. The potential for growth is boundless in other parts of the world, such as Asia and Europe, where bowling doesn't have the same stigma as in the United States. The PBA has gone to an arena format for some of their events, putting spectators closer and parallel to the lanes. They even built outdoor lanes for a few events. In forging alliances, the PBA is focusing on increased revenue. They are following NASCAR as a model, focusing on creative ways to identify and interact with consumers.

Exempt Tour

Beginning in October 2004, the PBA copied the PGA Tour and adopted an all-exempt national tour format with limited fields. The standard PBA event is now sixty-four players with fifty-eight exempt for the season, the other six filled by a qualifying round or weekly commissioner's exemption. One spot each week is reserved for the commissioner's exemption. It is the equivalent of a sponsor's exemption on the PGA Tour. The exempt player is usually selected for some type of association to the area where the event is being held. This helps promote the event and gives it a stronger local connection.

The purpose of the exempt tour is to make the tour more elite. It gives young bowlers something to aspire to and requires players to earn their way onto the tour. The exempt tour also narrows the field and creates a platform from which stars can emerge. In turn, this gives fans and viewers an opportunity to get to know the exempt players much better. The exempt tour uses the match-play format to emphasize head-to-head competition, which people understand better and relate to.

PBA Experience

One of the obstacles the revamped PBA Tour had to overcome was to explain to the bowling public just how difficult the conditions were during tournament competition. The lane conditions at the typical bowling alley are very easy compared to the oil patterns employed on the PBA Tour. Some fans were not watching the league games because they could bowl the same scores or better at their home lanes. To get this point across to the bowling public, the PBA established the PBA Experience, which allows bowlers to face the exact lane conditions found on the PBA Tour. The PBA uses five distinct lane patterns during competition, each providing a different challenge. Scoring will be lower on these lanes compared to standard lanes and will provide participants with a true test of their ability.

PBA and Broadcast Media

Professional bowling had its best ever TV ratings in the 1970s and 1980s, drawing audiences of 8 to 10 million per tournament. The PBA Tour was long known for its Saturday afternoon broadcasts prior to ABC's *Wide World of Sports*. The Pro Bowlers Tour on ABC lasted from 1961 to 1997 with Chris Schenkel as the main sportscaster. From 1984 to 1991, NBC Sports televised the PBA Fall Tour. In 1998, the PBA moved its telecasts to CBS, where it stayed for only two years. Since 2000, the PBA has exclusively been televised on ESPN.

Although viewership of the PBA is considered low, averaging around one rating point, it wasn't always that way. There were only three serious deliverers of TV sport in the 1960s and 1970s, and Nielsen surveys show that the PBA had more viewers than almost every athletic event it broadcast against for several decades. The fight for viewers became much tougher with the explosion of cable TV channels, proliferation of new sports and leagues, and saturation of entertainment options. The PBA still garnered larger TV audiences than college basketball, golf, and other sports, but advertisers stayed away because bowling fans tended to spend less on their products. The PBA is now associated with ESPN, and ratings are beginning to rise again. In 2002, the PBA averaged 775,354 homes per telecast. In 2003, the PBA reported a 6 percent increase in viewership, despite broadcasting against the NFL on thirteen of the twenty telecasts. Ratings increased another 10 percent from 2003 to 2004. During the 2005–2006 season, 63.1 million people tuned in to the PBA on all the ESPN networks, an increase of 23.5 percent from the previous year. The year also saw a 12.5 percent increase in ratings in the coveted eighteen to thirty-four male demographic.

The PBA reached new audiences in 2005, when it was featured in the sports documentary *A League of Ordinary Gentlemen*. The documentary, filmed during the 2002–2003 season, enjoyed a limited release in theaters before being released in a DVD format in March 2006.

The Final Score

The Professional Bowlers Association has experienced many ups and downs during its fifty years of existence. The league was once seen as a powerhouse in the field of televised sport but lost its TV presence in the late 1990s. The league was resistant to change: they never changed the presentation of their product or updated their marketing strategies. The brand was dying a slow death. By 1999, the PBA was performing so poorly that they filed for bankruptcy protection. In 2000, three former Microsoft executives came in to save the league and bought the PBA for $5 million.

The new owners face many challenges presented by prior mismanagement and changes in the culture of sport, but they have set out to revamp the PBA and restore it to its former glory. They have implemented new marketing strategies and developed both short-term and long-term goals. Most of the changes revolve around making the PBA a profitable venture and developing the bowlers into stars whom fans want to identify with and support.

The PBA must improve their image and reconnect with the public to grow the brand. Of the many changes that needed to be made, the new owners identified four areas for immediate improvement. They are:

- Create a defined bowling season
- Establish a television presence
- Develop an online presence
- Bring attention to the sport

To prosper, an organization must develop a successful strategic marketing plan. Gaining credibility, becoming profitable, increasing visibility, and connecting with a more meaningful segment of the market are the cornerstones of the PBA's marketing plan. Gaining credibility for the sport may be the most difficult aspect, but developing a target market that meets the demands of advertisers and sponsors is perhaps most important—without preferred consumers, it will be hard to convince stakeholders that their business enterprise with the PBA will produce a desired return on investment.

With all the changes sport has experienced in recent years, especially with respect to the modernization of sport media, it will be very difficult for the new ownership to return the PBA to its glory days. It is still too early to tell if they can continue to build the brand and prosper. However, they seem well on their way to making the PBA a successful venture.

Post-Game Comments

- The PBA is an example of an organization that refused to change with the times and almost became extinct.

- New owners are attempting to revamp the PBA and turn it into a successful sport league.
- The PBA seeks to grow the brand by developing stars and being creative in promotion of the sport.
- Publicity will be key. Relationships with the media are paramount in obtaining this objective.
- The PBA is making great strides but there are still many obstacles to overcome.

Web Resources

http://www.pba.com/corporate/pressroom.asp
http://www.pba.com/resources/basics/bowling101.asp
http://www.wired.com/wired/archive/12.09/kingpin.html

Additional Resources

Archibald, J. (2002). Arresting development. *Bowling Digest, 20*(5), 28–33.

Atkin, R. (2001). He sees pro bowling as back on a roll. *Christian Science Monitor, 12*(228), 12.

Baehman, S., & Miller, S. (2003). When you run PBA, it's always spare time. *Street & Smith's Sport Business Journal, 6*(27), 40.

Carney, S. (2003). Pro bowling takes a walk on the wild side. *Street & Smith's Sport Business Journal, 6*(21), 20.

Chen, A. (2005). Up from the gutter. *Sports Illustrated, 103*(21).

Feemster, R. (2002). Two leagues bowling for dollars to grow sport. *Street & Smith's Sport Business Journal, 4*(48), 21.

Pezzano, C. (2006, October 8). PBA tightens purse string with prize money. *The Record.*

Schoenfeld, B. (2001). Microsoft-Nike swagger takes to the lanes. *Street & Smith's Sport Business Journal, 4*(3), 42–43.

Chapter 12

The Rebranding of a Franchise: The Tampa Bay Buccaneers

Fritz G. Polite,
University of Tennessee

Steven N. Waller,
University of Tennessee

Team: The Tampa Bay Buccaneers
Location: Tampa, FL
Internet Address: www.buccaneers.com

Discussion Questions

- Discuss the history of the Buccaneers.
- What are the key points toward turning the organization around?
- What distinguishes this team from others?
- What characteristics are associated with the rebranding of the Buccaneers organization?

The Line-Up

Located in the beautiful city of Tampa, Florida, the Tampa Bay Buccaneers have established itself as one of the most successfully operated sport business franchises in the National Football League. The franchise has been referenced by sport executives as an extremely positive brand and value. Its business practices have provided a model for other professional groups. The reclamation and resurrection of the brand along with its sound business practices have raised the exposure of the franchise tremendously. The unique aspects of Raymond James Stadium include a host of unique features designed to provide an exhilarating game experience. The organization emphasizes atmosphere in relationship to the organizational brand. The Tampa Bay Buccaneers have gained positive valuable brand extension via strong marketing practices, sound business practices, and innovative concepts.

Timeline of Events

1967

- Tampa Stadium opened with an initial seating capacity of 45,000. The original tenant was the University of Tampa Spartans football team. The first sporting event was hosting the University of Tennessee football team on November 4, 1967.

1974

- The NFL awards the league's twenty-seventh expansion franchise to the city of Tampa (The Tampa Bay Buccaneers). The cost of the franchise is a record $16 million and the team is scheduled to begin play in 1976.

1975

- Expansion project adds 27,000 end-zone seats; This was a part of the NFL expansion bid and made the stadium one of the largest in the league. It became known as the "Big Sombrero" because of its sloping hat-like structure.

1976

- Head Coach John McKay reveals a five-year plan to bring the franchise into an elite status. His body of work eventually led to the success of the franchise.

1995

- Team is purchased by Malcolm Glazer for $192 million from the Culverhouse family. This was a record for a professional franchise at the time.

1996

- Tony Dungy hired as the head coach. Goes on to become the winningest coach in team history (56–46).

2002

- Won divisional playoff (v. San Francisco 49ers); won conference championship (v. Philadelphia Eagles); won Super Bowl XXXVII (v. Raiders).

The Franchise

The story of the Tampa Bay Buccaneers as an NFL franchise has been one of highs and lows. The city of Tampa and owner Hugh Culverhouse were awarded the NFL's twenty-seventh franchise in 1974 for $16 million. The city conducted a contest and chose the name Buccaneers in honor of the yearly Gasparilla Pirate Festival in Tampa, with the colors of sherbet orange and white. The owner was known as a flamboyant millionaire and wanted his team to reflect his personality. The team quickly became known as consistent losers. They lost their first twenty-six games and played a style that became known as "Yucs Football." The franchise was unable to maintain quality players because Culverhouse was unwilling to pay larger salaries to top players.

John McKay was hired as the franchise's first head coach. He was a very successful collegiate coach, having earned four national championships at the University of Southern California in sixteen years and was considered one of the top collegiate football coaches in history. McKay unveiled a five-year plan to bring the franchise into the top tier of the NFL. Despite his past successes, the team appeared to be unprepared: they fumbled, threw interceptions, missed tackles, fumbled snaps, and showed an inability to score points. On September 12, 1976, the Buccaneers played their first regular season game in Houston against the Oilers, and were shut out 20–0. They became the first team in NFL history to lose all fourteen of its regular season games (1976). They failed to score at all in five games, and had the worst defense and offense in the conference. The media was harsh, and the fans' patience was short. Attendance began to decrease, and many labeled the Bucs losers. Last second losses, strange plays, bungled draft picks, and failed personnel moves further entrenched the Bucs as losers. In 1976, the Bucs reached a franchise low for attendance (36,930).

After two difficult years, things began to turn around. In 1977, the Bucs won their first franchise win against the New Orleans Saints (33–14). In 1978, they went 5–11, and in 1979 they went 10–6 and tied for the Central Division (v. Bears) championship. They appeared in the playoffs in 1981–82, but their improvement did not last. They did not return until fifteen years later.

The Transformation

Hugh Culverhouse was initially held in high esteem by the citizens of Tampa for bringing a professional team to the city. The fans later despised him because of his frugal ways. The Bucs consistently had the league's lowest payroll, which contributed to the inability of the franchise to compete at a high level. Even though they were consistent losers, had a low attendance, and played in an out-dated stadium, the Bucs were still able to turn a minimal profit. The rental contract with city officials allotted for generous profit sharing by the Bucs franchise.

The Stadium

The franchise originally played in Tampa Stadium. It took over three years of specialized research and development before the new stadium became reality. A major part of the brand transformation was the reconstruction of a new stadium complete with special amenities. Considered one of the jewels of the NFL, Raymond James Stadium has a capacity of 66,000. It is a combination of classic history, modern technology, and state-of-the-art equipment. The stadium is considered one of the most exciting and electric places to watch a game. It has a special feature called the Buccaneer Cove, which adds to the overall experience of the game by creating a magical environment, complete with a $3 million pirate ship. The Cove is located in the north end zone. It is over 20,000 square feet and engulfs the entire back portion of the end zone. There are food stands, merchandise shops, tables, and resort-type amenities. It features a replica of a historic pirate ship complete with cannons, deck, skull, swords, smoke, attack flags, ship flag, and an extensive audio system. There are eight cannons that fire when the team scores or when they reach the red zone (inside the twenty-yard line). The dock serves as a meeting point for corporations and organizations to gather. The theme is centered around adding to the total fan experience.

Practice Facilities

In 1975, the franchise built a simple practice facility to accommodate their new team. As new franchises entered the league with state-of-the-art training facilities, the Bucs still had their original complex. Their annual training camp was held at the University of Tampa. Only recently, the training camp was moved to the Walt Disney's Wide World of Sports facility in Orlando, Florida. The new complex was completed in 2006. Composed of two natural grass practice fields, press room, movie theater, kitchen, expansive weight room, multiple swimming pools, Jacuzzi, medical center, and one of the largest locker rooms in the league, the facility is one of the most cutting-edge training centers in the NFL.

Team Colors

Another important part of the brand transformation was the changing of the team colors, mascot, and cheerleaders and the restructuring of the front office.

The colors were changed from the orange sherbet and white to pewter, red, black, and white. Bucco Bruce, the original mascot, was replaced with the skull and swords logo and was received favorably by the local fans as well as nationally.

Leadership Changes at the Top

The front office was restructured to include a new head coach. Tony Dungy was hired when the new ownership took control (Glazer family). In 1996, the team went 6–10. Coach Dungy brought a level of focus and direction that the franchise had not experienced before. A defensive specialist, even tempered, and with a solid religious foundation, Dungy provided the team with a strong presence to build on. He went on to set the franchise all-time total wins record in only six years (56–45). They reached the playoffs four out the six years of his tenure. The franchise had not appeared in the playoffs for fifteen years prior to Dungy's arrival.

The front office was also a pivotal aspect of the process of rebranding the franchise. Malcolm Glazer became the owner, and he appointed his three sons to guide and lead the franchise.

The Value of the Franchise

The Buccaneers are one of the most valuable teams in the NFL. *Forbes* ranked the franchise as the twelfth most valuable team in 2008, despite being considered a smaller market team. The team is valued at $1.1 billion and has revenues in excess of $220 million. The team's value has increased by nearly $1 billion since Malcom Glazer purchased the team in 1995 for $192 million.

The owners also negotiated one of the most profitable deals in the NFL. The (organization) owners get all profits for events in the stadium. This includes college games, concerts, exhibitions, and special events; profits include ticket sales, parking, concessions, merchandise, naming rights, and negotiated advertising rights within the stadium. This unique financial deal makes the franchise one of the most profitable in the league. The city of Tampa operates the facility and receives a lease payment from the franchise. The franchise does not own the facility and did not take out any loans or debt for it but utilizes it as a major source of income for multiple events aside from football. This is a unique and extremely profitable agreement that has contributed significantly to the success of the franchise. The stadium was built from a community tax that also incorporated city improvements, including public facilities, roads, and schools. In essence, the owners acquired use of a major facility with no incurred costs with the opportunity to use the facility for a limited lease and receive the majority of all profits and revenues. This created a model for other sport owners. Having a stadium built for you and receiving all proceeds from events held is almost unfathomable.

The Final Score

When attempting to assess the brand value of a professional franchise, there are several factors to consider comprising franchise value, brand equity, spectator attendance, season ticket sales, and general revenues. It is evident that the Buccaneers franchise has extended its value as a dominant franchise by vastly improving in these areas. By rebranding, the team has increased its brand value, brand equity, and overall positive brand essence by changing the face of the organization. From the change in colors, logo, and business model, it has established itself as one of the most profitable franchises in the NFL. This is evident in its increase in franchise value since the Glazers purchased the team ($192 million) to its current value ($1.1 billion). The crowning of the team as World Champions in 2002 is a testament to its overall success from its humble beginnings as one of the worst franchises in NFL history to the upper echelon of U.S. professional football. By retooling the leadership, redesigning the branding mechanisms, refocusing the brand, and involving the community, the organization experienced a remarkable turnaround. The increase in attendance and season ticket sales lead credence to its newfound success.

The transition from one of the worst NFL franchises to one of the most successful was accomplished by a keen sense of strategic moves encompassed around new leadership and exemplary visionary processes. The expanded positive brand image of the organization is attributed to sound business practices, sound marketing practices, and cutting-edge leadership. This case study exemplifies the skill sets necessary to turn a floundering franchise into one of a leading one. Via these identified traits, one can attribute positive brand equity and value by focused and concerted efforts. This franchise has been rebuilt into a profitable and well-established entity. This example is a positive one in that it effectively displays the necessary process to turn around a poor and dismal franchise into a profitable and competitive one. The current challenge for the Buccaneers is how to continue to build on their current status. In a growing and competitive field, this will be the barometer that past and present franchises will be measured against.

Web Resources

http://www.buccaneers.com/rjs/rjsmain.aspx
http://www.buccaneers.com/rjs/cove.aspx
http://www.buccaneers.com/rjsmain.aspx
http://www.forbes.com/lists/2008/30/sportsmoney_nfl08_Tampa-Bay-
    Buccaneers_306470.html
http://www.profootballhof.com/history/release_id-1285
http://www.sportslogos.net/team.php

Chapter 13

World Baseball Classic: Major League Baseball Attempts to Build Its Brand Internationally

Mark S. Nagel,
University of South Carolina

Matthew T. Brown,
University of South Carolina

Event: World Baseball Classic
Internet Address: www.worldbaseballclassic.com

Discussion Questions

- What were the potential structural, political, and economic issues surrounding the creation and implementation of the first World Baseball Classic?
- What marketing issues does the World Baseball Classic have to overcome in the following geographic areas to grow the event?
  - China
  - Europe
  - Japan
  - Latin America
  - South America
  - South Korea
  - United States
- Should the 2013 World Baseball Classic finals be played outside the United States? Why or why not?

- What activities can Major League Baseball and other sanctioning bodies implement to make future World Baseball Classics generate increased worldwide attention and greater revenue?
- As the sport of baseball develops around the world, will there be any resistance to the World Baseball Classic, since it is primarily operated by Major League Baseball and not an independent international organization? What concerns could arise?

The Line-Up

The World Baseball Classic (WBC) was the first international baseball tournament that permitted countries such as the United States, Canada, Japan, South Korea, Mexico, Cuba, and the Dominican Republic to send professional players to compete for a "world" championship. Japan defeated Cuba 10–6 in the 2006 finals to claim the inaugural title. However, more important than the outcome on the field was the platform that the WBC provided for Major League Baseball (MLB) to showcase its product and its brands beyond North America. As the sport and the business of baseball continue to develop around the world, MLB owners have investigated opportunities to maximize their position as the leading organization for delivering on-field baseball-related entertainment, as well as baseball-related products. For MLB owners, the profits from the initial tournament not only signified a short-term financial success but also encouraged future investment in the rapidly expanding baseball environment. The development of future World Baseball Classics will certainly present structural, political, and economic challenges, but if those are overcome, MLB owners believe that a worldwide brand, similar to the Olympic Games or FIFA World Cup, could be established.

Timeline of Events

1888
- Albert Spalding and the Chicago White Stockings complete a world baseball tour, with stops in Paris, Dublin, London, Rome, and Egypt.

1904
- Baseball is played as a demonstration sport at the third modern Olympics held in St. Louis. Although it will be played again as a demonstration sport at seven future Olympiads, it was not established as a medal sport until the 1992 Barcelona Games.

1908
- The Cincinnati Reds become the first U.S. professional team to travel to Cuba for a tournament.

1927
- A team of Negro League all-stars becomes the first professional team to play in Japan.

1931
- A team of MLB all-stars including Lou Gehrig, Lefty Grove, and Lefty O'Doul tours Japan.

1936
- First World Cup of Baseball is held. Overall, the thirty-six World Cups of Baseball have garnered limited media attention because most of the participants are little-known amateur players.

1969
- The Montreal Expos become the first MLB team in Canada.

1996
- The San Diego Padres and New York Mets play a three-game series in Monterrey, Mexico.

1999
- The Baltimore Orioles and the Cuban national team play an exhibition home-and-away series.

2000
- The Boston Red Sox and Houston Astros play two spring exhibition games in the Dominican Republic. Thousands of seats are empty because many fans cannot afford tickets.
- The Chicago Cubs and New York Mets open the regular season with a two-game series in Tokyo.

2005
- In May, the World Baseball Classic was announced for spring 2006. That July, the International Olympic Committee votes baseball and softball out of the 2012 Olympics.

2006
- First World Baseball Classic contested. Games are played in Japan, Puerto Rico, and the United States. Japan wins the inaugural games.

2009
- Second World Baseball Classic is played. Japan wins the WBC for the second time.

Planning the World Baseball Classic

Since 2000, MLB's record attendance numbers and increasing popularity in the United States have spurred a heightened demand for media contracts and other related MLB items. However, despite the positive short-term revenue achievements, baseball owners have noted that many American children are not playing or consuming baseball as they once did. Other emerging sports (such as the X-Games) have begun to attract attention, causing some to wonder if future generations will lose interest in attending or watching baseball games.

In addition to concerns regarding its future American customers, MLB owners have noted the dramatic increase in international initiatives by other American companies. Certainly, MLB has long been interested in growing the game globally. Since 1888, professional players have participated in exhibition games in foreign countries and, more recently, MLB-sanctioned regular season games in Mexico and Japan. While more American companies were becoming focused on maximizing global markets, MLB needed an event to help launch its brand and its brand extensions (such as media contracts, licensed merchandise, and sponsorships) into emerging markets. With a desire to create a worldwide baseball event similar to the Olympic Games or the FIFA World Cup, the first World Baseball Classic was staged in 2006.

Attracting Participants: Initial Problems

The WBC was designed to be the first international baseball tournament that would bring the best players from around the globe to compete for a "world" championship. However, attracting the best players involved myriad problems. The first obstacle was determining a time to hold the tournament. Some MLB owners and Nippon Professional Baseball (NPB) (Japan) owners expressed concern that the event could not be held during the late summer after the regular baseball seasons had commenced because this would potentially detract from their leagues' postseason championships. Eventually, March was chosen as the time of year to compete, but special considerations were enacted to attempt to alleviate specific concerns. Because March is the traditional time for spring training practices, some team owners were reluctant to permit their best players to leave to participate for their country. In addition, owners feared that high-level competition during a time of the year when most players were returning to baseball activity could result in injuries. Measures such as strict pitch counts were implemented to protect the players. Only Mexican pitcher Luis Ayala of the Washington Nationals was lost for the 2006 MLB season due to a WBC injury.

MLB also agreed to stage the WBC with drug testing designed to mimic the Olympic Games' testing program. For many years, MLB had few rules or testing protocols for steroids, resulting in some international skepticism regarding performance-enhancing drug use in professional baseball. Many players, such as Barry Bonds, who had been rumored to have previously used steroids, did not compete in the WBC. (Numerous players from a variety of countries also noted that other factors, such as needing time to prepare for the upcoming season, contributed to their election not to participate in the WBC; therefore, it is difficult to measure how much, if any, impact the drug testing rules had on the WBC participants.)

Staging an international event also resulted in other participation issues. For over forty years, the United States has considered Cuba to be a rogue state and has extended an economic embargo to Fidel Castro's island nation. Although U.S. citizens are permitted to travel to Cuba, direct commercial flights are not available. Although the Baltimore Orioles had been permitted to stage an exhibition game in Cuba in 1999, the U.S. Treasury Department initially denied a request by MLB for a waiver for the Cuban national team to participate in WBC games in U.S. territory. Eventually, the Treasury Department granted the Cuban team an exemption to participate, but required them to forgo any financial gain from the tournament.

With the Cuban team permitted to participate, the initial WBC commenced on March 3, 2006, with sixteen countries competing (Exhibit 13.1). Although Japan eventually defeated Cuba 10−6 to win the first championship, measuring the success of the growth of the WBC brand would involve investigating attendance levels, media ratings, as well as sponsorship and licensed merchandise sales.

Exhibit 13.1 Countries Participating in the 2006 World Baseball Classic

Australia	Netherlands
Canada	Panama
China	Puerto Rico**
Cuba	South Africa
Dominican Republic	South Korea
Italy	Taiwan
Japan*	United States***
Mexico	Venezuela

  * Hosted first-round games.
  ** Hosted first- and second-round games.
  *** Hosted first- and second-round games as well as semifinals and finals.

World Baseball Classic Success: Measuring Revenue Sources

Attendance

MLB estimated that 800,000 fans would attend WBC games. During the first games held in Japan, it appeared that the attendance would fall woefully short of projections as the three opening games that did not involve the home team (South Korea, China, Taiwan) had a total attendance of only 13,695. Fortunately, once games began in the United States and Puerto Rico, attendance increased. A total of 737,112 customers attended, with the final in San Diego between Japan and Cuba drawing 42,696. The games in the United States were particularly able to attract fans for non-U.S. competitions because recent immigrants of Hispanic descent attended games played by their home countries. Many fans also traveled to the United States to attend the WBC games.

In addition to the number of fans, MLB was encouraged by the passion exhibited at games in the United States and Puerto Rico. While other international baseball competitions certainly have elicited interest and enthusiasm, the WBC was able to take fan fervor to a new level. At many games, fans cheered and sang songs as if they were attending a FIFA World Cup match, bolstering MLB hopes for enhancement of future tournaments.

Media

Because live attendance was only one factor determining success, MLB also measured consumption of games through TV ratings. In the United States, the twelve WBC telecasts on ESPN had a 1.1 rating (1,205,600 households),[1] whereas the twenty telecasts on ESPN2 had a 0.6 rating (657,600 households). Of particular interest for the future growth of the WBC was the 1.8 rating (1,972,800 households) for the WBC final as the American team had been eliminated in the second round. Although the U.S. ratings were solid but not spectacular, the number greatly exceeded anticipated interest. However, the ratings for the semifinal game between South Korea and Japan were tremendous: 36 percent of people in Japan watched the game, despite it being shown at a less than desirable time of day.

---

1. *Rating* represents the number of households watching a TV program, whereas *share* measures the percentage of televisions that are on that are watching the selected show. Each rating point is roughly 1 percent of the total 109,600,000 households in the United States.

MLB had reason to believe that the WBC would attract a strong TV audience as the consumption of MLB via media outlets has been growing steadily. In 1990, MLB generated $10 million total from all revenue sources outside North America, and in 2005, MLB generated $120 million. ESPN launched a version of ESPN Classic in Europe that now reaches 8 million homes in Great Britain and an additional 8 million homes on the Continent. ESPN's European presence likely helped double MLB's European rights fees to $20 million over five years, with greater increases anticipated for the future. Ireland-based North American Sports Network (NASN), a company that initially was formed to service expatriated North Americans' desire to watch American-based sports, discovered that 70 percent of their subscribers were native Britons! This contributed to ESPN purchasing NASN in late 2006. Although television is currently the dominant media forum, MLB has already established a subsidiary, Major League Baseball Advanced Media (MLBAM), to extend the presence of MLB operations around the globe via the Internet.

Corporate Sponsorship

MLB hoped to attract numerous international corporations as sponsors of the World Baseball Classic. Soon after the WBC was scheduled, MasterCard signed as a sponsor. Tom Murphy, vice president of sponsorships for MasterCard, noted his company's interest in the potential of the WBC: "The Classic is a great way to extend our established ties to baseball, and it's one of the very few global sports properties." In addition to MasterCard, Konami participated as the other WBC global sponsor. In total, twenty-six companies sponsored the WBC at the national or regional level. Among the U.S. companies were Anheuser-Busch, Gatorade, and MBNA. In addition, other companies such as Taco Bell who were not official sponsors bought considerable advertisement time on ESPN and ESPN Deportes (the Spanish-language version of ESPN) in an effort to target emerging demographics in the global marketplace.

The success of the initial WBC has attracted other companies to become possible sponsors. Major League Baseball, long aware of the potential of the global community, has increased its presence in foreign countries. Where MLB once only ventured to foreign countries to seek potential players, it now has established permanent offices across Asia and Central America to maximize revenue opportunities.

In some cases, establishing permanent offices has helped officials understand the unique legal and cultural expectations in different countries—particularly for sponsorships and merchandise sales. Historically, teams and leagues in the United States have discouraged or prohibited sponsor logos on uniforms but have typically placed logos throughout sport facilities. However, in professional sports leagues in Asia and Europe, uniform sponsorships are a common practice. MLB has also learned that sponsorships need to be tailored to the unique aspects of each potential country. MLB Vice President of International Marketing and Development Jim Small remarked, "The thing we've learned is that you can't just say we're going to do something across a region. Strategies have to be customized, country by country." MLB Vice President of International Business Paul Archey echoed Small's comments when he specifically discussed MLB's Asian sponsorship initiatives:

> Japan and Korea are as different as two cultures can get, they just happen to be in close proximity. But they speak different languages and they have different cultures and food. Certainly we shouldn't expect to be able to put the same strategy in Japan and take it to Korea or China and have it work just because it's Asia.

Licensed Merchandise

The differences between South Korea and Japan are also manifested in their traditions regarding licensed merchandise sales. In South Korea, there are over fifty "team" stores that account for the majority of sales of all licensed sports merchandise. However, in Japan, there are few team stores, and licensees simply produce and distribute merchandise through myriad different channels such as traditional department stores.

In addition to different distribution channels, MLB has also learned through the WBC that legal protections for trademarks may be nonexistent in some countries. WBC sales of licensed merchandise were brisk in Central America, but in many cases, "pirated" merchandise was sold rather than officially licensed products. Too often, counterfeiters have brazenly operated nearby officially licensed points of distribution, a potential problem MLB must address in the future.

Despite the U.S. team not making the WBC finals, merchandise sales at the championship game in San Diego generated a $10 per cap (average sales per person) for the 42,696 attendees, which compares favorably to a typical World Series game. For a regular season San Diego Padres game, the licensed merchandise per cap is $2. WBC sales of licensed merchandise in Mexico and throughout Latin America were exceptional—vendors often ran out of products before games were finished. Paul Archey was asked to assess the TV ratings and the sale of licensed products south of the U.S. border: "Our business partners in Mexico ... think this may be the biggest thing to happen for baseball down there since Fernando [Valenzuela]."

Future Tournaments

Future World Baseball Classics will be held in 2013 and then once every four years. Although some countries, as well as some American baseball officials, have suggested that the WBC should be played every two years, the four-year period between events allows baseball the opportunity to become a landmark event that garners worldwide attention. Future tournaments will have more participants and additional preliminary rounds. MLB officials obviously dream that eventually the WBC will attract the same level of interest and attention as the FIFA World Cup. However, most officials understand that merely growing the game to the point that countries on every populated continent participate and begin to develop elite players and baseball consumers would be considered a huge success for the WBC brand.

Perhaps the most important signal that baseball has truly emerged as a global brand will occur once the semifinals and finals of the WBC are held away from the United States. Cuba expressed an interest in hosting the 2009 finals, but baseball officials were concerned that the U.S. government would never sanction such an activity for an American business in Cuba. Japan has also noted their desire to host the 2009 finals, but MLB was concerned that few Japanese customers would pay to attend games not involving the Japanese team. Although the 2009 tournament finals were played in the United States, there is a strong possibility that beginning in 2013, the finals will begin to rotate among participating countries.

The Final Score

Despite initial issues regarding attendance, sponsorship, and media rights, the 2006 WBC was a success. Prior to the start of the championship game between Cuba and Japan, MLB Commissioner Bud Selig noted, "Anything you do for the first time is not going to be perfect. But by any stretch of the imagination, this tournament exceeded my expectations in a myriad of ways." After initially worrying that the event might lose money, a $10 million profit was realized. Half of the profits will be divided evenly between MLB and the MLB Players Association. The other half of the profits will be divided among the participating teams, with half of each team's share required to be given to its baseball governing body to grow the game.

In addition to generating initial profits, the WBC has positioned MLB to be the leader in growing the game of baseball and the commercial aspects of the sport throughout the world. As baseball grows and, more important, as the American brand of baseball grows, it will be interesting to watch the world-wide reaction—particularly if MLB begins to generate huge profits overseas. Since the Olympic Games and other prominent international competitions are governed by an international board, the WBC may be viewed with some skepticism because it is primarily operated by Major League Baseball. Other prominent American brands such as Coca-Cola, Nike, Disney, and McDonald's have been both embraced and scorned as they have ventured beyond the United States. MLB will have unique challenges and tremendous opportunities as it attempts to expand its potential marketplace from 300 million U.S. consumers to the over 6 billion across the planet.

In some countries, such as most of those in Europe, baseball is not a popular participation sport, let alone a spectator sport that customers would consume. In countries throughout Latin American and parts of South America, playing and watching baseball are popular pastimes, but limited financial resources for most potential consumers limits MLB's ability to sell extension products (licensed merchandise, media rights, etc.). In Japan and Korea, baseball is popular, but MLB faces challenges to sell its product because both countries have extensive professional leagues as well as baseball cultures that are already established. Perhaps MLB's greatest but most difficult marketing opportunity is in China. Unfortunately, not only is there limited understanding of baseball, there are also generations who deny the existence of the game as a suitable pastime since former Chinese Chairman Mao Zedong had once declared it illegal.

Despite these challenges, MLB desired to expand into the global marketplace by attempting to build a baseball tournament that would bring the top world competitors together much as the Olympics and World Cup do every four years. MLB hoped that it could overcome political, social, and cultural barriers and begin to build an event that would not only generate short-term revenues but would create profits throughout the year from other critical sport revenue streams, such as global sales of sponsorships, media rights, and licensed merchandise. At this point, it appears that the WBC has provided a tremendous platform to continue to enhance MLB's brand.

Post-Game Comments

- Since the initial WBC, MLB teams have further enhanced their international initiatives. The Boston Red Sox paid a record $51.1 million for the rights to negotiate with Japanese pitcher Daisuke Matsuzaka. After some tenuous negotiations, Matsuzaka signed a six-year $52 million contract to leave Japan. The Red Sox, as well as MLB, see the signing as another opportunity to sell media rights in Japan.

- Some have speculated that despite the initial $100 million outlay, the Red Sox will easily recoup their financial investment—even if Matsuzaka does not become one of the top pitchers in MLB.
- As more MLB teams sign Japanese players, more games are broadcast live in Japan despite the time difference, resulting in games often starting in the middle of the night locally. In addition, Red Sox merchandise is likely to join that of the Seattle Mariners (who have Ichiro Suzuki) and New York Yankees (who have Hideki Matsui) as the top sellers in Japan.
- LB also has continued its efforts to enhance baseball in China. Each year, MLB owners have invested millions of dollars to develop local leagues and establish instructional clinics.
- Although China is probably at least ten years away from having a player make a tremendous impact in the Major Leagues, owners are hopeful that someday a "Yao Ming" baseball player will develop, with a significant portion of the one-billion-plus Chinese population embracing MLB games and products as a result.

Web Resources

http://sports.espn.go.com/mlb/worldclassic2006/news/story?id=2371083
http://www.worldbaseballclassic.com

Additional Resources

Fisher, E. (2006, March 27). Japan wants final, but doubts persist. *Sports-Business Journal*, 62.
WBC silences its critics. (2006, March 27). *SportsBusiness Journal*, 58.

Part III

Primarily Non-Sport Entities That Use Sport to Enhance Brands

Chapter 14

FedEx: Access to the World

Kimberly S. Miloch,
Texas Woman's University

Company: FedEx
Location: Memphis, TN
Internet Address: www.fedex.com

Discussion Questions

- What market trends are evident in the historical growth of FedEx?
- How has the company marketed itself throughout its history?
- What key elements of branding are evident in the company's advertisements and slogans?
- How has FedEx used its sport partnerships?
- What are the primary focal points of the company's sport partnerships?
- What types of programs and promotions have been developed to activate and further enhance the value of the company's sport partnerships?
- How do the company's sport partnerships reinforce its brand equity while also promoting the brand of the respective sport property?
- What has been a main factor in the successful development of FedEx's sport partnerships?

The Line-Up

FedEx is a worldwide leader in the shipping and freight industry. It is widely recognized in the United States and around the globe. The company prides itself on being customer- and employee-focused and uses integrative and up-to-date technology in providing access to the world. Established in 1971 as FDX Corporation, FedEx encompasses FedEx Express, FedEx Ground, FedEx Freight, FedEx Kinko's Office and Print Services, FedEx Custom Critical, FedEx

Trade Networks, and FedEx Services. The company provides service to the United States and more than 220 countries. Its daily volume tops an average of 6.5 million shipments. Just as the company revolutionized the shipping and freight industry, it has also developed a highly recognizable brand image, which continues to drive consumer and business choice for its service. Part of this recognition has been driven by FedEx's sport partnerships and the manner in which they have been activated. Through these partnerships, the company has successfully marketed its service to the masses while reinforcing its overall brand message.

Timeline of Events

1971
- FDX Corporation established in Little Rock, AR.
- Relocation to current corporate headquarters in Memphis, TN.

1978
- Becomes a publicly traded company.

1979
- Implements real-time computer system.

1981
- Begins international shipping.
- Begins overnight letter delivery service.

1983
- Generates $1 billion in revenue.

1984
- Launches its PC-operated system for shipping called PowerShip.

1986
- The SuperTracker is launched—a hand held data system.

1994
- Launches "FedEx" as its primary brand name.
- Establishes www.fedex.com.

1996
- Consumers gain ability to access shipments online.

1999
- Implements its EuroOne Network.

2000
- FDX Corporation officially become FedEx Corporation.

2004
- Purchases Kinko's stores and launches FedEx Kinko's.

2007
- Provides technology to allow consumers to access the company's printing services online.

"Relax, It's FedEx"

Tapping into consumer and business professionals' psyche, FedEx has established and branded itself using many slogans that illustrate its customer-focused commitment. Knowing that a key facet of its service is to deliver packages and freight on time and reliably, the company has been creative and firm in its brand message to consumers. Exhibit 14.1 highlights the company's historical branding slogans.

Exhibit 14.1 FedEx Timeline of Branding Slogans

1978–1983	"Absolutely, Positively Overnight"
1987–1988	"It's Not Just a Package, It's Your Business"
1991–1994	"Our Most Important Package Is Yours"
1995	"Absolutely, Positively Anytime"
1996–1998	"The Way the World Works"
1998–2000	"Be Absolutely Sure"
2001–2002	"This Is a Job for FedEx"
2002–2003	"Don't Worry, There's a FedEx for That"
2004–present	"Relax, It's FedEx"

Source: timeline located at www.about.fedex.designcdt.com/our_company/marketing_and_advertising.

A key facet of its branding strategy is to elicit confidence in its target market, which primarily includes other businesses but also individual consumers. These slogans embody the FedEx brand and serve to reinforce its value to its key constituents.

Building the Brand by Providing Access through Sport

As a leader in the global shipping industry, FedEx has used its involvement with sport to not only feature its services but also reaffirm consumer confidence in its brands. Recognizing that sport appeals to a worldwide audience, the company has targeted specific sport partnerships to enhance its branding efforts. While FedEx is a global company, most of its sport partnerships are limited to North America. These partnerships are highlighted in Exhibit 14.2.

Exhibit 14.2 FedEx Sport Partnerships

The National Football League	Official sponsor FedEx First and Goal Challenge
National Basketball Association	FedEx Global Scouting Report FedEx Follow the Global Leader Sweepstakes Global Top 10
FedEx Cup (Golf)	FedEx Cup Fan Challenge Opening Shot Delivered by FedEx FedEx Cup Nine
FedEx Field	Home to the Washington Redskins
FedEx Forum	Home to the Memphis Grizzlies Home to the Memphis Tigers
FedEx Orange Bowl	One of college football's premier BCS championships
FedEx Racing	FedEx Racing Fan Mail FedEx Racing Lawn Mower Challenge
FedEx and the Southern Heritage Classic (College Football)	Presenting sponsor Signature college football game featuring Jackson State University versus Tennessee State University

Through its partnership with the NFL, FedEx serves as the official delivery service sponsor for the league, the Super Bowl, and the Pro Bowl. FedEx shares the values of the NFL brand as illustrated on the company's Web site. "We have partnered together because we share key attributes of leadership, excellence, speed, precision, reliability, and global reach" (Fed Ex and the NFL: Air and Ground Game, 2008, para. 1). This shared vision is highlighted throughout the partnership and strategically designed to place the quality of both brands at the forefront of consumers' minds. The company creatively aligns itself with the NFL and uses the commonalities of the two brands to its advantages when positioning itself in the marketplace. Its marketing materials consistently point to those commonalities. For example, this excerpt of FedEx's Web site notes:

> Is it possible to have a better game plan? FedEx and the NFL think so. That's why FedEx and NFL teams work so hard to improve the plays that will get them to their destination. Both the air and ground game plans must be coordinated. Through the air, Minnesota Vikings had the leading passer of 2004 with 4,717 yards, while on the ground, the New York Jets had the leading rusher of 2004 with 1,697 yards. As the FedEx leader in the air, FedEx Express now has a powerful new ground game in FedEx Ground to serve you better ("FedEx and the NFL" 2009, para. 1).

Key to this marketing strategy is the "Air and Ground Game." The 2008 FedEx Air and Ground Game teamed with Safe Kids USA by providing funds to local programs in NFL communities. FedEx donated $1,000 each week during the NFL season to the local communities of the NFL players selected as the Air and Ground NFL Player of the Week. Additionally, the company conducted workshops focusing on pedestrian safety for elementary students in NFL communities. As part of this initiative, FedEx also identified areas where it could make improvements to benefit the local community. It donated $25,000 to Tampa for the installation of speed tables around an elementary school. The company also identified an elementary school in Dallas as the location for future workshops on pedestrian safety. This location was selected based on the number of motor pedestrian accidents in the area of the school.

These programs not only strategically align FedEx's brand values with those of the NFL, but also reach consumers at the local level by supporting community enhancement efforts. These programs allow the company to benefit and interact with consumers in a way that has significant value to communities.

FedEx promotes its Air and Ground promotion via its Web site with interactive tools, such as video downloads and mobile NFL ringtones and themes. Consumers may download player interviews and features, game highlights, and listen to short video features hosted by former NFL standouts like Marshall Faulk and Terrell Davis. This interactive marketing allows the company to market to its consumer while also engaging the consumer. Interactive messaging may have more of a lasting impact on the consumer than traditional advertising.

The company's partnership with the NBA also reinforces its brand image and focuses on the global nature of its services and the internationality of players and fans of the NBA. Positioning itself via this partnership as the "Global Leader in Assists," FedEx strategically aligns itself with the NBA. Through the

FedEx Global Scouting Report, consumers can follow international leagues and international players whose rights are held by the NBA. Such a partnership is ideally suited for both the NBA and FedEx because it allows each entity to highlight their international appeal. Through this partnership, FedEx reinforces its ability to provide reliable and fast delivery around the globe, and the NBA reinforces its international appeal by building its international fan base. Through this partnership, NBA fans and consumers can link to the NBA and FedEx Web site to participate in the Global Leader Sweepstakes and enter to win a international trip. Consumers must provide contact information to enter the sweepstakes. This allows both FedEx and the NBA to enhance its database of potential and current consumers, which enhances direct marketing efforts. While visiting the site, consumers can participate in polls featuring international players and read the weekly Global Top 10, which is a recap and feature of the league's international players. Video highlights are also available and consumers may sign up for e-news.

With FedEx Racing, consumers can obtain videos from races and track drivers' progress in the series. As one of the company's most interactive partnerships, fans can download clips and other media and play games like the Lawn Mower Challenge. These type of promotions link the FedEx brand to its respective sports partner in the mind of the consumer. Ideally, consumers that identify with racing will also identify with the FedEx brand. The interactivity of this partnership is highly appropriate given the nature of the company's services and consumer's familiarity with interactive media. Often, an interactive message is more lasting for consumers because they are actively engaged with the product.

Similar to FedEx Racing, the FedEx Cup partnership is also leveraged through significant interactivity and engagement. Consumers can play the FedEx Cup Nine, interact with a caddie, access the press tent, and stay up-to-date on the standings via e-mail. This capitalizes on consumers' emotional attachment to golf while also enhancing the likelihood of positive brand image transfer between FedEx and the PGA. Research has shown that this partnership has enhanced brand awareness for the company, particularly among PGA fans. Partnerships like this reach consumers in meaningful ways and, in doing so, increase brand awareness. This increase in brand awareness is often highly advantageous to companies in maintaining favorable brand presence.

FedEx has also been strategic in its official partnerships with the Orange Bowl, the FedEx Forum, FedEx Field, and the Southern Heritage Classic. These partnerships reinforce the company's commitment to quality while reinforcing the brand in a favorable manner. Its efforts have resulted in greater brand recognition and strong brand equity.

The Final Score

FedEx has creatively and strategically partnered with various sport properties to enhance its visibility and generate a favorable brand image. Fully aware
of its target consumer, FedEx has selected sport partnerships that not only
reach its target consumer but do so in a manner that reinforces the consumers'
image of the brand. FedEx has been careful to develop promotions and activation strategies that reflect its values and that of its sport partners. It clearly
links itself to its sports properties in meaningful and interactive ways. Its Air
and Ground theme with the NFL, its Global Leader in Assists with the NBA,
and its racing and golf partnerships appropriately link the company to those
respective sports. The partnerships incorporate the ideals of the sports properties and serve as effective cross-promotions for both entities.

When activating its sport partnerships, the company uses various strategies, but these strategies center on the maintenance and enhancement of the
brand. Whether it's the partnership with the PGA, the NFL, or the Southern
Heritage Classic, FedEx has been strategic in disseminating its brand message
to its key constituents. Its sport partnerships not only highlight the company's
service and reliability but also allow consumers to be exposed to the product
in a way that has meaning. This exposure serves to further build its brand equity while also reaffirming consumer confidence in the services provided by
FedEx.

Not only do these partnerships advance the brand mission of FedEx, they
also enhance the mission of the respective sport entities. The partnerships market both FedEx and their sport partners to the masses in a subtle and fun manner. This type of brand development is unobtrusive and often has a more
lasting impact on the consumer. For example, with FedEx Cup Nine, consumers can play "nine holes" on the virtual greens in the computerized game.
This allows the consumer to have an interactive experience, which both promotes the PGA and FedEx, while also reinforcing consumers' brand image of
FedEx. Similar partnerships with the NBA and NASCAR also serve to promote
both entities. FedEx Global Scouting Report and the FedEx Around the World
Sweepstakes promote the international flavor of the NBA, while enticing fans
to use their knowledge of NBA players to win prizes. This educates fans on the
NBA and its players while reinforcing FedEx's global services. The Lawn Mower
Challenge and Racing Fan Mail are also designed to be fun and educational. Each
of these partnerships has been structured and activated in such a manner that
consumers may not realize they are the targets of advertising. This subtle message management can be ideal when building a strong brand image in a cluttered marketplace.

As FedEx continues to enhance the global services it provides, it will likely increase its involvement with sport. The company has established itself as a top brand in its product service category and has structured its sport partnerships for maximum brand exposure and reinforcement. This type of brand development is key to achieving sustained success in a cluttered marketplace.

Post-Game Comments

- FedEx is a global leader in the shipping and freight industry.
- The company has experienced tremendous growth in its thirty-seven-year history.
- Advertising for the company has focused on generating consumer confidence in the reliability of its services.
- To continue to build its brand and reinforce its corporate values, FedEx partners with several sport properties, mostly in North America.
- The company has been strategic in the development and activation of its sports partnerships. It links its brand values to those of its sport partners using interactivity and marketing strategies that have significant meaning to the daily lives of consumers.
- Many of its sport partnerships are designed to subtly reinforce consumers' favorable brand image of FedEx and its services.
- Its sport partnerships have been key in its brand development and market both the company and the respective sport property.

Web Resources

http://about.fedex.designcdt.com/access
http://about.fedex.designcdt.com/files/factsheet_corporate.pdf
http://about.fedex.designcdt.com/our_company/company_information/fedex_
    corporation
http://about.fedex.designcdt.com/our_company/company_information/fedex_
    history/fedex_timeline
http://about.fedex.designcdt.com/our_company/fedex_innovation
http://about.fedex.designcdt.com/our_company/marketing_and_advertising
http://about.fedex.designcdt.com/our_company/vision_and_leadership
http://www.nba.com/fedex
http://fedexcup.van.fedex.com
http://fedex.com/us/sports/nfl/attack.html?link=4

http://fedex.com/us/sports/nfl/ [denoted as "Fed Ex and the NFL"]
http://fedex.com/us/sports/nfl/teamstats/?link=4
http://football.fedex.com
http://football.fedex.com/rulesandregs.aspx
http://www.fedex.com/us/sports/fedexfield
http://www.fedex.com/us/sports/fedexforum/?link=4
http://www.fedex.com/us/sports/fedexracing
http://www.fedex.com/us/sports/nfl/attack.html?link=4
http://www.fedex.com/us/sports/orangebowl
http://www.fedex.com/us/sports/shc

Additional Resources

Brees, Peterson voted FedEx Air and Ground players of the year. (2009, January 28). NFL Press Release. Retrieved March 15, 2009, from http://www.nfl.com/partner?partnerType=players-air-and-ground.

Broughton, D. (2008, October 27). Playoff sponsorship raises FedEx's profile. *Street & Smith's SportsBusiness Journal, 11*(26), 36.

FedEx and the NFL: Air and Ground Game. (2009). FedEx.com. Retrieved March 15, 2009, from http://www.fedex.com/us/sports/nfl/attack.html?link=4.

Chapter 15

Home Depot: It's Time to ...

Kimberly S. Miloch,
Texas Woman's University

Company: Home Depot
Location: Atlanta, GA
Internet Address: www.homedepot.com

Discussion Questions

- How have Home Depot's sport partnerships enhanced its overall brand image?
- Why was staying true to its core corporate values critical to Home Depot's brand success?
- How has the Olympics movement been beneficial for the brand development of Home Depot?
- What impact does Home Depot's involvement with ESPN's College Game-Day have on its overall brand image?
- How has the Home Depot brand stayed true to its core values while also representing its global growth and expansion?
- Why should companies such as Home Depot be selective and strategic in choosing sport partners?
- What can other companies learn from Home Depot's strategic brand develop via its sport partnerships?

The Line-Up

Founders Bernie Marcus, Arthur Blank, Ken Langone, and Pat Farrah opened the first Home Depot stores in Atlanta, Georgia, in 1979. Their mission was to provide a one-stop shopping environment for home improvement, while focusing on eight core values. These eight values embody what the company refers to as its "orange-blooded" culture and center on:

1. Taking care of people.
2. Giving back to the community.
3. Doing the right thing.
4. Excellent customer service.
5. Creating shareholder value.
6. Building strong relationships.
7. An entrepreneurial spirit.
8. Respect for all people.

The company operates using an inverted pyramid structure, which places the primary focus on the consumer and a secondary focus on management. By using this structure, the company strives to not only provide excellent customer service but also educate and train the consumer on how to make their home improvements. Cultivating and maintaining a strong brand identity among consumers is an integral step in creating brand loyalty to the product. Home Depot has always evaluated its brand image to ensure its message is being properly disseminated to the masses (Viveiros, 2006). This is evident in the company's overall marketing strategy as well as in its sport marketing efforts.

Home Depot uses its sport partnerships to distinguish its brand from competing brands, like Lowe's. From its Olympic Job Opportunities program to its NASCAR and NFL affiliations, Home Depot has consistently developed and activated sport partnerships with wide-ranging impact on its consumers. As illustrated in the timeline, the company's sport associations have increased as it has grown its brand.

Timeline of Events

1978
  • Company founded by Bernie Marcus and Arthur Blank.
1979
  • First store opens in Atlanta.
1980
  • Implements "how to" training seminars in stores.
1981
  • Becomes a publicly traded company.
1990
  • The Olympic Job Opportunities program is launched.

1993
- Employs more Olympic athletes than any other company.

1994
- Sponsors the Canadian Olympic Team and establishes the Canadian Olympic Job Opportunity program.

1995
- Introduces line of home improvement books.

1996
- Sponsors the Centennial Olympic Games in Atlanta and the Paralympic Games.

1997
- Announces its commitment to sponsor the Olympics through 2004.

1998
- Begins partnership with Joe Gibbs Racing.

2000
- Goes online with www.homedepot.com.
- The company launches its Olympic Job program in Puerto Rico.

2003
- The company becomes the naming rights sponsor of The Home Depot Center on the campus of California State University in Carson.
- Sponsors the Mexican national soccer team.
- The company begins awarding the NCAA Division I-A Home Depot Coach of the Year Award.

2005
- Establishes partnership with the International Speedway Corporation.
- Home Depot becomes the Official Home Improvement Retailer of motorsport facilities.
- The company partners with Major League Baseball.

2007
- Home Depot becomes the exclusive sponsor of the NFL Network's Post Game Show.

Note: The timeline of events was developed from the company's interactive timeline located online at http://corporate.homedepot.com.

Reinforcing "It's Time" through Sport

"It's time." This is the slogan used by Home Depot when encouraging consumers to select the company for their home improvement and design needs. The company focuses on the "weekend warrior" or the do-it-your-self home owner. Advertising for the company reminds consumers that "it's time" by using variations of the slogan, including "it's time to sweat," "it's time to get messy," "it's time to try something new," "it's time to dream big," "it's time to have the coolest house on the block," and "it's time to start." These slogans, combined with the company's commitment to its mission, maintain and reinforce the brand vision and values established by its founders.

As the timeline illustrates, the company has been committed to cultivating and reinforcing its brand through sport. It should also be noted that one of the company's founders, Arthur Blank, is owner of the Atlanta Falcons. This link has proved beneficial for the company as it has turned to sport to enhance its brand. The company expanded its sports ties on a global scale as it expanded its global reach. This is evident through its expansion of its Olympic Job Op-portunities program and its sponsorship of the Mexican national soccer team and the Canadian Olympic Team.

As with many companies, Home Depot has used sport to generate aware-ness among consumers and to reinforce and maintain its brand image. Since its inception, the company has partnered with the Olympics, the Paralympics, NASCAR, the NFL, and ESPN. As Home Depot grew, it also developed more sport partnerships. These partnerships are highlighted next, and they illus-trate how sport can be a major advantage to companies in generating aware-ness in a cluttered marketplace.

The Olympic Movement and the Olympic Job Opportunities Program

For sixteen years, Home Depot partnered with the Olympics movement. As part of this partnership, the company instituted the Olympic Job Op-portunities program in North America. For the duration of this program, Home Depot employed more Olympic hopefuls than any other company. As part of this program, the company allowed Olympic and Paralympic ath-letes a flexible part-time work schedule with full-time pay and benefits. The company recognized the time and commitment necessary for promising athletes to train and develop the skills needed to succeed at the Olympic level. Although the company recently ended this program, it supported and recognized Olympic hopefuls while celebrating the company's core values at the same time.

The Home Depot Center

In addition to the Olympic Job Opportunities program, Home Depot funded and built the Home Depot Center. Located on the campus of California State University in Carson, the facility has the purpose of providing Olympic hopefuls in various sports with a state-of-the-art training facility.

NASCAR and Joe Gibbs Racing

Through its partnership with NASCAR and Joe Gibbs Racing, Home Depot reinforces its values through the establishment of KaBOOM! and the Racing to Play program. Both programs are designed to meet the company's mission of giving back to its community. Through KaBOOM!, Home Depot strives to build playgrounds for American children. The goal is for playgrounds to be built within walking distance of children's homes. Linked to KaBOOM!, Racing to Play was developed to positively impact at-risk youths living in NASCAR communities. In conjunction with partner Joe Gibbs Racing, Home Depot strives to build racing-themed KaBOOM! playgrounds.

This partnership has also provided the company with numerous cross-promotional opportunities with other brands, including Coca-Cola and DeWalt Tools. These cross-promotional opportunities allow for more effective activation of the sponsorship and give the brand a broader consumer appeal.

National Football League

As the official home improvement sponsor of the NFL, Home Depot has access to the NFL's community affairs activities and serves as the presenting sponsor of NFL interactive theme park, The NFL Experience. Additionally, the company is the exclusive sponsor of the NFL Network's Post Game Show and is developing and managing a community service-focused program that is highlighted on the network's *Total Access* series. The company also partners with the NFL's Atlanta Falcons, Tampa Bay Buccaneers, Washington Redskins, and Denver Broncos.

ESPN

As part of the company's partnership with ESPN, Home Depot is the presenting sponsor of College GameDay. "ESPN College GameDay built by Home

Depot" allows the company to have a strategic brand presence in almost all of ESPN's college sports coverage.

Other Sport Partnerships

Home Depot also sponsors the Mexican national soccer team and partners with other individual franchises. These include agreements with MBL teams: Atlanta Braves, Boston Red Sox, Cincinnati Reds, Los Angeles Angels of Anaheim, San Diego Padres, and the Seattle Mariners. Partnerships in the NBA include the Phoenix Suns and the Atlanta Hawks. Its NHL sponsorship includes the Atlanta Thrashers. The company is also affiliated with the University of Hawaii and the Georgia Institute of Technology. Minor league partnerships include those with the Kane County Cougars and the Yakima Bears. The company also gives out the NCAA-Division I-A Coach of the Year Award.

The Final Score

Home Depot continues to embody the mission its founders envisioned by utilizing its sport partnerships to market its services and to develop programs that reinforce its key values and corporate culture. These partnerships and programs allow the Home Depot to build on its corporate culture and infuse its brand values not only through its company but also through its community. These brand management strategies have allowed the company to strengthen the brand in North America. As the company entered the Canadian and South American markets, it increased its sport partnerships in those regions, as well. As the company expands on a global scale, similar tactics must be implemented to maintain the strength of the Home Depot brand.

These partnerships illustrate the value of a comprehensive marketing strategy that focuses on brand management. Home Depot has used its sport partnerships to both heighten brand awareness and encourage repeat consumption. It has marketed to consumers in a manner that exposes mass audiences to its products and services by developing sport partnerships that have been well received. The company has maintained a key focus on its brand image; regardless of its tremendous growth, it has consistently reminded consumers that "it's time" to pursue whatever home improvement project they desire.

Post-Game Comments

- Home Depot's selection of sport partners allows the company to build on its existing corporate culture.
- The company's program extensions through its partnerships are ideal because they afford the company the opportunity to synergize its marketing efforts while continuously reinforcing its brand values.
- As the company has grown and expanded, it has continued to make its values a focal point. In doing so, the company has generated significant brand awareness.
- In selecting sport partners and in developing program extensions, the company stayed true to the mission of its founders. By not deviating from its mission, the value of the Home Depot brand has been greatly enhanced.
- Home Depot has a storied history with the Olympics, which has allowed it to enhance its corporate culture and brand image while also giving back to the community.
- The company engages in sport partnerships that will allow it to reinforce its existing brand image, programs, and values.
- Home Depot stays true to its core mission and eight key values when activating its sport partnerships.

Web Resources

http://corporate.homedepot.com
http://corporate.homedepot.com/wps/portal/Sports_Sponsorships
http://ir.homedepot.com/ReleaseDetail.cfm?ReleaseID=224939
http://ir.homedepot.com/releasedetail.cfm?releaseid=186191

Additional Resources

Home Depot sizes up sponsorship. (2003, July). *Retail Merchandiser, 43*(7), 42.
Sponsors and Licensing. (2009, March). *Sportstravel, 13*(3), 8.
Viveiros, B. (2006, November 1). Brand makeovers. *Direct, 18*(13), 14.

Chapter 16

Coca-Cola: Demand the Genuine

Kimberly S. Miloch,
Texas Woman's University

Company: Coca-Cola
Location: Atlanta, GA
Internet Address: www.coca-cola.com

Discussion Questions

- What are some of the brand strategies used by Coca-Cola to establish its brand presence in North America and globally?
- How has Coca-Cola's partnership with and support of the Olympics movement impacted the brand's global presence?
- What technological advancements have been central to the establishment of the Coca-Cola brand in North America and Europe?
- How have the company's selection of sport partnerships impacted its brand presence? Would the company have the same brand presence if it had selected different sport partners? Discuss and support your opinions.
- How has the company maintained its brand presence in the face of an ever-changing global economy?
- Why is Coca-Cola's global brand presence integral to its long-term success and financial viability?
- How does the NASCAR affiliation support the brand and encourage repeat consumption of the brand's products?
- In your opinion, which of the company's sport partnerships are most effective? Discuss and support your opinion.

The Line-Up

Since its inception in 1886, the Coca-Cola brand has engrained itself in American culture and expanded its reach globally. It is one of the world's most recognized brands, and was rated number 1 in Interbrand's list of top global brands in both 2006 and 2007. The company has launched some of the most memorable advertising campaigns in history. From one of its earliest campaigns—"Demand the Genuine," to "I'd Like to Buy the World a Coke," "Have a Coke and a Smile," "Always the Real Thing," and "Catch the Wave"—and its more current campaigns like "The Coke Side of Life," the beverage company has always sought to distinguish its brand from that of its competitors.

The product was created by pharmacist Dr. John Pemberton in Atlanta. In conjunction with his business partner, Frank Robinson, the trademark Coca-Cola was written and has remained unchanged since its development. Although the company has expanded from its small, downtown Atlanta roots to a company with significant global presence, Coca-Cola has maintained true to Pemberton's idea of providing a tasty, refreshing beverage for consumers. Regardless of its new product lines and its growth in foreign markets, the company has not deviated from its original brand identity.

Coca-Cola has a storied past, and many marketing experts credit the company for recovery from a key marketing blunder in the mid-1980s: New Coke. After tweaking the beverage's formula, the company launched a new version of the drink. Protests were waged and consumers were dumbfounded; some even stockpiled the "Old Coke." Shortly after its release, the company again began offering the original beverage, dubbing it Coca-Cola Classic. Although marketers widely criticized the company's launch of New Coke, executives at the company perceive this incident as a key point in the history of Coca-Cola. The launch of New Coke will forever be engrained in the minds of Americans. Consumers' response to its launch signifies the impact Coca-Cola has had on American culture.

Timeline of Events

1886
- John Stith Pemberton formulates the beverage.

1888
- Asa Candler purchases Coca-Cola.

1892
- The Coca-Cola Company is incorporated.

1895
 · The beverage becomes available in all states and territories of the United States.

1899
 · Bottling begins.

1916
 · Contoured bottle design developed.

1919
 · Ernest Woodruff and W. C. Bradley purchase the company for $25 million.
 · Becomes a publicly sold company.

1946
 · Bottling plants open internationally.

1955
 · Ten-ounce, twelve-ounce, and twenty-six-ounce cans are sold.

1960
 · Merges with the Minute Maid Company.

1977
 · Two-liter bottles sold.

1982
 · Diet Coke launches.

1985
 · New Coke debuts.
 · New Coke is removed from the market and Coca-Cola Classic returns.

1988
 · Landor & Associates name Coca-Cola as the world's best known trademark.

This timeline was developed using "The Chronicle of Coca-Cola" as a guide located at http://www.thecoca-colacompany.com/heritage/chronicle_birth_refreshing_idea.html. Additional timeline information is presented in Exhibits 16.1 and 16.2.

Coca-Cola and Brand Development

Throughout its history, the company has sought to remain true to its original message: the Coca-Cola beverage is fun and refreshing. Its commitment to its brand and its ability to remain true to this vision has dramatically contributed to the brand's success. See Exhibit 16.1 for examples of Coca-Cola's Advertising Campaigns over the years.

Exhibit 16.1 Coca-Cola Advertising Campaigns

1929	"The Pause that Refreshes"
1936	"It's the Refreshing Thing to Do"
1942	"It's the Real Thing"
1944	"Global High Sign"
1950	"Sign of Good Taste"
	"Be Really Refreshed"
	"Go Better Refreshed"
1963	"Things Go Better with Coke"
1969	"It's the Real Thing"
1971	"I'd Like to Buy the World a Coke"
1976	"Coke Adds Life"
1979	"Have a Coke and a Smile"
1982	"Coke Is It"
Late 1980s	"Can't Beat the Feeling"
1990	"Can't Beat the Real Thing"
1993	"Always Coca-Cola"
2003	"Coca-Cola ... Real"
2006	"The Coke Side of Life"
2009	"Open Happiness"

Exhibit 16.1 was developed by using "The Chronicle of Coca-Cola," located at http://www.thecoca-colacompany.com/heritage/chronicle_moving_times.html.

Differentiating and Reinforcing the Coca-Cola Brand through Sport

The company has always been on the forefront of brand management. It uses numerous integrated marketing strategies to further its brand presence, including lifestyle, entertainment, and cause marketing. The company has altered its packaging to activate its sport partnerships and has developed interactive activities designed to connect people all over the world. In fact, one of its most memorable commercials involved "Mean Joe" Green of the Pittsburgh Steelers. Tied to its "Have a Coke and a Smile" advertising, the commercial featured a young boy and the linebacker. At the end, Mean Joe gives the boy his jersey, showing his "softer" side.

Recent research indicated that Coca-Cola was the most admired brand by sports fans. More than 26 percent of fans surveyed listed Coca-Cola as one of five brands they most admire (Mullman, 2007). Such favorable brand perception is likely a result of the company's involvement in grassroots programs combined with its association with large-scale events on both the national and international scales. "The brand is a huge backer of major sports, as the official soft drink of NASCAR and the PGA Tour, and as one of the largest backers of the NCAA and the Olympics. But its brand is nearly as ubiquitous on and around local community fields as it is in pro arenas, thanks in part to a longtime relationship with the Boys & Girls Clubs of America, among others" (Mullman, 2007, p. 22). Coca-Cola's support of Triple Play and the NCAA YES Clinics are part of its Balanced Living initiative. Triple Play, the national after school program of the Boys and Girls Clubs of America, encourages participation in sports by girls and strives to keep youth active by encouraging healthy and active lifestyles. The NCAA's Youth Education through Sports (YES) Clinics provide opportunities for teens to learn the fundamentals of numerous sports, including football, soccer, volleyball, basketball, track and field, and baseball.

The company has also relied on sport to enhance its brand reach and was one of the first companies to partner with the Olympics. Coca-Cola's partnership with the Olympics was established just a few years after the company's inception; most recently, the company announced its intention to continue the partnership through 2020. Although Coca-Cola engages in partnerships with numerous sport entities, its most prolific involvement has centered on its association with the Olympics.

The Olympic Movement and Coca-Cola

The Olympics and Coca-Cola have a long-standing partnership. Coca-Cola first began sponsoring the Olympics in 1928 and shipped the product with the U.S. team in Amsterdam that year. In 1979, Coca-Cola partnered with the U.S. Olympic Committee and founded the U.S. Olympic Hall of Fame. 2008 marks the eightieth year of Coca-Cola's Olympic involvement. A brief timeline of the company's Olympics involvement is provided in Exhibit 16.2.

As Exhibit 16.2 illustrates, Coca-Cola has always been committed to cultivating and reinforcing the goodwill of its brand through sport, specifically the Olympics movement. As its global reach expanded, so did its Olympics involvement. The Olympics symbolizes the best of the Coca-Cola brand, as illustrated in the longevity of the partnership.

Exhibit 16.2 Coca-Cola and The Olympic Games

1928 Amsterdam:	Shipped Coca-Cola with the U.S. athletes to Amsterdam.
1932 Los Angeles:	Provided a personal record keeper and the beverage to attendees.
	Olympic Gold Medalist in swimming, Johnny Weissmuller, endorsed Coca-Cola.
1936 Berlin:	First served as Olympic sponsor.
1948 London:	Provided product for the Games.
1952 Oslo:	Donated a helicopter for use during the Games.
1952 Helsinki:	Provided the beverage as well as other souvenir items.
1956 Melbourne:	Coca-Cola was sold at the Games, and the company provided souvenir sun visors to event attendees.
1960 Rome:	Provided copies of the song of the day to attendees, event personnel, and athletes.
1964 Innsbruck:	Provided a "History of the Olympic Games."
1964 Tokyo:	Distributed sight-seeing guides.
1968 Grenoble:	Sponsored TV broadcasts from the Games.
1968 Mexico City:	Sponsored TV broadcasts from the Games.
1972 Munich:	Created a collectors' series of coins titled "Great Olympic Moments."
1976 Innsbruck:	Produced the film titled *Olympic Harmony*.
1976 Montreal:	Provided a horse ridden by the captain of the Canadian Equestrian team.
1980 Lake Placid:	Produced numerous souvenir items and debuted figure skating robot.
1980 Moscow:	Served as the official soft drink for the Games.
1984 Sarajevo:	Provided approximately 1 million cans of product for the Games.
1984 Los Angeles:	Implemented youth programs and developed a series of collectible cans.
1988 Calgary:	Debuted the Coca-Cola World Chorus.
1988 Seoul:	Hosted trading centers for Olympic pin collectors.
1992 Albertville:	Provided radio facilities and equipment for broadcasts of Coca-Cola radio.
1992 Barcelona:	Sponsored the Olympic Torch Bearers Program (TOP).
1994 Lillehammer:	Provided the Pin of the Day for attendees.

1996 Atlanta:	Given the Olympics presence in its headquartered city, the company had a significant presence at these Games. The company served as presenting sponsor of the Olympic Torch Relay and provided attendees with art exhibits, pin trading centers, souvenir items, and other special events.
2002 Salt Lake City:	Celebrated its tenth anniversary as Torch Relay sponsor and provided numerous interactive venues for attendees.
2004 Athens:	Sponsored the Torch Relay and provided more pin trading centers.
2006 Torino:	Developed and hosted the "Torch Exhibition Tour" Launched a blog series titled "Tornio Conversations."
2008 Beijing:	Highlighted its "Live Olympic on the Coke Side of Life" campaign, which focused on the enduring global spirit of the Olympic Games and provided a series of five collectible cans encouraging consumers to "Bring Home the World."

This table was synthesized and developed from the information provided in "Coca-Cola and the Olympic Games: Our Partnership History," located at http://www.thecoca-colacompany.com/heritage/pdf/ Olympics_ Partnership.pdf.

To best capitalize on its Olympics partnerships, Coca-Cola familiarizes itself with local communities and cultures. Its most recent partnership with the 2008 Beijing Games focused on its "Live Olympic on the Coke Side of Life" campaign. This highlighted China as a country, and the company altered packaging to reflect the Chinese culture. The commemorative packaging included Chinese characters that meant "delicious happiness" in Mandarin. "Delicious happiness" was included on each package in the language of the country where it was distributed (Zmuda, 2008). "Packaging is the best way to interact with consumers. They might not watch TV or get on the net, but they're going to see Mandarin packing" (p. 6). Coca-Cola's understanding and commitment to the local cultures in which it sells its product has dramatically enhanced its ability to effectively brand its products.

NASCAR and the Coca-Cola Racing Team

Though not as long-standing as its Olympics partnership, Coca-Cola's affiliation with NASCAR and its racing team, branded as the Coca-Cola Racing

Team, also help differentiate and grow the brand. This affiliation is not on the global scale of the Olympics movement, but is equally effective. The racing team enhances the brand and encourages repeat consumption of the company's beverage through its online rewards program. Those that purchase certain Coke brands may enter the codes provided on the caps and earn points for redemption. Consumers can redeem points for a variety of rewards, including birthday e-cards from the Coca-Cola drivers and the opportunity to enter for a chance to win a trip to the Coke 600, held annually at the Lowe's Motor Speedway in Concord, North Carolina.

Although it doesn't have the global reach of the company's Olympics partnership, the partnership with NASCAR provides a unique opportunity for Coca-Cola to encourage repeat consumption of its brand and further educate the consumer on its products.

Coca-Cola and Soccer in Europe and Mexico

The company has also partnered with Euro 2008 Soccer and the Mexican national soccer team. As part of this partnership, Coca-Cola drinkers can digitally collect, trade, and share "sticker albums" featuring the athletes from participating teams. This partnership highlights the company's ability to reinforce its brand presence while at the same time allowing consumers to interact and connect to the brand through a common shared interest in soccer. Consumers all over the world can interact at the click of a mouse and share their passion for the sport, while enjoying the best the Coca-Cola brand offers.

Coca-Cola and the PGA Tour

This partnership allows the company to reinforce its brand presence by supporting the PGA. This partnership includes direct links to the tour championship and allows the company to focus on a grassroots approach through sponsorship with the Champions Tour and Nationwide Tour. Via sponsorship, Coca-Cola serves as presenting sponsor of the tour championships and is the official soft drink of the PGA Tour, Champions Tour, and the Nationwide Tour. Recently, the company has become a major sponsor of the Australian PGA Championship, which includes naming rights at the PGA's National Junior Development Program in Australia. Through the sponsorship, Coca-Cola will promote the social and health benefits of golf and provide scholarships to young PGA professionals (PGA tastes better with coke, 2009). Extending its affiliation with the PGA allows the company reach a wider audience and assists in maintain its favorable image worldwide. By focusing on the social and health benefits of golf, the company is tapping into the lifestyles of its consumers. This puts the brand in the forefront of the consumer's mind and reinforces brand associations of the beverage.

The Final Score

Coca-Cola has grown from a company with a small local reach to a global powerhouse. It has remained entrepreneurial in nature, while maintaining a consistent brand focus. Although its focus has remained consistent, the company has been creative in the manner in which it brands its products. This is evident not only in its sport partnerships but in its many other partnerships in music, entertainment, and community activities throughout the world.

The company has primarily used the Olympics movement to further its brand presence but has developed and continues to engage in other sport partnerships, including those with soccer, NASCAR, and the PGA Tour. Recognizing the diversity of its portfolio, the company has established a strategic platform for each partnership that reinforces its overall brand presence. It has done so by being innovative and creative in the manner in which it reaches the masses.

Post-Game Comments

- Coca-Cola remained true to its original brand strategy while also expanding its global presence.
- The company's long-standing relationship with the Olympics movement has allowed it to grow and adapt to global trends in consumer needs and brand management.
- Coca-Cola has been strategic in selecting its sport partnerships. It selects events and programs that enable it to reinforce its brand image both locally and globally. In doing so, the company has developed a historically strong and recognized global brand.
- The company has used its sport partnerships to both establish its brand presence and generate loyalty and repeat consumption of its products.
- Coca-Cola's understanding of the local cultures in which it sells its product has dramatically enhanced its ability to effectively brand its products.
- Coca-Cola has used technology to connect consumers to its brand and enhance their enjoyment of the activities that mean the most to them.

- By understanding the culture and lifestyles of its consumers, the company has developed sport partnerships that enhance not only its brand presence but also the brand of the sport property.

Web Resources

http://heritage.coca-cola.com

http://www.coca-cola.com/template1/index.jsp?locale=en_US

http://www.coca-cola.com/template1/index.jsp?locale=en_US&site=../football/mnt/
   main.html

http://www.cokeusa.com/triple_play

http://www.euro2008album.com

http://www.mycokerewards.com/index.jsp?adParam=1#windowType:pLanding/id:
   3/Skin:true/SkinType:pillar/SkinID:home

http://www.pgatour.com/tournaments/r060/sponsors.html

http://www.thecoca-colacompany.com/heritage/chronicle_birth_refreshing-
   _idea.html

http://www.thecoca-colacompany.com/heritage/olympicgames.html

http://www.thecoca-colacompany.com/heritage/olympicgames_partnership.html

http://www.thecoca-colacompany.com/heritage/ourheritage.html

http://www.thecoca-colacompany.com/heritage/pdf/Olympics_Partnership.pdf

Additional Resources

Mullman, J. (2007). Sports fans root for the home team—but also cheer for Coke. *Advertising Age, 78*(45), 22.

PGA tastes better with Coke. (2009, February). *Golf Australia*, 240, 18–19.

Zmuda, N. (2008). Coke unleashes Olympic blitz. *Advertising Age, 79*(27), 6.

Chapter 17

McDonald's: I'm Lovin' It

Kimberly S. Miloch,
Texas Woman's University

Company: McDonald's Corporation
Location: Oak Brook, IL
Internet Address: www.mcdonalds.com

Discussion Questions

- How has McDonald's been strategic in selecting its sport partnerships?
- How do the company's sport partnerships reinforce its corporate values and charities?
- What specific brand management strategies have McDonald's used to establish itself as a premier global brand?
- How have the McDonald's sport partnerships allowed the company to develop its brand regionally, nationally, and globally?
- What impact do McDonald's products and brand images have on the sport consumer?
- What key challenges face the McDonald's brand in the future?
- Compare and contrast McDonald's sport partnerships with those of its competition.
- Examine the company's corporate values and mission. How do its sport partnerships and charities reflect those values and mission?

The Line-Up

McDonald's has been a mainstay in the American fast food industry since Ray Kroc opened his first store in Des Plaines, Illinois, in 1955. Since then, the popularity and growth of the fast food giant has soared, and the company now serves more than 52 million people per day in more than 100 countries.

McDonald's established itself as one of the world's top brands and has some of the world's most recognized products and brand images, including the Big Mac, the Happy Meal, the Golden Arches, and Ronald McDonald. Always on the forefront of integrated marketing, the company has consistently been listed in the top ten of Interbrand's best global brands. Considered the leader in the industry, McDonald's is keen on corporate responsibility and the betterment of its local communities. Through its Ronald McDonald House charities, the company focuses on the well-being of children. Both the McDonald's brand and its charitable arm are widely recognized on a global scale. Part of this recognition is due in large part to the company's association and involvement with sport. They were one of the first to recognize the impact sport affiliations can have in building brand recognition and have long relied on these relationships to generate awareness and position the brand in the United States and throughout the world. From its Olympics partnerships to its sponsorship of the McDonald's High School All-American Basketball games, McDonald's has developed and used sport partnerships to relate to consumers and enhance the strength of its brand.

Timeline of Events

1950s
- In 1955, Ray Kroc opens first McDonald's in Des Plaines, IL.
- McDonald's sponsors local Little League championships.

1963
- Ronald McDonald appears on television.

1968
- The Big Mac debuts.
- Hamburgers airlifted to Olympic athletes.

1974
- First official sponsorship of the Olympic Games.

1976
- In conjunction with the Philadelphia Eagles, the first Ronald McDonald House is opened in Philadelphia.

1977
- Inaugural McDonald's All-American High School Basketball team is named.

1979
- The Happy Meal debuts.

1984
- Secures title rights to the Olympic swimming venue in Los Angeles.

1993
- Begins affiliation with NASCAR.

1994
- Begins sponsorship of FIFA World Cup.

1996
- Places restaurants inside Olympic Village.

2002
- Inaugural McDonald's All-American High School women's basketball team is named.

2004
- Becomes an official AVP Pro Beach Volleyball sponsor.

2005
- Opens a flagship restaurant in Chicago to commemorate the company's fiftieth anniversary.

Building the Brand and I'm Lovin' It through Sport

McDonald's was one of the first companies to market its products to the masses through sport. In doing so, it has been strategic in the development of its sport partnerships and has fully integrated them into its overall corporate brand mission.

As illustrated in the above timeline and in Exhibit 17.1, the company has been proactive in its sport marketing efforts.

In the late 1970s, the company began sponsorship of the McDonald's All-American High School Basketball team. Since then, the event has grown tremendously and has featured some of basketball's top talents, including Magic Johnson, Michael Jordan, Shaquille O'Neal, LeBron James, and Candace Parker. In 2002, McDonald's added the women's basketball game. Remaining true to its charitable mission, a percentage of revenue derived from the game is allocated to the Ronald McDonald House Charities. The company recently formed the McDonald's All-American Advisory Council to help the event maintain its key focus points of showcasing the best high school basketball, a charitable focus, and mentorship of young basketball talent. The sponsorship not only enhances awareness for McDonald's but also reaffirms its commitment to youth.

As official sponsor of the 2006 FIFA World Cup, McDonald's continued to expand its global brand presence. Through this partnership, McDonald's established its Player Escort Program, which partnered youth with the players.

Player escorts walked hand in hand with players before each match, which again highlighted the company's commitment to the well-being of youth. In addition to this program, McDonald's established a fantasy game online and offered various promotions across the globe. These promotions included offering special sandwich promotions in Brazil, TV commercials in China, a text message contest in the United Kingdom, and a souvenir cup in the United States. This global activation of the sponsorship allowed McDonald's to continue to position its brand to global consumers.

As McDonald's continues to expand regionally, nationally, and globally, so have its global sport partnerships, as illustrated through its FIFA relationship. Through this expansion, the company has not lost sight of its original brand mission and has maintained consistency in its images and brand messages to consumers throughout the world. It began its sport partnerships by sponsoring local Little League championships during the late 1950s. It has now grown into a global sport partner, and McDonald's is widely considered a key Olympics sponsor. Exhibit 17.1 highlights McDonald's Olympics partnerships.

Exhibit 17.1 McDonald's Olympics Partnerships

1968 Grenoble	Airlifts hamburgers to U.S. Olympic athletes
1976 Montreal	First time as an official Olympic sponsor
1984 Los Angeles	Builds and secures naming rights to the swimming venue
1988 Seoul	Sponsors National Olympic Committees
1992 Barcelona	Sponsors National Olympic Committees
1994 Lillehammer	Sponsors National Olympic Committees
1996 Atlanta	Provides restaurant in the Olympic Village
	Begins its worldwide sponsorship of the Olympics
	Becomes member of the Olympic Partner Program (TOP)
1998 Nagano	First worldwide sponsorship of the Olympic Games
2000 Sydney	Sponsors Olympic Youth Camp
2002 Salt Lake City	Debuts the Olympic Champion Crew Program
2004 Athens	Announces its "Go Active" fitness campaign
2008 Beijing	Debuts its McDonald's Champion Kids program

Provided in part by Lefton (2005) and in part by www.mcdonalds.com

---

Through its Olympics partnerships, McDonald's has truly established itself as a premier brand in the minds of global consumers. It has not only generated great brand equity in doing so, it has created global goodwill by maintaining true to its mission of serving youth. The Champion Kids Program is one of the key programs affiliated with its Olympics partnership. For the 2008 Beijing Games, kids traveled to Beijing and acted as reporters for their hometowns. The mission of the program was to once again focus on the well-being of youth.

McDonald's has long affiliated itself with the Olympics. Its official partnership began in 1976, and the company recently announced that its official affiliation will continue through at least the 2012 London Games. This partnership allows McDonald's to enhance its brand equity globally while also reaffirming its charitable focus on youth. As illustrated in Exhibit 17.1, McDonald's has used the Olympics to reinforce and enhance its existing brand images and values. From the Olympic Youth Camp and Champion Kids program to its Olympic Crew Program, the company has used the Games to meet its marketing needs by reinvesting in its brand and reaffirming its corporate responsibility. It brands itself both internally and externally. James Skinner, McDonald's vice chairman and chief executive officer, noted:

> Throughout the 2008 Olympic Games in Beijing, China, our Olympic Champion Crew will represent their home countries to proudly serve McDonald's world famous food to the world's best athletes, coaches, officials, and media—our best serving the world's best.... The members of the 2008 elite team were selected based on local programs in which they demonstrated their commitment to restaurant operations, customer service, and teamwork.... This is their opportunity to be an ambassador for our brand, their country and their local restaurant. The managers and crew of this year's Olympic Champion Crew share the spirit, and ideals of the Olympic Movement and help bring those to life with our customers everyday. The Olympic Champion Crew Program generates excitement in our local markets and builds trust, camaraderie, and pride among our employees. Further, the program illustrates that McDonald's is not only a great place to work, but a great place with unique opportunities for those who work for us. While in china, the Olympic Champion Crew will work hard representing our Brand to the world (Skinner, 2007, para. 2–4).

Skinner's comments indicate the strategic nature in which McDonald's maintains and reaffirms its brand image. It is strategic by carefully developing and selecting various promotions and internal marketing activities that continuously reinforce the brand on a corporate, local, and international scale.

Through its partnerships with AVP, FIFA, NASCAR, the McDonald's All American High School Basketball Games, and its sponsorship of several NBA,

MLS, NHL, and NFL teams, McDonald's continues to reinforce its brand image among a wide array of consumers. Sport is an ideal avenue to reinforce brand messages, as it appeals to the majority of the masses. Sport fans share a common passion for sport, but they vary widely in their demographic profiles and lifestyle characteristics. By engaging in partnerships with varying sport entities, McDonald's ensures its brand messaging reaches diverse and large audiences worldwide.

The Final Score

The McDonald's brand has grown tremendously since Ray Kroc opened the first store in 1955. Kroc established the brand on the basis of fun, and that brand vision is what has helped the fast food giant establish itself as one of the world's premier brands and a staple of American culture. From the Golden Arches and Ronald McDonald to the Big Mac and Chicken McNuggets, McDonald's has been a leader in brand management and has used its sport partnerships as a primary vehicle to reinforce its dominance in a global marketplace.

The McDonald's All American Basketball Team combined with the company's development of programs like its Champion Kids and Go Active! have reinforced its value system of fun while also supporting the mission of its Ronald McDonald House Charities, which specifically focus on the well-being of youth. McDonald's has strategically linked its brand to the Olympic spirit and in doing so has also created innovative programs, like its Olympic Champion Crew. This not only reinforces the brand externally but also builds corporate brand equity while establishing a favorable internal brand image among its employees and shareholders.

Establishing a global brand image is challenging for any corporation, but McDonald's has relied on sport partnerships with entities like the FIFA World Cup and the Olympics to expose its products to global sport consumers. Its longstanding relationship with FIFA and the Olympics only solidifies its commitment to its brand values and enhances its brand equity worldwide.

In the United States, McDonald's has strategically partnered with the major sports leagues and has also established firm commitments with NASCAR and the AVP. Both NASCAR and the AVP continue to post strong and loyal followings. The unique manner in which the company reinforces its brand through these affiliations continues to set it apart from its competition.

McDonalds has always been at the forefront of brand management and serves as an outstanding example for other corporations to emulate. The company strives to use its sport involvement to enhance its global brand equity. It has selected its sports partnerships carefully to most represent its brand management needs. This alignment will continue as McDonald's continuously strives to maintain its strong brand presence on a global scale.

Post-Game Comments

- McDonald's is a leading global brand.
- The company has franchises in more than 100 countries.
- It is the leader in the fast food industry and continues to expand globally.
- By selecting key sport partnerships, the company has reaffirmed its "fun" brand image and exposed its products to billions worldwide.
- Through its sport partnerships, McDonald's has reinforced its commitment to its values.
- McDonald's has some of the most recognized logos and products in the world.
- Its Ronald McDonald House Charities have been enhanced via its sport partnerships.
- By maintaining a consistent brand image, the company has also build its corporate equity through an enhanced relationship with its employees and shareholders.

Web Resources

http://www.interbrand.com/best_brands_2007.asp
http://www.mcdepk.com/2008OlympicGames/index.html
http://www.mcdepk.com/2008OlympicGames/resourcematerials/McDonalds_
    Olympic_History.pdf
http://www.mcdepk.com/olympicresourcecenter/downloads/olympic_advert_
    facts.pdf
https://www.mcdocc.com/c/home.htm
http://www.mcdonalds.com/corp/about.html
http://www.mcdonalds.com/corp/about/factsheets.RowPar.0001.ContentPar.0001.
    ColumnPar.0006.File1.tmp/Community%20Fact%20Sheet.pdf
http://www.mcdonalds.com/corp/news/corppr/corprelease_2008/07_02_08_mcd_s
    _bringing.html
http://www.mcdonalds.com/usa/sports/basketball.html
http://www.mcdonalds.com/usa/sports/cup.html

http://www.mcdonaldsallamerican.com
http://www.nascar.com/2005/news/business/03/30/mcdonalds/index.html

Additional Resources

Lefton, T. (2005, May 30). How McDonald's has used sports to package the perfect pitch during most of its 50 year history. *SportsBusiness Journal, 8*(6), 15.

Skinner, J. (2007). Welcome to the McDonald's Olympic Champion Crew Program. Retrieved April 14, 2009, from https://www.mcdocc.com/c/home.htm.

Chapter 18

Mountain Dew: Taking Soft Drinks to the Extreme

Jason W. Lee,
University of North Florida

Company: Mountain Dew (a subsidiary of PepsiCo, Inc.)
Location: Purchase, NY
Internet Address: www.mountaindew.com

Discussion Questions

- How has Mountain Dew's image changed since its inception?
- Whom does Mountain Dew target and why?
- What type of presence does Dew have in the world of action sport? Has this been a successful approach?
- Is Dew synonymous with action sports? Why or why not?

The Line-Up

Mountain Dew transcends merely being a soft drink. The image of the Dew has become a cultural icon. Mountain Dew is a classic example of cultural branding in which a target audience is identified within a market example of an identity brand. Such methods can be enacted through reaching out to "myth" markets. Mountain Dew has been able to tap into these myths from its inception. Through its duration, the Dew has relied on myths from the cultures of hillbillies, being country cool, and going to the extreme.

Mountain Dew's popularity has spread from the hills of Tennessee to become a global phenomenon. This treat that could "tickle your innards" is now clearly affiliated with the risk-taking, thrill-seeking world of extreme sport.

The question begs to be asked: how does a company go from identifying itself with the hills of Tennessee to being the drink of choice for X Gamers? This chapter sheds some light on the issue.

Timeline of Events

1940s
- Mountain Dew's origins can be traced back to the hills of Tennessee. The precursor beverages are marketed in this decade.

1954
- The Tri-City Beverage Company in Johnson City, TN, is the first franchisee of an early version of Mountain Dew.

1964
- Mountain Dew goes national after being purchased by PepsiCo.

1970s
- The BBDO advertising agency helps usher in a new phase of Mountain Dew.
- Hillbilly images remains on bottles into this decade, however, in the mid-1970s a shift from the earlier hillbilly imagery to a "Country Cool" theme is emerging.

1980s
- Mountain Dew promotes a Country Cool image throughout the decade
- MD used slogans such as "Give me a DEW," "DEW it to it," and "DEW it Country Cool."

1993
- Featured in commercials, Mountain Dew's Dew Crew shows their affinity for extreme activities including sky surfing, mountain biking, and bungee jumping.

1995
- Mountain Dew is a proud sponsor of the inaugural X Games.

2002
- Mountain Dew kicks off the Free Flow Tour.

2005
- The Dew Action Sports Tour begins.
- MD Films releases the snowboarding motion picture *First Descent.*
- Dew signs motorsport driver Brian Vickers to a multiyear contract.

2007
- Dale Earnhardt Jr. sponsored by Mountain Dew and AMP Energy Drinks (Mountain Dew's line of energy drinks).

What Is Mountain Dew?

Mountain Dew is a caffeinated, citrus-flavored soft drink that is owned by PepsiCo. Dew is among Pepsi's most popular brands, and is only surpassed in the soft drink industry by brand giant colas Coke and Pepsi (see Exhibit 18.1). With annual sales of $4.7 billion, Dew is an enormously popular brand, and much of the success associated with this drink has been tied to its appeal to young, active consumers.

Mountain Dew's beginnings can be traced back to the hills of Tennessee in the 1940s. The name Mountain Dew was a euphemism used in Southern culture for moonshine; the caffeinated sugar beverage was gladly associated with this image in its early days.

Exhibit 18.1 Mountain Dew and the Crowded Citrus Soft Drink Market

Mountain Dew is by no means the only product of its kind. Other citrus-flavored soft drinks on the market include:
- 7-Up
- Fanta
- Fresca
- Mello Yello*
- Orange Crush
- Sprite
- Squirt
- Sundrop
- Sunkist
- Surge**
- Sierra Mist
- Vault

 * Mello Yello is produced by Pepsi's rival soft drink bottler Coca-Cola, and is perhaps the most similar to Mountain Dew.
** Surge is no longer produced.

The Images of Dew: From Hillbilly to Country Cool to the Extreme

The genesis of this "zero-proof moonshine" was categorized by country (more specifically hillbilly) themes. During the early years of the beverage's existence, such images were used in a variety of ways, including:

- Sketches of "Willie the Hillbilly" on signs and bottles.
- A tactic in which names of individual bottlers, sellers, and towns were written under the name of Mountain Dew on bottles in efforts to make the product seem more of an "illegally cooked" batch of moonshine.
- Animated advertisements featured a character named Clem, who replaced Willie the Hillbilly.
- Hillbilly images remained on bottles into the 1970s.

The 1970s saw a bridge between the hillbilly image and today's extreme sport image in the form of a country cool theme. This theme was categorized by such slogans as "Doin' It Country Cool." The appeal has been compared to that of the popularity of other country themed entities, such as TV series *The Dukes of Hazzard* or the immensely popular Southern rock culture, featuring acts like Lynyrd Skynryd and the Charlie Daniels Band.

Mountain Dew's marketing target today is radically different. It is mainly marketed to people aligned with a young, energetic profile. Being tuned in to the importance of image and identity, the powers that be decided that the brand image of their soft drink needed to be something that could appeal to the current generation of target users. The late 1980s and early 1990s saw, in various forms, a new mentality that appreciated doing things "your own way" and carving one's own niche. Mountain Dew sought to capitalize on images of a "been there, done that" mentality. This mindset made sports that took things to the extreme a perfect vehicle for promoting its extreme beverage. Dew was at the forefront of outlets that provide a visible and relevant medium for reaching those that identified with an "extreme" ethos. The association with extreme sport is clearly displayed through the most visible marketing efforts used by Dew.

Dew and Action Sports

In 1995, Mountain Dew became a sponsor of the inaugural X Games. They have been a primary corporate sponsor in the world of alternative sport since then (see Exhibit 18.2). Additionally, Dew has positioned itself within the sport world due to its title sponsorship of the extreme sport competition series the Dew Tour.

The company's involvement with Dew Tour has helped enhance the product in many ways. The Dew Tour enhances its association with the action sports community, a very important base for the company. The tour complements the company's continuing support of the X Games. According to Pepsi representative Melanie Watts, "There is no better way to get a halo effect from a property like the [Dew Tour] than by becoming the tour's title sponsor" (Lee, 2006, p. 44).

Dew is currently involved in a long-term agreement for the naming rights of the tour. Through title sponsorship of the Dew Tour, the company hopes to build off the association with the excitement and the "on the edge of your seat" intrigue of the Tour.

Exhibit 18.2 Other Areas of Sport Involvement

Mountain Dew is involved in concentrated efforts aimed at projecting a high-energy, action-packed image to consumers. Among such marketing endeavors are:

- The sponsorship of the Mountain Dew Vertical Challenge, a series of snowboard and ski races, is a great example of their efforts.
- Mountain Dew's marketing arm, MD Films, recently produced a wide-release motion picture, *First Descent* (a documentary chronicling the rise of snowboarding).
- Mountain Dew has a long-standing sponsorship commitment to ESPN's X Games and Winter X Games franchise.
- In 2002, Mountain Dew kicked-off the Free Flow Tour, a sixteen-stop amateur skateboarding competition.
- Mountain Dew had a presence in the basketball community as a sponsor of the And 1 Mix Tape Tour and Mountain Dew Street Hoops.

Mountain Dew has been able to gain association with numerous notable athletes. Among the associations are product endorsers, which have included many current top action sports stars (highlighted in Appendix 3). Through its AMP Energy Drink brand, the Mountain Dew family is now aligned with one of the biggest names in all of sport, Dale Earnhardt Jr. When Junior left DEI racing for Hendrick Motorsports in 2007, he received a new no. 88 car and a new primary sponsorship by the AMP brand—this was quite the coup. Dew had previously sponsored Hendrick Motorsports driver Brian Vickers. Before that, the company had been associated with NASCAR legend Darrell Waltrip.

The Final Score

As stated before, Mountain Dew is more than just soft drink. The image of the Dew has become a cultural icon. Mountain Dew is a classic example of cultural branding in which the target audience lay the foundation for a product to become an identity brand. Such methods can be enacted through reaching out to myth markets. Myth markets are based on ideas or themes that exemplify or symbolize certain characteristics of a culture. Mountain Dew has been able to tap into these myths from its inception. Through its duration, the company has relied on myths from the cultures of hillbillies, being country cool, and the current, highly successful approach of going to the extreme.

Mountain Dew's drive to brand itself as a product choice for those inclined to an action-packed image has been quite successful. A company marketing representative stated that the image of Mountain Dew is about individuality, a slight irreverence, and living life to the fullest. Seeking to rebrand the corporate image has turned out to be ingenious, as the name Mountain Dew and the associated images of its brand are now synonymous with the world of extreme sport. They have crafted this image through high-profile associations with events such as the Dew Tour and the Summer and Winter X Games. Furthermore, connections with prominent extreme athletes such as snowboarder and skateboarder Shaun White have further solidified the Dew as a major player in the extreme sport genre. Tapping into popular sport personalities such as White will provide further exposure for the company while continuing affiliation with pivotal figures in the world of action sport.

"Doing the Dew" has become a euphemism for high-energy activity that is primarily embraced by youth consumers and those who are young in spirit. Though this has turned out to be a tremendous success, the risk that Mountain Dew took when they became affiliated with action sports should not be discounted. The drive to take things to the extreme was a drastic change from earlier country-themed images. Additionally, the association with Dale Earnhardt Jr. allows the company to benefit from associations with one of the most marketable (and marketed) entities in all of sport.

The success and notoriety of Mountain Dew is a model that many companies aspire to follow. Their company's creative efforts and skillful positioning have been truly remarkable. Though jumping on board with the popular world of alternative sport is not a huge gamble in today's market, Dew was at the forefront of this movement. The association could have easily turned out much different. What if extreme sport had not reached the level of popularity that has been surmounted to date? What if the majority of "Dewers" backlashed against the new image of their favorite soft drink? Questions such as those pose interesting propositions. Though these and other similar questions raise good points, it is hard to argue with the results. The company's decisions to embrace such sports and those who identify with this lifestyle clearly has positioned them as one of the premiere brands in the highly competitive soft drink market.

Post-Game Comments

- Mountain Dew maintains the presence of a strong mega-brand image.
- Mountain Dew's action sports-oriented marketing focus has allowed this brand to be easily associated with sports (and life) that goes to the extreme.
- Though action sports are the primary focus of Dew's sport marketing efforts, the company still seeks to have a presence in various other sport offerings.
- Dew's marketing efforts focus on a young, energetic target audience.
- Though today's Dew is associated with images of the extreme, the brand image has had drastic changes since its debut.

Web Resources

http://www.ampenergy.com
http://www.ast.com
http://sports.espn.go.com/espn/wire?section=auto&id=3028531
http://www.mountaindew.com/#/aboutdew/history.php
http://www.mountaindew.com/#/sports
http://www.mountaindew.com/#/sports/actionsports/index.php
http://www.mountaindew.com/#/sports/dewreport/index.php
http://www.mountaindew.com/#/timeline.php
http://www.md-gear.com/vintage.htm

Additional Resources

Holt, D. B. (2004). *How brands become icons: The principles of cultural branding*. Boston: Harvard Business School Press.
Lee, J. W. (2006). Insider's perspective: Melanie Watts, marketing analyst, Pepsi Sports. Available at: http://www.thesmartjournal.com/ip1.pdf.

Other information was obtained from the now-defunct Soda Museum (formerly available at http://www.sodamuseum.bigstep.com).

Appendix 1 Other Brands in the Mountain Dew Family

- Diet Mountain Dew
- Mountain Dew Code Red
- Mountain Dew Livewire
- Mountain Dew Baja Blast
- AMP Energy Drink
- Mountain Dew syrups have also been used in a variety of Slurpee flavors

Appendix 2 Some Memorable Advertisement Campaigns by Mountain Dew

Additionally, Mountain Dew has had a number of memorable advertisement campaigns and slogans. Among some of the more memorable are:

- Yahoo! Mountain Dew!
- Thar's a Bang in Every Bottle
- Yahoo Mountain Dew … It'll Tickle Yore Innards
- Get That Barefoot Feelin' Drinkin' Mountain Dew
- Dew It to It
- Doin' It Country Cool
- Do the Dew
- Follow the Code (associated with Code Red flavor)

Appendix 3 Notable Athletes Associated with Dew (Past and Present)

Dale Earnhardt Jr. (NASCAR)
Darrel Waltrip (NASCAR)
Brian Vickers (NASCAR)
Shaun White (snowboarding/skateboarding)
Paul Rodriguez (skateboarding)
Hannah Teter (snowboarding)
Chad Kagy (BMX)
Danny Davis (snowboarding)
Allan Cooke (BMX)
Luke Mitrani (snowboarding)

Chapter 19

Red Bull New York: To Build or Not to Build Off of the Parent Company's Image?

Greg Letter,
Adelphi University

Brian Rothschild,
Adelphi University

Parent Company: Red Bull GmbH and Red Bull New York
(Major League Soccer team)
Location: Fuschl am See, Austria (Red Bull GmbH headquarters);
Secaucus, NJ (RBNY team headquarters)
Internet Address: www.redbull.com; http://web.mlsnet.com/t107

Discussion Questions

- Besides ownership and the name, what products do team Red Bull New York (RBNY) and Red Bull GmbH beverage have in common?
- What are the major positives and negatives associated with aligning RBNY branding efforts with the established Red Bull brand?
- Does RBNY need to separate itself from the existing Red Bull image?
- Should Red Bull GmbH attempt to shed its racy image of the antibrand, which could be its major competitive advantage, for the purpose of future growth?
- What will become of the "underground" feel associated with Red Bull, which is and was a large part of the success for the product, since the company is moving toward a mass marketing appeal?

The Line-Up

The following statements are regularly found, sometimes in whole or parts, in various self-promoting sources on the Internet and traditional mediums. Specific references from the Red Bull messages include the fact that it is not a soft drink—it is an energy drink. It is for times when individuals are under increased physical and mental stress, and it is said to improve endurance, alertness, concentration, and reaction speed. Other declarations the company makes include that it revitalizes body and mind. Furthermore, many people, including top athletes, value this product.

Red Bull GmbH (Gesellshaft mit beschränkter Haftung, German for "limited liability company") produces the world's leading energy drink. Billions of cans are sold in nearly 100 countries each year. The product is classified as an energy drink, or functional beverage, a category it was largely responsible for building; Red Bull owns a 70 percent market share of the category. Red Bull's dominance in the fastest-growing segment of the soft drink market in a number of countries has created a frenzy of followers. Although the concoction began as a popular elixir for blue-collar workers in Thailand, marketing is aimed at trendy young people with active lifestyles. As a company, Red Bull continues to build a brand and incessant market share domination; it appears they are walking a fine line between the antibrand consumers niche to a mass marketed, common consumer product. This issue is vital to address because it may require the company to shed the anti-brand image. As Red Bull aligns the corporation with traditional sport sponsorship, as well as its existing involvement in nontraditional art, music, and extreme sporting events, will the antibrand become more insipid in its brand image? This market penetration strategy needs to be further analyzed to see how the traditional sport sponsorship strategy of Red Bull New York will affect a brand image developed by its initial connection with nontraditional sport and entertainment.

Timeline of Events

1982
- T.C. Pharmaceuticals in Thailand, owned by Chaleo Yoovidhya, bottles a cheap tonic called Krating Daeng ("red bull" in Thai) in a brown bottle.

1984
- Red Bull GmbH is created in Austria and is credited with creating the energy drinks category.

1987

- Austrian FDA approves Red Bull energy drink. The main ingredients of Red Bull include taurine, glucuronolactone, caffeine, and vitamin B, which creates some confusion over the product as a medicinal drink, so several outlets refuse to sell Red Bull. The product is mostly sold in gas stations to truck drivers due to the high caffeine content. Soon after, outdoor enthusiasts see the reviving benefits from the ingredients. These benefits open a new market. The product eventually is used during social situations, either as a stand-alone drink or as part of a mix with alcohol, specifically vodka. This concoction becomes popular over the next several years.

1991

- Flugtag event is held in Vienna, Austria. The concept of the event allows anyone to register as long as they follow Red Bull criteria. Teams launch their homemade flying contraptions off the ramp and are judged in three categories: distance, creativity, and showmanship.

1992

- Distribution moves to foreign territories, including Hungary and Slovenia.

1994

- Further expansion into Germany and Switzerland.

1996

- Red Bull sponsored rower Xeno Müller from Switzerland, who won an Olympic gold medal in the single sculls.

1997

- Arrival in United States for select distribution in California, while expanding throughout the entire United States over the next five years.

1999

- Big Wave Africa surfing competition established.

2000

- Red Bull Barako is a professional team of the Philippines Basketball Association.

2001

- Red Bull Rampage, a free-riding mountain bike contest to a finish line 1,500 vertical feet below, launched and held in Virgin, Utah.

2003

- Red Bull X-Fighters kicked off in Valencia. Several thousand wild Spanish freestyle motocross fans came to the bullfighting arena to watch their heroes fly through the air.
- U.S. market contributed to 40 percent of international sales. Red Bull yearly sales figures approach 1.5 billion cans.

- Red Bull Trolley Grand Prix created. Competitors built vehicles based around a theme and raced down a 700-meter track. They are evaluated on originality of the vehicle's concept, time to complete course, and quality of performance (including excitement of crashes).
- The Red Bull Air Race World Series established. The event is an international series of air races in which competitors navigate a demanding obstacle course in the air in the fastest time.

2004
- Red Bull sold in over 100 countries. Company numbers show the product category "energy drinks" as entering a maturity stage. Red Bull faces first sales and marketing challenge to continue growing and maintaining the buzz.

2005
- Red Bull Elevation, an event for BMX dirt jumping, created and recognized by elite cyclists as a must attend event.
- SV Salzburg soccer team purchased and renamed Red Bull Salzburg.

2006
- Red Bull Racing Team joined NASCAR Sprint Cup Series as well as the NASCAR Craftsmen Cup Series.
- The Major League Soccer organization New York/New Jersey MetroStars is purchased and renamed Red Bull New York.

2007
- Red Bull Brasil, a football (soccer) team from São Paulo in the Federacao Paulista de Futbol League, is formed.
- Red Bull links up with Freestyle Games to develop the games for consoles such as Xbox 360 and PlayStation 3.
- Groundbreaking on Red Bull Arena in Harrison, New Jersey. Red Bull Arena is a thirteen-acre site, with a state-of-the-art soccer facility, which will also include the organization's offices.

"Red Bull Gives You Wings"

Dietrich Mateschitz was born in Austria in 1946. As a student in Vienna, he focused his studies on world trade and commerce. In 1982, Mateschitz visited Thailand and began to regularly sample an array of energy drinks. He said in an article in *The Economist* that he preferred a product called Krating Daeng after it eased his jet lag. He consumed up to eight of the drinks a day.

Krating Daeng, which is Thai for "red bull," was popular among truck and cab drivers and other blue-collar workers. Krating Daeng was originally produced in the early 1970s by T.C. Pharmaceutical, founded in Thailand in 1962 by Chaleo Yoovidhya. T.C. Pharmaceutical eventually formed the subsidiary Red Bull Beverage Co. Ltd.

Initial product research and development efforts in 1982 reported mixed feelings regarding the taste of the drink. Mateschitz found the report not at all disturbing because half of the participants highly approved of the drink. Mateschitz and primary partner Chaleo Yoovidhya founded Red Bull GmbH in Austria in 1984 and each became 49 percent owners, with Yoovidya's son assumed the remaining 2 percent ownership. The company went forward with product development and initial launching even after the reviews could have clipped their wings prior to launching. Sales and marketing of the Red Bull drink began in Austria in 1987; a million cans were sold in that year.

The original formula was altered for Western palates. Some ingredients were dropped, and carbonation was added. Ingredients of the elixir included B vitamins, glucuronolactone, sodium, and caffeine. A rumor regarding one synthetically derived ingredient, the amino acid taurine, was supposedly from bull testicles, a ploy designed to create attention for the product. Red Bull's sales scheme promoted the drink as amplifying stamina and mental concentration, making it a natural for one of the original target users: long-distance drivers. The taste of the viscous yellow beverage, said to be similar to liquid gummi bears, further differentiated the brand. The effects of the ingredients in Red Bull were instrumental in developing additional creative monikers for the product, such as Liquid Cocaine, Speed in a Can, and Crack in a Can, to name a few.

Marketing Strategies

Red Bull GmbH was first established as an "antibrand" through an effective viral marketing campaign (see side-bar). Red Bull continued to move forward with the carbonated caffeine drink by using several viral marketing strategies. First, Mateschitz restricted supply of product and refused to advertise. This created a youth-oriented "underground" perception among the targeted consumers. Following this effort, Mateschitz focused on the hot spots (night clubs) of mostly Austria and Germany, paying students, disc jockeys, and influential personalities to host activities while serving Red Bull, which naturally took on a mixer role along with alcohol, mostly vodka. It became the rage of the after-hours crowd, while assisting in building product recognition and loyalty. These individuals, either action sport participants and/or all-night "ravers," spent long days recovering from the night before pursuing such activities as snow boarding, skiing, or simply recovering to dance all night again, all the while drinking Red Bull for its caffeine and cultural influence. Red Bull relied heavily on this atmosphere to enhance product recognition and consumer loyalty. Cocktails associated with Red Bull became so popular that bartenders knew them by names, such as Deca Voddy Bull, Jägerbomb, Belushi Ball, and Quad Vod. The cocktails mixed with Red Bull further differentiated it from other cocktails because they appeared to glow green under the fluorescent lights; consumers found that the glow of their drinks attracted attention.

Exhibit 19.1

Antibranding is a philosophy and a practice of an anticorporate movement. This anticorporate sentiment takes on many forms, by individuals as well as activist groups, for either environmental, human rights, and/or political issues. Antibrands are against the corporate dominant world and more concerned with consumer needs.

Viral marketing describes any strategy that encourages individuals to pass on a marketing message to others, creating the potential for exponential growth in the message's exposure and influence. Like viruses, such strategies take advantage of rapid multiplication to explode the message to thousands or even millions (Wilson, 2005).

Mateschitz wanted to create a connection with a "style of life"—in marketing terms psychographics, often referred to as state of mind. In marketing strategies, understanding the power the state of mind component has on consumer behavior, we see the Red Bull concept as one that penetrates the consumers' mindset as a product or accessory that aids in the development of the consumers' image. Trendy libations are common in all demographic and psychographic groups, whether it is children at the soccer field or school cafeteria, or adults at the gym or social gathering places. Mateshitz didn't invent the idea, but he used it to influence a core segment of future trendsetters. Consumers sought an alignment with the branded image associated with Red Bull because it was so influential on the consumer's desired image. This transference occurs instantaneously through an association of what a product represents, therefore enabling individuals to become part of the culture simply by using the product. Although this may appear simple, it is a dynamic process that requires a synergistic effect and relies on a mutual dependent relationship. Viral marketing efforts are one example of this relationship.

Red Bull GmbH placed a special emphasis on the branding strategy to entrench their product as the premier member of the energy drink category, which Red Bull is credited with creating and dominating from its beginning.

Gobe (as cited in Rodgers, 2001) states, "The beauty of Red Bull is that it's the antibrand brand ... Red Bull doesn't have any of the commercial trappings of a traditional, off-the-shelf product. It's underground, even when it's above ground, and that appeals to the young people who drink it." The success of the marketing efforts maintained an antibrand concept. The viral marketing concept was one that was necessary during the introduction of the product to position with the targeted consumers and to build an image. This practice became a core tactic during all product expansion phases while Red Bull sales representatives continued to seek out local hipsters in key neighborhoods, gyms, and night clubs in the new markets.

History shows that consumers indirectly influenced the branded image of products which assisted in the development of brands, but not until researching more about Red Bull did it become apparent how much the events, requiring direct involvement from consumers, achieved this concept. After the initial introduction through viral marketing strategies, the product's image was coming into its own, and that image allowed Mateshitz to move into the engagement, or experiential marketing (see side-bar), a strategy to continue the growth stage of the product and support the desired product image. While Red Bull's market growth—actually, market domination—continues, Mateshitz has implemented strategies to reinforce the established image. Engagement or experiential marketing practices took center stage, as well as the majority of the marketing budget, which focused on the clever idea of bringing individuals together through low-budget sport, art, and music event sponsorships to build an existing event or start a new one. This strategy was perfectly aligned with Mateschitz's hopes of creating a product image that becomes part of a lifestyle. This became a positioning and promotional tool that allowed consumers to invent the event alongside the Red Bull staff. These local off-the-cuff events are now considered almost international events. The antibrand has a very complex Web sites, all the while displaying social images and streaming videos of previous events.

Exhibit 19.2

Experiential marketing requires corporations to design activities that necessitate direct involvement from the targeted consumers. The design of these activities, which can include an array of events, should allow participants to enter by choice and inadvertently assist in the development of the entire event, meanwhile allowing the corporation to place and promote their products, therefore achieving several of the main corporate marketing objectives.

The creativity of these events varied greatly but all focused on a "hands-on" approach, including an abundance of product trials. A fairly unique approach used by Red Bull included events created by the company to connect these hands-on experiences with art, dance, music, and cutting-edge, adrenaline filled, action-based experiences. All the while, Red Bull focused these events toward the core culture of a young, trendy lifestyle. According to Sports Business Institute research, consumers of these activities tend to be more active than passive and open to newer sports. Most of the events require participants to commit themselves to acts of danger—from paragliding up to 1,500 feet and attempting flips in Chicago on Lake Michigan, to wake-boarding through rocky caverns in Missouri, to flying in a homemade machine over San Francisco Bay. Other events include the Red Bull Art of the Can Competition—an international art competition in which artists use the Red Bull can to create works of art— and the Red Bull BC (Breakdance Championship), and the Red Bull Music Academy for DJs in New York City. Consumers of these action-based social environments enjoyed plenty of product trials and at times mixed the product with adult beverages, which usually included vodka or Jägermeister. These event tactics were carefully planned and contributed to the widespread association that Red Bull drinkers live on the edge, are full of energy, live life to the fullest, and participate in action sports. Red Bull GmbH was extremely concerned with the consumers' needs, which is part of the experiential marketing programs that were implemented to create Mateschitz's vision of a product that offered a *style of life*. All the while, Red Bull knew that these action-oriented activities were beginning to gain popularity with the aid of expanded media coverage, providing the company with more access to targeted consumer segments.

A more traditional marketing campaign that aimed to reinforce Red Bull's image began with the sponsorship of sport figures and basketball teams, motorsports sponsorships throughout the world (including Formula 1), NASCAR (including Craftsman Truck Series), as well as what is considered the world's most followed sport, soccer. Red Bull also used other traditional marketing strategies, mostly paid advertising on television, which included animated cartoons promoting the theme that "Red Bull gives you wings" and, more recently, commercials including action footage of the Red Bull-sponsored events.

Merging the Branding Strategy into Sport Sponsorship of Red Bull New York

Red Bull GmbH has achieved insurmountable success in the energy drink category, and it appears the Red Bull New York team, and possibly the sport of soccer, may benefit from the success of branding. Initially, numerous negative concerns came from the original New York/New Jersey MetroStars fans—one included the removal of the Metro identity, while another came about from the corporate branding associated directly with Red Bull, and a third concern came from dropping New Jersey and associating the franchise with only New York. The fans associated well with the Metro brand and wanted to speak out with regards to corporate naming of the team. Are the fans of this soccer team anti-corporation when it comes to involvement with sports teams, and does the negative feedback regarding the nickname associated with the team cause due concern? Because the team officially plays in New Jersey and the teams' headquarters are there, Red Bull New York had to make good public relation moves to regain the fans' loyalty.

The Major League Soccer (MLS) team hired renowned former U.S. International team coach Bruce Arena and is the only team in MLS to use two "designated player" slots, league protocol that allows a team salary cap exemptions, and therefore the ability to sign several big-name players. This is seen as an attempt by RBNY to add instant credibility to a team that was floundering prior to Red Bull GmbH ownership. Another step in the RBNY plan was to add a fan-friendly soccer complex suited for professional games. Soccer purists saw the prior stadium as a horrible venue to view soccer, and the players also complained—they were considered the third priority in their use of stadium, behind the NFL New York Giants and New York Jets. Currently, Red Bull is developing a new 25,000-seat soccer only facility in Harrison, New Jersey, called Red Bull Arena. Early attempts by RBNY were seen as a commitment to the league and the followers of professional soccer in the tri-state area. Following these business decisions, RBNY proposed to put in place a youth-development structure, which is seen as socially responsible and a good public relations tactic.

The traditional marketing strategy of sport sponsorship in some cases appeared aligned with prior marketing practices, because speed and danger were involved in the sports. However, the image associated with the three soccer teams Red Bull GmbH purchased (the others are in Brazil and in Austria) appears disengaged with prior strategies. The teams benefit from the presence of the established logo on each uniform and the revenue streams from the Red Bull GmbH parent company, but how else does RBNY benefit from brand association? Remember, Red Bull has a well-established branded image that makes people think of endurance, speed, getting a rush, daredevils, and socially engaged images.

Soccer is an endurance sport that at times requires speed, and the athletes have committed themselves to years of physical training to increase their speed and endurance. From start to finish, the game of soccer is nonstop action, requiring consumers and players of the sport to keep up with the pace. As for getting a rush and socially engaged images, soccer is the most widely followed sport in the world, and as the fans show their enthusiasm in an array of celebratory ways for ninety-plus minutes, it appears a sea of individuals have come together to build this fan experience. Although in America, soccer stadiums do not generate the enthusiasm that the Premier League or Bundesliga fans regularly achieve during their soccer matches, RBNY consumers are involved and regularly contribute to the total experience. The marketing efforts during the introductory years of RBNY include more typical and traditional methods, because they are more practical for a soccer team. Currently, a traditional advertising campaign features a theme of "flying high," while including team players and a charging Red Bull character within the advertisement. Using different means to an end does not prevent RBNY from connecting with the Red Bull GmbH brand image. As RBNY continues to penetrate the market, they can continue to use the established brand image of Red Bull GmbH as a leveraging tool to gain more attention and eventually fans.

The Final Score

RBNY cannot disassociate itself from parent company Red Bull GmbH and the image associated with its legacy in the energy drink category. For nearly two decades of the company's existence, the public has witnessed an extremely successful product launch and continuous market domination. The viral marketing concepts used during the introduction phase, along with their experiential marketing concepts during the growth stages, have created an extremely recognizable product, as well as a brand notably affiliated with action sports. The current direction of the marketing efforts includes a focus on team sponsorship and stadium naming rights in soccer and several professional auto racing teams in multiple circuits throughout the world, which aims to fend off competitors in the energy drink category. This strategy attempts to prolong the maturity phase of the product life cycle and extend the growth stage, but it comes with branding concerns.

Since Red Bull GmbH penetrated the market, targeted consumers have helped build the allure of an antibrand product. This impression was partially responsible for Red Bull's success, but it appears to no longer be feasible. With extended market reach came increased sales, which created a change in the targeted consumers and an increasingly mass marketing concept was established to build the Red Bull GmbH Corporation. Red Bull GmbH still uses most of its original concepts, which include the events, sales tactics, and more traditional sport sponsorship, while using little advertising, but the product

Chapter 2 Akadema

Figure 2.2
Joe and Lawrence Gilligan

Figure 2.1
Joe Gilligan

Chapter 4 Life is good

Figure 4.1
Jake

Figure 4.2
Rocket

Figure 4.3
Jake and Rocket

Figure 4.4
Life is good Festivals logo

Figure 4.5
Life is good 4th of July

Figure 4.6
Assorted Life is good images

Chapter 5   Mossy Oak

Figure 5.1
Toxey Hass, founder and CEO

Figure 5.2
Bear 10 yards from hunter's stand

Figure 5.3
Hunter wearing Mossy Oak

Figure 5.4
Mossy Oak pattern Break-Up

Figure 5.5
Mossy Oak pattern Obsession

Figure 5.6
Mossy Oak pattern Duck Blind

Figure 5.7
Mossy Oak pattern Brush

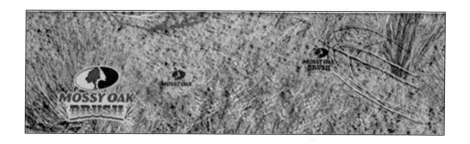

Figure 5.8
Mossy Oak pattern Treestand

Figure 5.9
Mossy Oak pattern Break-Up Infinity

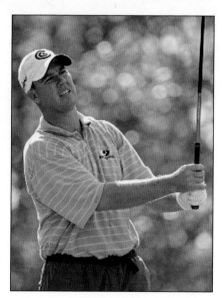

Figure 5.10
Professional golfer Boo Weekley, member of Mossy Oak's Prostaff

Chapter 9   Montgomery Biscuits

Our Mission Statement:

The Mission of the Montgomery Biscuits is to provide affordable, innovative entertainment and positively outrageous service while building a lasting relationship with our community.

Our Operating Principles:

People We will employ only talented, idea-oriented people with high standards, who demonstrate respect for other people, exhibit a sense of competitive pride, display an eagerness to excel and learn, and put our customer's interests before their own.

Environment We will maintain a climate, in terms of working conditions, human relations, opportunities for growth, self-expression, and monetary rewards, that will attract the best people and provide them with the most stimulating, rewarding and enjoyable career in minor league baseball.

Customer Service We will remember at all times, that our customer is the reason we are in business. Each and every employee of the organization must realize that it is their job to provide POSITIVELY OUTRAGEOUS SERVICE. That means treating every customer with respect, recognizing any complaint as a challenge to improve, immediately addressing any concern a customer might have, honoring any reasonable request, and ensuring the complete satisfaction of each customer.

Product We will always remember that we are in the entertainment business. From the moment a fan first comes in contact with the club, to the moment they leave the stadium after a game, they should have a wildly positive and entertaining time.

Value We will provide a great value to our customers. We realize, however, that value means more than low prices — it means a great product at a fair price.

Reputation We will strive to be recognized as the best organization in minor league baseball based on our ability to provide a terrific product to our customers, the quality of our people, and our cutting-edge, idea-oriented philosophy. We will be a good member of our community.

Innovation We will look to innovate in everything we do. If there is a better way to do something — we will find it.

Integrity We will operate, at all times, in an ethical and moral manner.

Power Every employee has the authority to do whatever they believe it takes to ensure each customer has a wonderful experience.

Figure 9.1
Montgomery Biscuits Mission Statement

Chapter 10 The National Hot Rod Association

Figure 10.1
NHRA's Geographic Reach

Chapter 22 Mitchell & Ness

NOSTALGIA CO.

Mitchell & Ness

PHILADELPHIA, PA.

Figure 22.1
Mitchell & Ness logo

Chapter 29 Bass Pro Shops

Figure 29.1
Bass Pro Shops logo

Figure 29.2
Outdoor World in Springfield, Missouri

Figure 29.3
Interior, Outdoor World in Springfield, Missouri

Figure 29.4
Big Cedar Lodge

Figure 29.5
Interior, Big Cedar Lodge

Figure 29.6
Dogwood Canyon Nature Park

Figure 29.7
Dogwood Canyon Nature Park

no doubt ably has established a mass market appeal. Koehn (as cited in Rodgers, 2001) declares, "Red Bull is building a beverage brand without relying on the essential equipment of a mass-marketing campaign. Perhaps the indispensable tools of marketing aren't so indispensable after all." The deliberate positioning strategies have changed for the purpose of corporate growth, which slightly changed the culture associated with the users of the product, therefore possibly disturbing brand image. Brand image is an invaluable source of corporate affluence, but it can also contribute to the corporation's demise.

Red Bull GmbH today still owns a dominant piece of the energy drink market share. Although consumers now have a choice of over a dozen competitors—with the likes of KMX, Adrenaline Rush, and Red Devil to name a few—it appears that this competition is what prompted Red Bull GmbH to react and develop a mass marketing campaign. However, most of the tactics used in this mass marketing campaign are atypical; specifically, they avoid traditional advertising mediums. It is for this reason that an underground feel can continue, therefore reinforcing the desired brand image.

As for the future, Red Bull GmbH and RBNY seem to have a mutually beneficial relationship. RBNY has an enormous task ahead of them: continuing to develop and strengthen ties to the brand image, but the foundation has been established. Once these ties become apparent to more consumers, RBNY should be able to build a larger and more loyal fan base. Red Bull GmbH continues to achieve several corporate marketing objectives regularly through its support of the MLS soccer team and, most important, remaining consistent with its established branding. Klein (1999, p. 21) states, "the products that will flourish in the future will be the ones presented not as 'commodities' but as concepts: the brand as experience, as lifestyle."

Post-Game Comments

- Red Bull GmbH strategically sequenced a viral marketing concept that was extremely influential in the development of the brand image and was soon followed with the experiential marketing practices that successfully reinforced that image.
- Without using traditional advertising tools associated with a mass marketing campaign, Red Bull GmbH has successfully created a mass marketing appeal to enhance sales growth.
- RBNY should benefit from building brand associations with Red Bull GmbH to further establish the fans' experience, thereby enabling the soccer team to become part of the fans' lifestyle.

- RBNY is effectively using more traditional advertising and marketing means to connect with the brand image developed by Red Bull GmbH.

Web Resources

http://www.drivearoundtheworld.com/sponsors/redbull.htm
http://www.fastcompany.com/articles/2001/10/redbull.html
http://www.nytimes.com/2007/03/03/sports/othersports/03ice.html

Additional Resources

Klein, N. (1999). *Money, marketing, and the growing anti-corporate movement: No logo.* New York: Picador.

Rodgers, A. L. (2001, September). It's a (Red) Bull market after all. Fast Company.Com: Where Ideas and People Meet. Retrieved October 22, 2008, from http://www.fastcompany.com/articles/2001/10/redbull.html.

Wilson, R. F. (2005, February 1). The six simple principles of viral marketing. *Web Marketing Today.* Retrieved October 22, 2008, from http://www.wilson web.com/wmt5/viral-principles.htm.

Part IV

Media, Memorabilia, People, and Places

Chapter 20

Madden NFL: Bringing the League to the Consumer

Galen Clavio,
Indiana University

Product: Madden NFL from EA Tiburon
Location: Orlando, FL (EA Tiburon)
Internet Address: http://maddennfl.easports.com

Discussion Questions

- What has made the Madden NFL franchise so successful among gamers?
- How important is the emphasis on realism is to the franchise's popularity?
- Do you think the series would be as successful if the NFL was not so popular?
- How do you feel about the franchise's expansion into in-game licensing?
- What lessons could other sports games take from the Madden series?

The Line-Up

You could make a compelling argument that sports video games wouldn't be anywhere near as prominent in today's entertainment culture without the Madden brand. The Madden Football video game series is the longest-running game franchise of any sort, starting in 1989 and still going strong. The name brand popularity of John Madden, a Hall of Fame football coach and the most popular football commentator on television for decades, has made this franchise *the* football simulation for gamers. Furthermore, the ability of the franchise to sign big-name endorsement deals with popular NFL stars, such as the recently retired Brett Favre, continues to ensure the pop culture relevance of the game.

Throughout its history, the Madden franchise has relied on the increasing popularity of the National Football League, marrying the passion and pageantry of the league to a simulation that is both realistic and enjoyable to fans of all ages. Along the way, the game has added a wide array of features, allowing gamers to immerse themselves in a world of sports fantasy. Additionally, what is so remarkable about this franchise is that it has continued to abide by its own lessons, while so many competitors have failed to learn from them.

Timeline of Events

1984
- Electronic Arts (now EA) commissions a football game to go along with their successful line of sports video games. John Madden refuses to authorize the game because of its unrealistic portrayal of the game of football.

1989
- Following the release of the more powerful Sega Genesis system, Madden agrees to license his name to a football game through EA, provided that the game is realistic. The release of John Madden Football marks the game's entrance into the cultural mindset.

1993
- The franchise name changes from John Madden Football to Madden NFL, further cementing the ties between the game and the league it portrays.

1994
- The first portable version of Madden NFL is created for the Nintendo Game Boy system.

1995
- The Madden NFL franchise makes its first appearance on the Sony PlayStation, the most popular of the thirty-two-bit consoles. The upgrade in available hardware allows for more lifelike graphics and better simulation control.

2004
- EA Sports announces an exclusive licensing deal with the NFL. The deal ensures that the Madden franchise will be the only professional football game that can use the team and player names of NFL franchises until at least 2008.

2005
- Madden NFL adds the Superstar feature, which allows the user to play as a single player instead of controlling a team. Superstar mode includes

several role-playing elements, such as character creation and interaction with other nonplayer characters.

"If It's in the Game, It's in the Game"

The Madden phenomenon is perhaps the most recognizable element of video gaming today. While certain nonsports titles can generate larger sales for a single year, no other video game franchise has built the passionate and long-standing following that the Madden series enjoys. With 51 million copies sold over the life of the franchise, and with perhaps the highest name recognition of any video game in the United States, the Madden phenomenon is a formidable force in the industry.

The Madden NFL series began its life as the brainchild of Electronic Arts (EA) in the mid-1980s. EA, now a preeminent video gaming giant, was looking for a football title to add to its successful line of sports games and had settled on famous coach and broadcaster John Madden as its spokesperson. However, due to the constraints of technology at the time, game play in the original version of the title only featured seven players per team, far short of the eleven players per team that take the field in actual football. Because of this unrealistic portrayal of football, Madden withdrew his name and support. This attention to detail and accuracy later helped give birth to the Madden phenomenon.

As gaming technology advanced, the developers at EA were able to construct a realistic version of football with the requisite number of players on the field. With this condition satisfied, Madden threw his full support behind the project. He expected the game to become a strategic tool for football coaches to use. Surprisingly, the franchise became an immediate success, with its blend of entertaining action and realistic strategy. More than any other football game that came before it, the Madden NFL series allowed users to truly feel as if they were part of the NFL's universe.

In the newest versions of the game, the virtual players will go so far as to complain about a lack of playing time if they are not utilized enough and will suffer drops in performance as a result. Users can do practically anything a real-life owner or general manager would do, from raising or lowering stadium concessions prices to firing coaches, trading players, and signing free agents. As one fan recently stated, "It looks just like a real football game on TV. The players act and move just like they do in real life." That level of realism has set the Madden NFL series apart from its competitors.

Part of the demand for that realism comes from the advancing age of video gamers. Once considered the domain of the young, developers and retailers are finding that their audiences are no longer kids. In 1990, the average age for a video game user was eighteen. By 2003, that average age had increased to twenty-nine. While arcade graphics and violent tackles alone might be enough to satisfy the tastes of a younger crowd, the more mature video game audiences of today require a more personal investment, which Madden NFL is more than happy to deliver.

Ironically, one feature that was originally created for the Madden NFL series translated into an innovative and highly successful feature of real-life football. To assist users with making first downs in the game, a line was added to the field that represented what yardage marker would earn a new set of downs. The feature was so successful in the game that the NFL itself, in conjunction with its TV broadcast partners, added the line to game broadcasts. The now-ubiquitous "first down line" has become a crucial part of television broadcasts (it doesn't actually appear on the field) of NFL games over the past decade.

Marketing Strategies

While the popularity of the NFL is a major boon for sales of football video games, it is by no means a guarantee of success. Throughout the 1990s and the early part of the next decade, several other NFL-based video games came into being, with varying degrees of success. None of these, however, could topple the dominance of the Madden series.

A major marketing strategy for the series was borne out of Madden's obsession with creating the most realistic version of football available. A famous example occurred as a result of Madden watching his grandson play a version of the game. He noticed that his grandson would consistently "go for it" on fourth down and would be successful more often than not. Fearing that this was inconsistent with how NFL games actually were played, Madden contacted the game developers and demanded changes to the game engine to make it harder to perform the actions that he had witnessed his grandson doing with ease. This dedication to the small details helped cement the Madden series' reputation as a serious football simulation, an important distinction in the sport video game marketplace.

By combining this nearly obsessive pursuit of realism with extensive in-game features, the Madden series went from being a cult phenomenon to a pop culture icon. Playing on the popularity of the league it promoted and the spokesperson who promoted it, the game became a true crossover platform, gaining social acceptance within a broad demographic of fans. Whereas video gaming was often derided as antisocial in nature due to its solitary nature in the 1980s and 1990s, the Madden NFL series used its booming popularity to forge a common connection between NFL fans and video gamers.

This connection saw its apex in 2004, when EA announced plans for a "Maddenoliday" to celebrate the release of the game. The company put out a press release imploring businesses to give their employees the day off from work so they could fully enjoy the newest version of the game on the day it was released. EA even went so far as to provide "sick notes" for employees to take to their bosses. While the suggestion was likely not taken seriously by employers, the cultural effect of the Madden NFL series had become readily apparent.

The Madden series has also shown a willingness to supply fans with the most up-to-date elements of the NFL world. With the advent of online gaming services on the Xbox 360 and PlayStation 3, users can download roster updates throughout the preseason, as players are dropped, added, and traded by their teams. EA Sports even went as far to change the cover of the game when necessary, as it was in 2008. The original cover of that year's edition of Madden featured a retired Brett Favre in a Green Bay Packers uniform. When Favre came out of retirement and was traded to the New York Jets, EA Sports announced that a new cover, with Favre in a Jets uniform, would be available for gamers to download and print.

The financial effect of video games in general had also become readily apparent by this time. Though traditional entertainment venues such as movies and television receive far more critical attention, video games have carved out a large niche in the entertainment spectrum. In 2001, video game sales accounted for $9.4 billion in revenue, $1 billion more than Hollywood box office receipts for the same year.

Sacking the Opposition

The last real threat to the Madden NFL series' hegemony in pro football video gaming came in the form of Take Two Interactive's ESPN NFL series. Beloved by critics who hailed it as a worthy competitor to Madden in terms of on-the-field game play, the ESPN NFL series further challenged Madden's position by selling at a highly reduced cost of $19.99, a full $30 below the asking price for Madden NFL.

One can only wonder whether the ESPN NFL series would have eventually pulled even with Madden NFL in terms of sales or popularity, because in the heat of the battle between the franchises, EA announced that it had signed an exclusive rights agreement with the NFL. This meant that gamers who wanted to play an NFL video game would have to buy Madden, since no other company was allowed to use the NFL trademarks. Furthermore, in the same year, EA announced a fifteen-year exclusive rights deal with ESPN itself, ensuring that no other developer could use the graphics and personalities of the sports television giant, including Take Two, who had built their game series' brands around the ESPN moniker.

Would the marketing power of ESPN have been enough to counter the built-up popularity of the Madden NFL series? Though it's enjoyable to speculate on such things, the reality is that the Madden series was already so ingrained in both sport culture and pop culture that it would have proven extremely difficult for the upstart series to compete. The momentum of fifteen years of steadily increasing sales, combined with the sheer popularity of the game among both regular video game users and NFL players, helped make Madden NFL more than just a video game. Despite it being the only series on the professional football video game landscape today, that built-up popularity elevates its sales far beyond other sport titles.

The Final Score

The Madden NFL series has managed a rare feat in the video game industry: maintaining its base of users while continuing to build market equity. Even more remarkable has been the franchise's ability to avoid serious competition, despite the crowded nature of the sport video game field. There's no doubt that the franchise has been helped along by the enormous marketing power of parent company EA, although as both sales numbers and product reviews have shown over the years, the EA brand is not impervious to competition. While other EA sport titles, such as the Triple Play baseball series, have struggled against inspired competition, Madden NFL managed to carve out its niche effectively and has been able to maintain its place. Even Take Two's ESPN NFL series, which combined entertaining game play, the ESPN brand, and a sales price that was less than half that of the Madden NFL series, was ultimately unable to make a dent in Madden's popularity.

In the early days of the Madden NFL brand, simply having a realistic simulation of football was enough to satisfy the demands of video game users. The franchise's simulation elements, combined with the name recognition of John Madden, made for smooth sailing for the franchise. As gaming systems evolved, a good football simulation was not enough, and to EA's credit, they have adapted their marketing philosophy to make the series more than just a game for its users. By allowing gamers to act as coach, owner, or superstar player, Madden NFL created a personal element to the series that its competitors were never able to match effectively. As each edition of the franchise brought new and intriguing elements to game play, it became crucial for users to acquire the newest version. Although critics have argued that the core game itself has not changed much, the newer elements, such as Owner Mode or Superstar Mode, give users the impetus to spend $50 or more every year on the franchise. Gameplay innovations, such as the Hit Stick, which allows for users to line up their opponents for bone-crushing tackles, added flash and excitement to the defensive side of the ball. The series has also branched out into spin-off games, such as the revamped NFL Head Coach franchise, which will be packaged together with the newest version of Madden.

With the exclusive licensing deal now in effect between EA and the NFL, the Madden NFL series is guaranteed to be the only pro football simulation around until the end of the decade. The new challenge for the franchise will be to remain innovative despite the lack of competition. The series' popularity seems assured at this point, having survived and thrived in the video gaming industry's leap into the HDTV-focused Xbox 360 and PlayStation 3 eras, as well as the hands-on approach offered by the Nintendo Wii. Just as it was incumbent on the popular gaming franchises of the late 1990s to use the new technology of the PlayStation 2 and original Xbox in innovative ways, so it is now incumbent on these game franchises to take the same innovative leaps with the newest technology. If past history is any indication, the Madden NFL series will not only survive the technology jump but thrive in it. After all, Madden NFL has survived two major technology changes during its career, and with the exclusive NFL license in its back pocket, one would expect the franchise to maintain its mantle as the preeminent sport video game.

Post-Game Comments

- Madden NFL is the most popular and most recognizable sport video game.
- Madden NFL's emphasis on realism has made it stand out among all sport games, particularly football games.
- EA's exclusive licensing deal with the NFL gives the Madden series the highest possible brand awareness in the sport video game genre.
- Madden NFL has maintained its audience while adding new users every year, thanks to a variety of new innovations such as Owner mode, the Hit Stick, Superstar mode, and online play.

Web Resources

http://maddennfl.easports.com
http://www.gamespot.com/gamespot/features/video/hist_football
http://www.maddenauthority.com
http://www.mobygames.com/game-group/madden-series
http://www.tiburon.com

Additional Resources

Bishop, G. (2004, December 29). The game outside the game. *Seattle Times*, p. D1.

Clark, C. (2004). The principles of game based learning. Paper presented at the NETC/LSC Conference, Crystal City, VA.

Fritz, B. (2006, November 3). "Madden" sales drive up EA revs. *Daily Variety*, News, p. 6.

Haberkorn, J. (2006, August 23). Men go mad for Madden NFL 07; Game retailers ready for rush. *Washington Times*, p. C08.

Hartlaub, P. (2003, August 17). No more child's play: As gamers grow up, top-selling titles sport aging pitchmen. *San Francisco Chronicle*, p. E1.

Hartlaub, P. (2004, August 17). Madden remains the untouchable football franchise that transformed video games into pop culture. *San Francisco Chronicle*, p. E1.

Chapter 21

Nintendo Wii: Revolutionizing the Video Game Industry

Galen Clavio,
Indiana University

Product: Nintendo Wii
Location: Corporate headquarters in Kyoto, Japan;
American headquarters: Redmond, WA
Internet Address: www.nintendo.com/wii

Discussion Questions

- What aspects of the Nintendo Wii are significantly different from its competitors?
- Is fun more important than realism in video games?
- How do you explain the Nintendo Wii's increasing popularity?

The Line-Up

If you were attempting to predict the future of video gaming at the midpoint of the first decade of the twenty-first century, the smart money would have been on Internet-based interaction between gamers. The growth of broadband Internet access, coupled with the predominance of two major competitors in the video game console market (Sony and Microsoft), seemed to portend a future where games became increasingly complex, graphically intensive, and online-focused. The imminent appearance of the next generation consoles, specifically Sony's Playstation 3 and Microsoft's Xbox 360, had set the stage for a realism-based gaming technology war.

But something funny happened along the way. That something was the Nintendo Wii.

Sporting a revolutionary motion-based style of gameplay, a significantly lower price point than its competitors, and the familiar and historic characters of gaming yesteryear such as Mario and Luigi, the Nintendo Wii unexpectedly shot to the top of the sales charts not long after its introduction to the marketplace. Nearly two full years after its release, the Wii has maintained its popularity, outselling the flashier Playstation 3 and Xbox 360 by wide margins, both in the United States and in Japan. With an emphasis on fun, cooperative gameplay, and the novel experience of physically acting out the required tasks in its games, the Nintendo Wii represents a paradigm shift in the way consumers interact with video games.

Timeline of Events

2002
- Nintendo names Satoru Iwata as global president of company; Iwata focuses research and development of Nintendo on creating a console that will access untapped markets of potential gamers.

2006
- Nintendo announces that their next-generation gaming console, previously nicknamed "Revolution," will instead be known as the "Nintendo Wii."
- Nintendo Wii is released to retailers across the world. Console sells out its entire stock in North America in just three days.

2007
- Nintendo Wii far outsells its competitors during the busy December holiday shopping season, with over 1.3 million units sold during this time span.

2008
- As of May, Nintendo Wii continues its dominance of the marketplace, outselling both Xbox 360 and PlayStation 3 combined for three consecutive months in the United States.

Taking a Different Route

Nintendo is no stranger to the video game console market. The Nintendo Entertainment System (NES), which first appeared in the mid-1980s, dominated the American marketplace for several years, almost single-handedly resurrecting an industry left reeling in the wake of poor sales and subpar game design. Nintendo's advanced (for the time) graphics, and its games' casts of memorable characters, such as Mario, Luigi, and Zelda, made it the top-selling gaming console in the world. Nintendo was subsequently able to follow up on the success of the NES with the Super Nintendo, introduced in the early 1990s.

However, by the mid-1990s, consumer tastes seemed to favor a gaming experience that provided more realism and graphical capability than what Nintendo could offer. The Nintendo 64, released in 1996 as the successor to the Super Nintendo, fell far behind Sony's PlayStation in total units sold. These poor sales numbers continued into the following generation of gaming consoles, the Nintendo Game-Cube; though it sold in greater numbers than the Nintendo 64, it lagged behind both the PlayStation 2 and Microsoft's Xbox in units sold.

These failures in the marketplace prompted Nintendo to take some radical steps to regain their prominence in home video gaming. First, rather than maintain the branding established with the release of the GameCube, Nintendo chose to select the name Wii for their console. Originally, the console was named Revolution, and initial press releases referred to it as such. However, at the E3 Conference in spring 2006, the company announced that they were changing the name of the console, stating, "While the code-name 'Revolution' expressed our direction, Wii represents the answer. Wii will break down that wall that separates game players from everybody else. Wii will put people more in touch with their games ... and each other" ("Revolution renamed Wii," 2006, para. 2).

In addition to the new brand name, the designers of the Wii took the unusual step of fundamentally altering the console's controllers. Instead of the standard type of controllers, which have been a part of video gaming as far back as the original Nintendo eight-bit system, the company decided on creating a smaller, more streamlined controller that used motion controls instead of large numbers of buttons and control sticks. As one commentator noted soon after the launch of the console, the Wii's controllers looked more like TV remotes than traditional game controllers (Greenwald, 2006).

However, the biggest and most radical step that Nintendo took during the development of the Wii was to change the way that the company looked at the marketplace. Satoru Iwata, the global president of Nintendo, took over the company in 2002. At this point he decided to reevaluate the way that Nintendo attracted people to their products. In an interview with BBC News, Iwata noted, "Five years ago when I was appointed, I thought that if we didn't do anything but took the same route, there would be no bright future for the entire industry. So we decided we needed to increase the number of people gaming" (Waters, 2008, para. 6).

Capturing a New Market

Iwata's plan did not include trying to compete with Sony and Microsoft, who had staked their claim on the existing video gamer marketplace. The GameCube had attempted to do that, and the sales figures showed that such a strategy was untenable. Instead, the focus of the Wii was on capturing the market of people who might be interested in playing games, but were not at the time. Iwata noted, "We started thinking about people who weren't playing games and asking ourselves why they were not interested. And why had some people stopped playing despite playing in their youth?" (Waters, 2008, para. 7).

The answer, as it turned out, was enjoyment. Many video gamers, who had grown up in the less complex gaming world of 1980s-era Atari and Nintendo, may have felt uncomfortable with the uncompromising realism of the current generation of games and consoles. The Wii, by focusing on simpler themes and physical involvement, struck a chord with those users, as well as with those who might not have experienced home video gaming before. As one trade publication noted, "[The Wii is] strange, it's different, and it's not as powerful as its competitors, but the Nintendo Wii succeeds in its primary mission: it's fun to play" (Greenwald, 2006, para. 2).

In addition to being fun to play, Nintendo also made sure that the Wii was affordable to a larger percentage of consumers than the competition's consoles. The Wii was released with a retail cost of $200, which was $100 less than Microsoft's Xbox 360, and $300 less than Sony's PlayStation 3. The combination of a lower pricepoint, wider marketing net, and advanced buzz about the console led to a remarkable console launch in North America. Within three days of the Wii's appearance in retail stores, consumers had purchased every available console, which numbered close to 600,000 units.

By comparison, Sony's PlayStation 3 sold fewer than 300,000 units in almost double the timeframe. In fact, the Wii proved so popular and successful that for months after its launch, Nintendo was unable to manufacture enough units to meet demand.

That popularity has continued unabated. With the release of the popular Wii Fit add-on game, sales numbers continued to soar, a full eighteen months after its release. In a three-month period from March to May 2008, the Wii sold over 2 million units in the United States alone, far more than the combined sales totals of both the Xbox 360 and the PlayStation 3. As of June 2008, Nintendo had sold over 28 million Wii consoles worldwide.

Nintendo's design for the Wii didn't just revolutionize the gaming market; it also had a remarkable effect on the company's bottom line. Thanks to the runaway success of both the Wii and the handheld DS gaming system, Nintendo became one of the five largest Japanese companies by market value in 2007, a position the company had never held before.

New Frontiers

While Sony and Microsoft concentrated much of their next-generation console efforts on creating virtual meeting spaces where people could play games with users online, the Nintendo Wii reintroduced the concept of people getting together in person and playing games. By making their games relatively simple, accessible, and broadly appealing and by allowing participants' physical skills to enter into the gaming equation, Nintendo was able to make its new console appealing to a large number of people who might not have considered purchasing any other gaming system.

The inclusion of the Wii Sports Pack with each console was another smart marketing strategy. Bundling popular games with the console was an old trick for Nintendo; indeed, they had used the strategy to great effect with the original NES system, which came bundled with the immensely popular Super Mario Brothers, as well as the game Duck Hunt. By including the Wii Sports Pack, users could immediately use the system and do so with a game that allowed for basic movements that translated to their one-screen counterparts. With the Sports Pack, users could experience virtual bowling, baseball, tennis, boxing, and golf. Adding another player required nothing more than an additional controller, which could be purchased separately from most electronics stores. The ease of entry into the hardware system led to the initial purchasers of the Wii taking their consoles to the homes of friends and family, thereby giving those individuals a free demonstration of the console's capabilities.

Further evidence of the revolutionary nature of the Wii can be found in the ways that the system has reached into areas that would have seemed incongruous with video gaming just a few years ago. One of the best examples of this is the Wii's extension into the fitness market. Some gyms have started to integrate the Wii into their personal training regimens. At one gym in New York City, personal trainers have integrated the Wii Sports Pack, which contains simulations of boxing, tennis, and golf, into their clients' activities. As a trainer stated in an interview, "[The Wii] may have little to do with the real sports, but we get people's heart rates up to 140 to 150 beats per minute ... We think of this as just another tool at the gym" (Olshan, 2008, para. 9).

The Wii has also been utilized in the field of physical rehabilitation. In one instance, a rehabilitation hospital in Edmonton, Canada has reported significant improvement in patients. As one occupational therapist said while discussing the development of his patient, "We could have him do therapy for an hour and he wouldn't mind one bit. Now, when I see him playing today, it's incredible to think back to where he was" (CBC News, 2007, para. 8). The Wii has even found a use among medical surgeons—a preliminary study found that practicing on the Wii helped surgical residents hone their fine motor skills.

The Final Score

The Nintendo Wii pulled off two rare feats in its first two years of existence. It was able to revolutionize the gaming world with its motion-based gameplay, and it was able to single-handedly bring Nintendo back into a position of prominence in the gaming world. Nintendo's analysis of the marketplace indicated that there were potential users out there who had been lost in the next-generation video game console shuffle, and their innovative approach to capturing that marketplace had yielded results that cannot be argued.

The Wii has proven wildly successful during its first two years, and it will be interesting to see whether it can maintain its momentum. Although Nintendo was able to create a brand-new sector of the video gaming marketplace through its technological and marketing innovations, the traditional video gaming market still exists, and the fact remains that both the Xbox 360 and the PlayStation 3 are far more suited to cater to that audience, both through complexity of game design and processor capability. The next marketing challenge for Nintendo is to create a large core audience out of the new generation of gamers they have found, while using the unique elements that the Wii possesses to make its games attractive to traditional gamers.

Post-Game Comments

- The Nintendo Wii is the most unique video game console in today's marketplace.
- The Wii's emphasis on fun and physical activity has made it stand out from its competitors.
- Nintendo's ability to bring popular characters and games to the Wii, such as the much-celebrated Super Mario Galaxy, gives it an advantage over its competition.

- Nintendo managed to create a new audience of gamers by evaluating what former gamers and people who didn't play video games wanted to see in a console system.

Web Resources

http://www.nintendo.com/wii
http://www.nintendo.com/wii/virtualconsole/games
http://www.gamespot.com/games.html?platform=1031&type=games
http://www.wii-gamer.com

Additional Resources

CBC News. (2007, May 11). Wii-habilitation has Edmonton patients on their toes [electronic version]. Retrieved July 20, 2008, from http://www.cbc.ca/canada/calgary/story/2007/05/11/wii-therapy.html.

Goldstein, J. (2008, January 17). Surgeons Hone Skills on Nintendo Wii [electronic version]. *Wall Street Journal*. Retrieved August 4, 2008, from http://blogs.wsj.com/health/2008/01/17/surgeons-hone-skills-on-nintendo-wii.

Greenwald, W. (2006, November 13). Nintendo Wii [electronic version]. CNet. Retrieved August 4, 2008, from http://reviews.cnet.com/consoles/nintendo-wii/4505-10109_7-31355104.html.

Nintendo Wii sells out in North America. (2006, November 21). Playfuls.com. Retrieved August 4, 2008, from http://www.playfuls.com/news_05259_Nintendo_Wii_Sells_Out_In_North_America_And_Canada.html.

Olshan, J. (2008, August 4). Gym's Wii-zy money [electronic version]. *New York Post*. Retrieved August 4, 2008, from http://www.nypost.com/seven/08042008/news/regionalnews/gyms_wii_zy_money_122934.htm.

Revolution renamed Wii. (2006, April 27). *GameSpot*. Retrieved August 4, 2008, from http://www.gamespot.com/news/6148462.html.

Smith, T. (2008, June 13). Nintendo Wii US sales 3x PS3, XBOX 360. *Register Hardware*. Retrieved August 4, 2008, from http://www.reghardware.co.uk/2008/06/13/us_console_sales_may_08.

Tomassi, K. D. (2006, May 11). Analyst: Wii will cost $200 [electronic version]. *Forbes*. Retrieved August 4, 2008, from http://www.forbes.com/digital entertainment/2006/05/11/nintendo-microsoft-sony_cx_kt_0511wii.html.

Waters, D. (2008, July 17). Taking the Wii to the next level [electronic version].
    BBC. Retrieved July 27, 2008, from http://news.bbc.co.uk/2/hi/technology/
    7511215.stm.
Yam, M. (2007, July 27). Nintendo now the fifth largest company in Japan
    [electronic version]. *DailyTech*. Retrieved July 20, 2008, from
    http://www.dailytech.com/Nintendo+Now+the+Fifth+Largest+Company+
    in+Japan/article8209.htm.

Chapter 22

Mitchell & Ness: The Evolution of the Premier Retro Sports Apparel Provider

Coyte G. Cooper,
University of North Carolina at Chapel Hill

Company: Mitchell & Ness
Location: Philadelphia, PA
Internet Address: www.mitchellandness.com

Discussion Questions

- What tactics did Mitchell & Ness use to build their brand image in the 1920s?
- What was the first team that Mitchell & Ness provided an off-field apparel deal to?
- What was the overall impact of the deal?
- What was the impact of including retro jerseys in the product line for Mitchell & Ness?
- What professional sport leagues have product license label deals with Mitchell & Ness? How has this impacted the success of the company?
- What steps have Mitchell & Ness taken in the 2000s to help improve their brand image among customers?
- What is the significance of Mitchell & Ness hosting a high school tournament at Rucker Park in New York City?
- What is the significance of the scholarship foundation formed by Mitchell & Ness with the University of Michigan?

The Line-Up

Located in Philadelphia, the Mitchell & Ness sporting goods store was founded by Frank P. Mitchell in 1904 (see Figure 22.1 in image insert). Mitchell, a former AAU tennis and wrestling champion, partnered with a Scottish golfer named Charles M. Ness, who shared his passion for sports. Together, the men decided to form a sporting goods store that would feature high-quality golf clubs, tennis racquets, and other sport equipment. Though their sales in sport equipment proved to be a great success, the company clearly made their mark as a top sporting goods provider when they positioned themselves as a uniform provider for college and high school athletic programs in the 1920s.

The move into the uniform apparel business turned out to be a major turning point for Mitchell & Ness. In the early 1980s, the company made a decision that changed their image forever—they decided to offer retro jerseys in their product line. Following the decision, Mitchell & Ness quickly became known as the top provider of retro jerseys when Major League Baseball granted them the Authentic Cooperstown Collection license. The partnership proved to be a huge milestone for the company as other professional leagues lined up to offer vintage licenses to Mitchell & Ness. As a result, the company is known as the premier retro apparel company in today's sporting goods industry.

Timeline of Events

1904
- The Mitchell & Ness sporting goods store is founded on Philadelphia's Arch Street by Frank P. Mitchell and Charles M. Ness. The company initially focuses on providing golf clubs, tennis racquets, and other sport equipment.

1925
- Following the decision to enter the uniform business, Mitchell & Ness quickly becomes the uniform provider for many of the high school, college, and semi-pro teams in Philadelphia and the surrounding areas.

1933
- The company receives their first professional contract with the newly formed Philadelphia Eagles as a uniform provider.

1938
- The company creates their first professional baseball contact as the Philadelphia Athletics decide to wear the Mitchell & Ness distinctive wool flannels during games.

1946
- The Phillies wear distinctive wool flannels during their record-breaking season.
- The Eagles wear the company's sweaters and jackets during off-field activities.

1978
- The USA National Field Hockey Team wears the Mitchell & Ness script label during their qualification into the Olympics.
- The Redskins and Giants wear a wide range of on-field and off-field merchandise produced by Mitchell & Ness.

1983
- The company decides to create retro jerseys.

1987
- Mitchell & Ness are featured in *Sports Illustrated* in a "Baseball Flannels Are Hot" article. The article is the company's first appearance in the publication.

1989
- Major League Baseball grants Mitchell & Ness the license to its Authentic Cooperstown Collection label. This allows the company to create vintage MLB jerseys with player's numbers.

1998
- The NBA grants Mitchell & Ness the license to its Hardwood Classics label.
- The NFL grants Mitchell & Ness the license to its NFL Throwback label.

2000
- The artist Big Boi launches a MTV video wearing a 1980 Nolan Ryan #34 Houston Astros jersey. The video created a huge interest in vintage jerseys within the entertainment industry.

2001
- The NHL grants Mitchell & Ness the license to its Vintage Hockey label.

2005
- The CLC College Vault License allows the company to feature many of the top colleges' vintage apparel.

The Early Key to Success: Team Affiliation

The Mitchell & Ness brand is known as one of the premier providers of retro sports apparel across the world. Though the company is well known for their intricate designs, their ability to form positive relationships with teams and leagues has vaulted them to the top of the sport apparel industry. The company initially realized success with this strategy when becoming the uniform provider for high school, college, and semi-pro teams in the Philadelphia area in the 1920s. The initial exposure to many of the teams allowed them to build their brand with customers in the area, and as a result they were able to build new relationships with professional teams in the area.

The Mitchell & Ness brand received a major boost when they became the official on-field outfitters for the Philadelphia Eagles in 1933. The ability to create a relationship with an NFL team proved to be an essential stepping stone for the company because it legitimated the Mitchell & Ness brand. As a result, Mitchell & Ness were able to provide their distinctive wool uniforms to the MLB Philadelphia Athletics during the 1938 season. The Eagles also named Mitchell & Ness as their off-field apparel provider in 1946.

In addition to their affiliation with teams in the Philadelphia area, the Mitchell & Ness brand received further recognition through their partnership with the 1978 national field hockey team. The deal provided the company with international exposure as the team wore the Mitchell & Ness script label during the Olympics. The deal marked the first exposure for the company outside of the United States.

Creating a Stronger Brand Image: The Vintage Appeal

During the 1980s, the Mitchell & Ness company focused a great deal on the creation of high-quality uniforms for their clients. Though the focus of their business was on uniform production, the company also provided additional services, such as a uniform repair service, to improve customer satisfaction. Over twenty years later, it is clear that the uniform repair service is at least partially responsible for the success Mitchell & Ness has realized in the retro sports apparel business.

In 1983, a gentleman came to the company in hopes of having two vintage jerseys repaired. In an attempt to find materials to repair the jerseys, the company went to a factory and found 12,000 yards of useless wool flannel. The visit inspired the owners to create an entirely new product line: retro jerseys. The goal of the product line was to produce jerseys with styles and patches that had not been seen in many years.

The company's production of vintage jerseys proved to be a huge success. In fact, the vintage line led the company to its first appearance in *Sports Illustrated* on July 6, 1987, when the publication featured a story on the company's jerseys called "Baseball Flannels Are Hot." In addition to the focus on the grow-ing popularity of sportswear as fashion, the article also highlighted the in-depth research used by the company when creating their intricate jersey designs.

A Professional Touch: League Affiliation

Building on the visibility of the *Sports Illustrated* article, Mitchell & Ness ce-mented their place in the retro sport apparel industry when they were granted the license to the Authentic Cooperstown Collection by Major League Baseball. With the deal, the company was allowed access to all the former players who par-ticipated in MLB. The deal provided the groundwork for the control of the retro attire for each of the four major professional leagues for Mitchell & Ness.

In 1998, Mitchell & Ness further strengthened their brand image when cre-ating deals to add former player's jerseys from two professional leagues: the NBA and the NFL. The NBA granted the company the license to their Hard-wood Classics label, and the NFL granted the company the license to their Throwbacks label. Additionally, the company added their fourth professional league in 2001: the NHL granted the rights to their Vintage Hockey label.

The addition of the licenses from the four professional leagues did not stop Mitchell & Ness from attempting to extend their product line. In 2005, the company expanded on their retro apparel line again when they earned the rights to the CLC College Vault License. The deal was crucial for the company because it provided the rights to vintage logos from top college programs, such as the University of Michigan and the University of Notre Dame. Subsequently, the company held the rights to the licenses from the college vault and the four major professional leagues.

Additional Interest in Retro:
The Hip Hop Appeal

In the early 2000s, the company began to fully realize the benefits of ac-quiring the rights to the vintage licenses from the professional leagues. The retro jerseys created a mass buzz among sport fans all across the country. In 2000, the company received an additional boost when hip hop artist Big Boi wore a 1980 Nolan Ryan Houston Astros jersey in a music video. The video turned out to be a significant moment for the company because it represented a move for Mitchell & Ness into mainstream America. The end result has been an in-creased demand in the newest retro products from R&B stars such as Fabulous (1970s New York Yankees; 1980s San Francisco 49ers), P. Diddy (1974 Hank Aaron, Braves; 1969 Tom Seaver, Mets; and 1973 George McGinnis, Pacers), and Jay-Z (1947 Sammy Baugh, Redskins). As a result, the company has been able to strengthen their brand image in new fan segments.

Recent Strategies to Expand Brand Image

In an attempt to continue to offer high-quality products, Mitchell & Ness has built on deals previously created with professional leagues. Recently, the company extended their deal with the NBA to include Hardwood Classics spanning over decades to form "the ultimate dream team." Such a dream team includes items such as Larry Bird's 1981–82 All-Star jersey and Wilt Chamberlain's 1963–64 San Francisco Warriors road jersey. Mitchell & Ness President Peter Capolino added the following about the new NBA retro product line: "We thought creating this limited edition collection of jerseys would be the perfect way to honor our relationship with the NBA while also providing basketball fans with a never-before-seen line of retro apparel they could truly appreciate" (Thomas, 2004, p. 16).

In addition to creating new innovative products, Mitchell & Ness has also attempted to capitalize on sponsorship opportunities to improve their brand image. In 2008, the company hosted a basketball tournament featuring twenty-four of the top high school players in the country at the legendary Rucker Park in New York City. An example of measures enacted by the company to continue to build its brand has been the creation of a retro line for the players to wear during this tournament.

The Final Score

Mitchell & Ness has experienced a tremendous amount of growth since its founding in 1904. Throughout the years, the company has made many decisions that have allowed them to position themselves as the premier retro apparel provider in today's sport apparel industry. The overall impact has been the creation of a brand image that is recognized across the world by individuals interested in retro sport apparel.

The first step that helped position the company as the premier retro apparel provider involved the decision to provide uniforms to sport teams in the Philadelphia area. Overall, the company's ability to create strong relationships with local sport teams helped Mitchell & Ness build a brand image that helped negotiate both on-field and off-field apparel deals with professional sports teams.

The success as an apparel provider for professional sport teams helped position Mitchell & Ness for their success in the retro sport apparel industry. Ultimately, when the company decided to create retro jerseys in 1983, they had already established themselves as a premier uniform provider for sport teams across the country. As a result, their decision to create retro jerseys turned out to be an easy transition for the company as they reached licensing deals with the four professional sport leagues. Additionally, their acquisition the license of the College Vault License in 2005 has turned out to be a valuable asset.

In today's sports apparel industry, Mitchell & Ness continues to build strong relationships with professional sport teams. The company continues to develop its brand image by creating relationships with new sport's entities. For example, the company recently formed a scholarship foundation with the University of Michigan that is supported by its sales of retro Wolverine jackets. The scholarship foundation is just one example of how Mitchell & Ness continues to build on its brand legacy.

Post-Game Comments

- Mitchell & Ness has grown from a local sporting goods store in Philadelphia to a retro sport apparel provider that is known worldwide.
- The Mitchell & Ness brand has been strengthened through its ability to create strong relationships with sport teams and leagues.
- Mitchell & Ness created a unique brand image when deciding to create a retro apparel line.
- Mitchell & Ness strengthened their brand image by forming licensing deals with each of the four professional sport leagues.
- The Mitchell & Ness line continues to expand through innovated product design.
- The company's ability to create unique events incorporating the brand's products has helped strengthen the image of the company in key target markets.

Web Resources

http://www.entrepreneur.com/magazine/entrepreneur/2006/july/159964.html
http://media.www.ncatregister.com/media/storage/paper277/news/2003/04/07/Ente
    rtainment/Throwback-408967.shtml
http://www.mtv.com/news/articles/1450431/20011030/jay_z.jhtml
http://www.popmatters.com/sports/features/030213-sportsfashion.shtml

Additional Resources

Demartini, M., & Grish, K. (1998). Mitchell & Ness getting nostalgic with replicas. *Sporting Goods Business, 31*(7), 17.

Herek, M. (2003). Philadelphia story: Jersey maker Mitchell & Ness defines retro. *Sporting Goods Business, 36*(4), 32.

Kim, A., & Kennedy, K. (2002). Vintage jerseys. *Sports Illustrated, 96*(23), 18.

Rushin, S. (2002). Throwback hip-hop style points: Some of the history's most hideous jerseys now happily colorize landscapes of urban America. *Sports Illustrated, 87*(18), 15.

Thomas, R. (2004). Mitchell & Ness extends NBA license. *Sporting Goods Business, 37*(10), 16.

Vorkapic, R. (2004). Throwbacks in the here and now: Old-time jerseys are all the rage, thanks to the loving work of the Mitchell & Ness Nostalgia Co. *Football Digest, October*, 1–3.

Wolff, A. (2004). Rockin' the retros: A streetwise Philly marketer, with some juice from hip-hop stars, has turned the throwback into a big-bucks fashion frenzy. *Sports Illustrated, 99*(24), 46–54.

Chapter 23

Steiner Sports: The Best in Authentic Memorabilia

Raymond G. Schneider,
Bowling Green State University

Company: Steiner Sports Memorabilia
Location: New Rochelle, NY
Internet Address: www.steinersports.com

Discussion Questions

- What are the products that Steiner Sports sells?
- What makes Steiner Sports unique?
- List and discuss the education and experience of select Steiner Sports employees.
- How does Steiner Sports guarantee their items are authentic?

The Line-Up

A graduate of the Martin J. Whitman School of Management at Syracuse University in 1981, Brandon Steiner established Steiner Sports in 1987. Since that time, his business has blossomed into a $50 million enterprise, with more than 100 employees. Steiner has capitalized on the increased demand for authentic signed memorabilia from the sport and entertainment industries. The key to the success of Steiner Sports is the connections Brandon Steiner has with the most popular names in the industry. Steiner has exclusive autograph contracts with superstars such as Derek Jeter, Carmelo Anthony, Joe Torre, Rex Grossman, and even the rock band KISS. However, Steiner Sports is more than just autographs. They also are a marketing firm, host an online auction, and have established Last Licks, a sport-themed ice cream store.

Steiner Sports prides themselves in their service, integrity, and quality. There is no question the products they provide are the most sought after in the sport memorabilia industry. How Steiner Sports became so prominent is a model that other businesses have attempted to emulate. This chapter details how Steiner Sports has rocketed to the top of the industry and profiles the individuals who are the leaders of this unique company.

Timeline of Events

1987
- Brandon Steiner establishes Steiner Sports.

1997
- Steiner partners with Joe Duetsch and forms Last Licks, a sports bar for kids that serves ice cream.

2000
- Steiner Sports is sold to Omnicom Group.

2001
- The company purchases all remaining autographed baseballs from the estate of Joe DiMaggio for $500,000.

2002
- Steiner teams with New York Mayor Rudy Giuliani to create signed memorabilia; proceeds go to the Twin Towers Fund.

2003
- Brandon Steiner publishes his first book, titled *The Business Playbook: Leadership Lessons from the World of Sports*.

2004
- The Yankees-Steiner collectibles partnership is established. Steiner becomes the exclusive dealer for game used New York Yankees memorabilia.

2005
- Steiner strengthens their role in providing authentic signed merchandise from prominent names by signing exclusive contracts with Tony Hawk and KISS.

2006
- Steiner parlays the success of the Yankees-Steiner collectibles partnership and creates the New York Mets-Steiner collectibles. This partnership gives Steiner Sports a stronghold on the most sought-after memorabilia in the industry, that being the New York Mets and Yankees game merchandise.

2007
- Steiner and Syracuse University create a partnership in which Steiner will assist the athletic department in an attempt to further sales of university memorabilia.
- Steiner Sports hosts University of Notre Dame football coach Charlie Weiss in a meet-and-greet with fans.

Steiner Sports Marketing

Founded in 1987, Steiner Sports marketing has transcended the world of sport memorabilia. The $50 million, 100-employee business is where collectors of authentic signed memorabilia go to purchase rare and unique items. Steiner Sports grew into an industry leader because of the leadership and business connections of Brandon Steiner.

Sport memorabilia enthusiasts recognize Steiner Sports as the leading producer of authentic, hand-signed collectibles. Steiner has established themselves as a leader because of their exclusive autograph contracts with stars as such as Derek Jeter, Joe Torre, Eli Manning, Carmelo Anthony, and Rex Grossman. Exclusive contracts with these athletes means that collectors seeking authentic signed items from these players must purchase them through Steiner Sports. When a collector purchases an item from Steiner Sports, they are guaranteed that the athlete actually signed the item. In addition to a photograph of the athlete signing the individual item, each piece includes a hologram and matching certificate of authenticity. With nonauthentic signatures prominent within the sport collectibles industry, Steiner's motto of "The Steiner Seal Means It's Real" has been embraced.

In addition to authentic autographs, Steiner Sports provides collectors with photographs from the most famous moments in sports. The staff at Steiner Sports conducts detailed research to obtain the highest quality photos to capture these unique moments. Events such as Carlton Fisk's famous World Series home run and Derek Jeter's World Series heroics are captured forever on the photographs available at Steiner Sports.

In addition to having secured exclusive contracts with top players, Steiner Sports has capitalized on collectors' demands for game used merchandise. In 2004, the New York Yankees and Steiner Sports announced the launch of an unprecedented multiyear agreement. This agreement allowed Steiner Sports to the exclusive rights to market Yankees game used merchandise to memorabilia as well as to provide fans with access to the players. This agreement has been so successful that Steiner Sports has signed similar agreements with the New

York Mets, Syracuse University, and the University of Notre Dame. For example, Steiner Sports and the athletic department at Syracuse cut the former playing surface at the Carrier Dome into small pieces, with plans for having former Syracuse stars sign the pieces. Proceeds from the sale of the floor pieces will go toward athletic scholarships at the university. News of this product has been received favorably by not only Syracuse fans but also collectors of rare and unique memorabilia.

It is also important to note that Brandon Steiner has embraced the idea of corporate philanthropy. Since forming the business nearly twenty years ago, Steiner has always attempted to assist those less fortunate. For example, Steiner estimates he was involved in over 1,000 fund-raising events in 2005.

Steiner Sports: Experience and Education

Though it is true that Steiner Sports offers a unique product in addition to having secured exclusive contracts with some of the top names, many who have studied the industry note that Steiner Sports's success is due to the education and experience of not only Brandon Steiner but the rest of his staff. When comparing educational backgrounds and real-world experience in the industry, Steiner's staff is unmatched. Although the company boasts over 100 employees, the fundamental success of the business can be linked to Brandon Steiner and a few other key individuals (see Exhibit 23.1). Brandon would be the first to admit that the success of his business can be traced back to the years of experience accumulated by himself and his staff.

Exhibit 23.1 Education and Experience of Select Steiner Sports Executives

JARED WEISS, President: Graduate of Harvard University, bachelor's degree in advertising and communication. Jarrod began at Steiner Sports with an entry-level position in 1992 and worked his way to president of the company in 2001.

MATTHEW LALIN, Executive Vice President: Graduate of the University of Albany business school, bachelor's degree in business administration. Matthew has worked in the industry for over a decade.

STEVEN LAM, Chief Financial Officer: Graduate of the University at Albany, degree in accounting. Prior to joining Steiner Sports in 2004, Steve had more than twenty years of experience as a CFO.

NICK THYRRE, Distribution Manager: Graduate of Syracuse University, bachelor's degree in transportation and distribution management. Before joining Steiner Sports, served as a mail order fulfillment manager for the Metropolitan Museum of Art.

TONY CAPPA, Controller: Graduate of Pace University, degree in accounting. Tony began working at Steiner Sports in 2004. Previously worked as a senior account manager for Heineken USA.

KEN MARTIN, Credit Manager: Earned MBA from St. John's University and bachelor's degree from Queens College of CUNY. Ken has more than twenty years in the accounts receivable management area and before joining Steiner Sports, was the director of credit for Snapple Beverage Group.

Final Score

Success in any business is extremely difficult. Becoming respected and trusted within the sport memorabilia industry is even more difficult. The increasing number of fraudulent pieces of sport memorabilia has shaken the confidence of collectors and investors. Brandon Steiner responded by creating Steiner Sports in 1987; since then, his business has become the place where many collectors purchase authentic sport memorabilia. His experience in the industry has allowed him to create relationships with stars, such as Derek Jeter, Mia Hamm, Michael Jordan, and hundreds of others.

Steiner has combined the exclusive contracts with rare photographs to produce memorabilia and collectibles that cannot be found elsewhere. The exclusive contracts allow the company to be the sole marketer of the various athletes' signatures. Despite the fact that other businesses have attempted to develop exclusive autograph contracts, Steiner Sports remains the leader in this area. As a matter of fact, the additional competition from other companies has only made Steiner Sports stronger. The fact that they have a large staff with tremendous experience in the industry allows Steiner Sports to produce the collectibles that are in demand.

Brandon Steiner and his company have realized that collectors want more than just an autographed item. To meet this demand, Steiner Sports has teamed with the top names in the industry, such as the New York Yankees, New York Mets, and Syracuse University, to create a partnership that will allow fans, collectors, and investors to acquire game used merchandise. Before Brandon Steiner created these partnerships, it was virtually impossible to obtain game used items from any team.

Finally, by completely understanding the demands of the sport memorabilia collector and investor, Steiner Sports has been able to effectively market authentically signed products and game used memorabilia, which allows collectors to feel as though they are part of the game.

Post-Game Comments

- Steiner Sports began in 1987 and has exploded into a $50 million enterprise.
- Despite competition for exclusive contract with the top names in sport, Steiner has been able to use his experience and connections to secure the players that are in the most demand.
- Steiner Sports understands the market for sports memorabilia and constantly offers new items to meet the needs of all collectors.
- Steiner Sports plans to continue to diversify brand offerings as consumer preferences change within the memorabilia market.

Web Resources

http://auction.steinersports.com
http://query.nytimes.com/gst/fullpage.html?res=9804E1DB1539F93AA3575AC0
        A9679C8B63&sec=&spon=&&scp=3&sq=Brandon%20Steiner%20&st=cse
http://sports.espn.go.com/mlb/columns/story?id=2965512
http://www.brandonsteiner.com
http://www.brandonsteiner.com/susc/susc.html
http://www.steinersports.com

Chapter 24

Topps: From Penny Gum to Priceless Trading Cards

Raymond G. Schneider,
Bowling Green State University

Company: The Topps Company
Location: New York, NY
Internet Address: www.topps.com

Discussion Questions

- What was the original product marketed by Topps?
- What initiated Topps to include baseball cards as a purchasing incentive?
- List and discuss the thirteen brands offered by Topps.
- What challenges will Topps face as they proceed into the next decade?

The Line-Up

With company headquarters located in New York City, The Topps Company began selling chewing gum priced at one cent and has become the leader in production of trading cards. Drawing from the knowledge they gained while watching their father run the American Leaf Tobacco Company, four brothers established Topps in 1938. The Shorin brothers could not have dreamed that seventy years later, the company would experience success in the trading card market. However, the success did not come easy. Topps faced challenges throughout its history, such as competition for player contracts as well as increased competition from additional trading card companies. Because of their constant attention to consumers' preferences, Topps has been able to produce desirable trading cards, despite the increased competition and saturation of the market. How the company did this is a remarkable story. This chapter explains how Topps transformed from bubblegum to valuable trading cards.

Timeline of Events

1890
- Morris Shorin establishes the American Leaf Tobacco Company.

1938
- Morris Shorin's four sons—Abram, Ira, Joseph, and Philip—rename the American Leaf Tobacco Company to Topps with the idea of becoming a company that produces chewing gum.

1950
- Topps attempts further the sale of bubblegum by combining the gum with trading cards of Hopalong Cassidy.

1951
- Topps produces its first baseball-specific cards. The two sets, Red Backs and Blue Backs, each contained fifty-two cards and were designed to be used to simulate a baseball game.

1952
- Topps includes baseball cards with its bubblegum for the first time.

1957
- Topps produces trading cards for all four major team sports: baseball, basketball, football, and hockey.

1972
- Topps offers stock to the public.

1974
- Topps discontinues the tradition of releasing several series throughout a baseball season and only produces one base set.

1984
- Forstmann Little and Company acquire Topps in a leveraged buyout.

1987
- Forstmann Little and Company makes Topps a publicly traded company.

1992
- Topps eliminates chewing gum from its packs.

2000s
- Topps responds to consumer demand and includes game used memorabilia in packs of trading cards.
- Topps launches eTopps, a brand that sells cards exclusively online through initial public offerings.

2003
- Topps produces Pokémon trading cards.

2007
- Topps is acquired by Michael Eisner's The Tornante Company, LLC, and Madison Dearborn Partners, LLC.
- Topps produces Turkey Red Baseball, featuring the artwork of Dick Perez.

2008
- Topps launches cards featuring Disney pop culture phenomenon's *Hannah Montana*, *Camp Rock*, and *High School Musical*.

The Topps Company

The beginning of The Topps Company can be traced back to 1890, when Morris Shorin founded the American Leaf Tobacco Company. Shorin's four sons—Abram, Ira, Joseph, and Philip—reconfigured American Leaf in 1938, after the company suffered as a result of the Great Depression. On analyzing various business opportunities, the Shorin brothers decided to manufacture chewing gum and to rename the company Topps, indicating they would be the "top" producer of the product.

Topps found success with the relatively new product Bazooka bubble gum. The unique marketing twist incorporated by Topps was to include a small comic on the gum wrapper. Soon, the comic became just as popular as the bubblegum. In 1950, the Shorins made a move that eventually contributed to the baseball card collecting craze. In an attempt to increase stagnant gum sales, they began including trading cards of Western star Hopalong Cassidy with the product. The trading cards were an immediate success.

Although Topps began producing baseball cards in 1951, they were not packaged along with the gum and were designed to be used to simulate the play of a baseball game. In 1952, baseball cards became the focus of the company. For the first time, Topps offered cards that included a picture of the player on one side and statistics and biographical information on the reverse. Within the baseball card industry, this is considered to be the first set of baseball cards.

Topps was not the first company to produce baseball cards. In fact, Bowman Gum had been producing trading cards packaged with bubblegum since the 1930s. When Topps entered the market, a furious rush to obtain the rights to the individual players occurred. Bowman had been signing its players to exclusive one-year contracts allowing them to sell the cards along with chewing gum. Topps, in an attempt to avoid a contract dispute, included caramel in the 1951 set. In 1952, as Bowman's contracts with the players expired, Topps was able to secure a majority of the rights to market baseball cards of players. Although the battle for player contracts, as well as market share, continued for the next several years, it ended in 1956, when Topps bought Bowman.

In the company's nearly seventy years of existence, Topps has been able to withstand not only fierce competition but also saturation of the trading card market. In the early 1980s, companies such as Fleer and Donruss attempted to garner a portion of the trading card market. In 1989, Upper Deck created a high-end trading card incorporating increased technology, such as a hologram on each card in an attempt to guarantee authenticity.

Topps: Standing Out from the Pack

Most collectors would agree that Topps's success has been due to their ability to continually diversify their brands and cater to the wide variety of collectors. No longer will you find just one set of Topps baseball product. Now, Topps has created collectible trading cards at both the low-end and high-end of the price range, as well as packs including memorabilia, rookies, or legends. No matter what the desire of the collector, he or she can find a Topps product to satisfy demand. The major brands offered in 2006 by Topps indicate how the company has changed to satisfy the consumer. The company offers thirteen different brands, including a wide variety of technology, price levels, and base set construction (see Exhibit 24.1).

Exhibit 24.1 Brands Produced by Topps

Bowman: Bowman is a trading card set that focuses on providing collectors with the most extensive collection of rookie cards. While the set features all players, it is most recognized for producing the first card of many players each year.

Bowman Chrome: Similar to the regular Bowman series, Bowman Chrome incorporates a popular chrome design on the face of the trading card.

Bowman's Best: Bowman's Best is at the upper end of the price range for trading cards. The set features randomly inserted memorabilia and autographed cards, in addition to high-quality card stock.

Topps Finest: Topps Finest features a stratified set base in addition to sequentially numbered cards for all rookies.

Topps Gallery: Featuring painted artwork of each player, Topps Gallery is said to be where art and sport intersect. This set is popular among collectors because of the beauty created by each painting.

Topps Gold Label: Topps Gold Label features 100 of each sport's pre-eminent players on its elegant, double-photo, gold-stamped, holographic card. Each player card delivers three distinct aspects of a player's game.

Topps Heritage: Topps Heritage is the only product in the hobby that still includes gum in each pack. This series includes current players but uses card designs from previous years.

Premier Plus: Focusing only on hockey, this high-end set includes game used relics as well as premium inserts for hockey collectors.

Stadium Club: With limited text on the front of each card, Stadium Club attempts to include the most visually pleasing photograph of each player to complete the set. This set is believed to have the best photography in the industry.

Topps: Basketball, baseball, football, and hockey collectors who seek to collect one series each year generally select the traditional Topps basic set. This set features average pricing and extensive inserts.

Topps Chrome: Topps Chrome incorporates the popular chrome design on the basic Topps set.

Topps Stars: Topps Stars features the best players of yesterday, today, and tomorrow.

Topps Pristine: Each triple-pack of Topps Pristine includes a Pristine Uncirculated card, a Relic card, and base cards of four Veterans and two Rookies. The Pristine Uncirculated card is securely held in a protective, plastic holder. Additionally, all Rookie cards are offered in three variations—common, uncommon, and rare.

Topps has also created the brand eTopps, where the company issues a card through an initial public offering online. The cards are stored at the company and are held in an individual collector's portfolio. While most collectors buy and sell the cards just like they would a stock, some collectors choose to have the card mailed to them. Topps developed eTopps in 2001 with the idea of treating and trading cards much like stocks. Prices are reflected by the actual trading value of the card on eBay and are updated throughout each day.

In 2001, The Topps Company, in conjunction with eBay, launched the Topps Vault, where the company offers some of the most sought-after items in the collectibles industry. The Topps Vault sells original and one-of-a-kind items, such as paintings, photography (including original negatives), artist proofs, and uncut sport card sheets. "People have waited years and years for an opportunity to own something from the Topps archives," said Warren Friss, director of the Topps Vault. "The Topps Vault contains tens of thousands of truly special and unique items that have a place in American sports and entertainment history."

As the 2000s progressed, so have the innovative products that Topps produces. For example, in 2008 the company produced trading cards featuring Disney hit shows *Hannah Montana, Camp Rock,* and *High School Musical.* Traditional sport card collectors were rewarded when Topps introduced Turkey Red Baseball Artwork. These were cards that featured legendary artist Dick Perez. Turkey Red Baseball remains a highly sought-after product.

The Final Score

To survive in business, a company must learn to adapt to the demands of the consumer. Because Topps has listened to the wants and needs of trading card collectors over the past seven years, it has been able to survive and flourish in a sometimes oversaturated market. When the Shorin brothers reorganized the American Leaf Tobacco into Topps, they never dreamed they would eventually produce highly sought-after trading cards. However, after the success of inserting Hopalong Cassidy cards into their bubble gum product, the idea was born.

Despite the fact that Topps flourished in the trading card market up to the early 1980s, increased competition forced them to refocus their brand offerings. Both Fleer and Donruss attempted to capture some of the market in the early 1980s, and Upper Deck joined the competition in 1989. Overall, the numerous companies producing trading cards created a saturation of the market. Because of the excess supply and ease of obtaining any card that a collector desired, the perceived value of baseball cards plummeted. Collectors were demanding that producers of baseball cards limit production numbers. Topps responded by being innovative and establishing brands to meet each of the consumer needs. By randomly inserting game used memorabilia, such as pieces of jerseys, baseball bats, and bases, in addition to including clay from the baseball field, Topps brands continued to be in demand. They were able to stay ahead of the other companies by securing the exclusive contracts to represent star players such as Alex Rodriguez, Barry Bonds, and Dwyane Wade, not to mention holding the exclusive rights to produce trading cards of Mickey Mantle.

Finally, by completely understanding the demands of the trading card collector, Topps was able to effectively market and create eTopps, a brand that allows collectors to buy and sell cards similarly to buying and selling stocks.

Post-Game Comments

- Topps is an example of a company that has established a variety of brands to meet consumer demand.
- Despite early challenges for player contracts and later saturation of the trading card market, Topps has been able to find success in a variety of product offerings.
- Differentiation, according to Topps executives, is the key to success in any industry.
- Topps plans to continue to diversify brand offerings as consumer preferences change within the trading card market.

Web Resources

http://www.beckett.com/default.osi
http://www.beckettpedia.com
http://www.etopps.com
http://www.topps.com
http://www.topps.com/product/PRDRLS.ASPX?sportsid=0&l=n
http://www.topps.com/sports/default.aspx

Chapter 25

David Beckham: Soccer's Global Brand

John Vincent,
University of Alabama

John S. Hill,
University of Alabama

Jason W. Lee,
University of North Florida

Internet Address: www.davidbeckham.com

Discussion Questions

- Will David Beckham's transfer to MLS provide him with the platform to rival Michael Jordan's position as one of the premier sports celebrity endorsers/pitchmen of all time? Or will soccer's status in the United States as a second-tier sport behind football, basketball, and baseball condemn this venture to failure?
- Do you think that Beckham is more celebrity style over sporting substance?
- Does Beckham's penchant for nonconformity and metrosexual tendencies make him more or less appealing in the United States?
- Is Beckham's move to the Los Angeles Galaxy a testament to his declining soccer-playing ability?
- Will Beckham be a good ambassador for soccer in the United States? Can he, as Timothy J. Leiweke, president and CEO of Anschutz Entertainment Group, suggested, build the bridge between soccer in America and the rest of the world?

The Line-Up

David Beckham's career has experienced various ups and downs; through it all, he has never been out of the media or public eye. Since his debut with the famed Manchester United, his soccer career soared. His brilliance playing for Manchester United and the England national team was only eclipsed by his crossover marketing appeal in a sport where the commercial rewards for elite soccer players increased exponentially in the global market place.

As Beckham turned thirty, his career experienced adversity, and his appeal seemed in decline. When his 2006 World Cup squad (viewed as being "England's greatest generation" of players since the country won the World Cup in 1966) were eliminated by a penalty shootout at the quarterfinal stage, Beckham re-signed his captaincy and was later dropped from the national team. Subsequently, the following season, he lost his regular first team status with famed Spanish soccer club Real Madrid. With these setbacks, Beckham's distinguished soccer career seemed to be in inexorable decline. His commercial appeal seemed to be slipping as he lost several lucrative endorsement contracts, including being dropped as a brand ambassador for Gillette and as the face man for Police sunglasses.

However, in January 2007, the next phase of "Brand Beckham" was launched as he signed with the Los Angeles Galaxy of Major League Soccer (MLS), in the United States. By signing an unprecedented contract (reputedly worth $250 million over five years), Beckham benefited from the newly passed "designated player rule" (consequently referred to as the "Beckham rule"), which permitted MLS teams to pay above the salary cap for two players. This stunning contract reflected Beckham's Hollywood good looks and his popular global appeal. This contract exceeded those of superstars in the traditionally mainstream U.S. sports of football, baseball, and basketball. This new deal allowed Beckham to benefit financially from his image rights, related sponsorships, and endorsements opportunities, sharing in revenue from team replica shirts and club ticket sales; in effect, Beckham's contract made him a partner with Los Angeles Galaxy owners, Anschutz Entertainment.

Beckham's jump to the MLS was motivated by the promise of generating interest in soccer in the United States. Beckham brings much more to the table than his soccer prowess; he also brings his persona. This persona entails an athletic, attractive superstar that comes with a celebrity wife, Victoria "Posh Spice" Beckham. This package seems to be the recipe desired for attracting interest for and to the Los Angeles Galaxy, MLS, and even Hollywood.

Timeline of Events

1975
- David Beckham born in Leytonstone, London.

1991
- Signs as a trainee for Manchester United.

1995
- Makes first team debut for Manchester United.

1996
- Scores from the halfway line in a Premier League game against Wimbledon.

1997
- Professional Football Association (PFA) Young Player of the Year.

1998
- Sent off playing for England in World Cup loss to Argentina. England eliminated in a penalty shootout. Beckham widely blamed for England's defeat.

1999
- Marries Victoria Adams, better known as Posh Spice of the pop music group Spice Girls; first son born.
- Wins the "treble" with Manchester United (Premier League, FA Cup, and Champions League).

2000
- Appointed England national team captain.

2001
- Voted BBC Sports Personality of the Year.

2002
- Makes cameo appearance in the film *Bend it Like Beckham.*
- Amidst Beckham mania, Beckham captains England to the quarterfinal stage of the World Cup finals, held in Japan and Korea.

2003
- Awarded OBE for services to football.
- Transfers to Real Madrid.

2004
- Google records that Beckham was the most searched for sportsman on their Web site.

2005
- Makes cameo appearance in the film *Goal!*

2006
- Captains England in the 2006 World Cup. Becomes the first-ever English player to score in three successive World Cup tournaments. Resigns the

captaincy in the aftermath of England's disappointing elimination by
Portugal at the quarterfinal stage.

2007
- Transfers to Los Angeles Galaxy for a five-year contract, reportedly worth
  $250 million in salary and commercial endorsements.

2008
- Makes his 100th appearance for the England national team.

Beckham: The Soccer Player

David Beckham became famous playing soccer for England's most celebrated club team, Manchester United. He emerged as a member of the Manchester United team that won the FA Youth Cup in 1992. He made his first
team debut for Manchester United as a seventeen-year-old in 1992, and went
on to make 394 appearances and score 80 goals. Beckham achieved notoriety
early in his career in a game against Wimbledon, when he scored a spectacular goal from the halfway line after he had spotted the opponent's goalkeeper,
Neil Sullivan, standing a long way out of his goal. Beckham went on to star
for Manchester United as a midfield playmaker for ten seasons, during an era
when the club was incredibly successful. Beckham's team won the English Premier League, which is generally acknowledged to be one of the best leagues in
the world, a staggering six times. His teams also won the FA Cup twice and
the European Champions League once. In 1999, Beckham was a standout in
the legendary Manchester United team that won an unprecedented three tro-
phies in one season: the English Premier League, the FA Cup, and the European Champions League. While playing for Manchester United, Beckham
became famous for his ability to score from his signature right-footed free kicks
from as far out as thirty-five yards from the goal by bending the ball around
and over defensive walls and into a corner of the net (known as "bending it
like Beckham"). He is also famous for his ability to unlock opposing defenses
with long, accurate, penetrating diagonal passes and crosses from wide areas.

Although Beckham made his name playing for his club team, Manchester
United, his soccer career and reputation were enhanced through many stellar
performances playing for the England national team. He made his debut for
the England national team in 1996, and as of March 2009, he has played for
his national soccer team on 108 occasions. This makes him one of only five
Englishmen to have represented the national team on 100 or more occasions,
which is a remarkable feat. Beckham played for England in three successive
World Cup final tournaments (1998, 2002, and 2006), and is the only Eng-

lishman to have scored goals in three successive FIFA World Cup final tournaments. He became the England team captain in 2000 and led his country in two World Cup final tournaments. As captain, Beckham led the team with many inspirational performances. Perhaps his finest hour playing for his country was his game-changing performance in a crucial World Cup qualifier against Greece. With England facing elimination, Beckham scored from a trademark bending free kick against Greece in the final seconds of the game. His goal secured the England national team's qualification for the 2002 World Cup finals. Such performances for the national team endeared him to the English public, and he was voted the BBC Sports Personality of the Year at the end of 2001.

Two months before the 2002 World Cup final tournament, Beckham broke a metatarsal in his left foot playing for Manchester United in a Champions League game against Spanish side Deportivo de La Coruna. This injury, which threatened to prevent him from leading England in the World Cup, was caused by a bad tackle by Deportivo's Argentinean player Aldo Duscher and caused consternation throughout the country. Beckham's injury featured more prominently in several newspapers than did the death of the Queen Mother. One notable tabloid newspaper, supported by Tony Blair, the British prime minister, urged its readers to pray for Beckham's metatarsal bone to heal in time for him to lead England in the World Cup. Although he had not fully recovered from his injury, as captain, he led the team in its attempt to win the World Cup in 2002, including scoring to defeat and eliminate archnemesis Argentina. Beckham's significant contributions to football (soccer) were recognized later in 2002, when he was selected as the thirty-third greatest Briton by the BBC and awarded the Order of the British Empire (OBE) in the Queen's Birthday Honours list the following year.

Although Beckham is perhaps the most famous football player in the world, he has had to overcome adversity on his way to becoming a postmodern soccer and celebrity icon. Early in his career, while playing for the England national team in the 1998 World Cup, he was sent off in a crucial game against Argentina when he kicked Diego Simeone after the Argentinean player fouled him. Beckham's sending off meant England was forced to play the reminder of the game with one fewer player than Argentina, and although they held Argentina to a draw, they were eliminated in a penalty shoot-out. England's bitter disappointment at being eliminated by archrival Argentina and the resulting damage to the national pride and psyche was widely blamed on Beckham. One popular English newspaper, the *Daily Mirror*, made Beckham a scapegoat for what it viewed as England's premature elimination from the World Cup and printed a dartboard with a picture of him in the middle. He was widely criticized by the English media and supporters alike; at the height of the vilification, an effigy of him was hung outside a London pub. The following season, Beckham had to endure taunts, abuse, hostility, and provocation from opposition supporters while playing for Manchester United. In some matches, every time he touched the ball, opposing supporters jeered him. However, his stoicism in the hostile environment and the quality of his performances gradually won over most soccer supporters in a season that culminated with Manchester United winning an historic treble (the English Premier League, the FA Cup, and the Champions League). His appointment as England captain in 2000 confirmed that he had successfully resurrected his soccer career two years after he became a pariah.

In 2003, under the glare of enormous publicity and media scrutiny, Beckham transferred to perhaps the only other soccer club in the world as famous as Manchester United—Spanish side Real Madrid—for a transfer fee of $41 million. Beckham joined Real Madrid as part of club president Florentino Perez's policy of buying one Galáctico (superstar) each year. Beckham joined a Real Madrid team filled with an array of global soccer superstars, including France's Zinedine Zidane, Portugal's Luis Figo, and Brazil's Ronaldo. The Los Galácticos policy proved to be a relative failure on the field, with the club winning only one trophy, the La Liga championship, during Beckham's four seasons. This spurred some critics to suggest that some Galácticos were selected based on their global marketing appeal rather than their playing form, which was also called the "Disneyfication" of Real Madrid. However, the Los Galácticos policy resulted in increased financial success based on their ability to leverage the legendary club's high marketing potential around the world, especially in Asia, where Beckham is extremely popular. Many commentators suggested that the "Beckonomics" of the deal helped Real Madrid overtake Manchester United as the world's richest soccer club in 2006.

Beckham's move to Real Madrid had obvious commercial synergies. Both parties benefited from their sponsorship deals with Pepsi and Adidas. Beckham's iconic global appeal enabled Real Madrid to sell over $1 million worth of replica shirts bearing his name and his number—23—on the day of his transfer and increase total merchandize sales by 67 percent in his first season. Real Madrid also leveraged Beckham's enduring iconic global appeal with preseason exhibition matches and promotional tours in Asia and the United States.

The Celebrity Crossover Star

In 2007, Beckham shocked the soccer world by signing with the Los Angeles Galaxy in the United States for $250 million, an unprecedented contract for a soccer player. The rationale given by the Galaxy's owners for signing him for such a significant amount of money was that he is such a significant figure in popular contemporary culture that he transcends the sport of soccer. He has been the most successful soccer player at crossing over to become a celebrity icon; based on his multifaceted global appeal and enduring popularity, he is well on the way to going from being a hugely successful celebrity endorser and pitchman to becoming a brand in his own right. Evidence of Beckham's pervasive global presence and celebrity status can be gleaned from the revelation from Google that he was searched for more than any other sport topic on their site in 2003 and 2004. Before he had even kicked a ball for the Los Angeles Galaxy, a poll in the United States conducted by marketing agency Davie Brown Entertainment found that 51.9 percent of Americans recognized Beckham, despite the fact that soccer significantly trails the big three traditional American sports (football, basketball, and baseball) in popularity. A further testament to his enduring global popularity is that the United Kingdom used Beckham as an ambassador for their successful bid for London to be the host city of the 2012 Olympic Games, and a similar future role is envisaged for him in Britain's bid to host the 2018 World Cup.

Beckham's Multifaceted Appeal

Beckham's enduring global popularity and brand appeal is underpinned by the fact that, unlike most sport stars, he does not appeal to just soccer fans— or just sport fans, for that matter. His multiple brand personalities appeal to many different demographic segments; in fact, he has almost universal appeal. The term "Bend it like Beckham," although ostensibly referring to his famed free-kick skill, could equally be applied to his multidimensional global commercial appeal.

World-Class Soccer Player

Beckham appeals to aspiring youth, men, and women alike. As a world-class soccer player, he is the quintessential Englishman, a humble, working-class lad who made good. He has lived a schoolboy's dream, serving as a premier soccer player and starring for the two most famous club soccer teams in the world. He has captained his national team with distinction. Unlike other prodigiously talented British soccer players from previous eras, such as Paul "Gazza" Gascoigne and the late George Best, whose alcohol-fueled partying lifestyles detracted from their soccer talent and commercial appeal as celebrity endorsers, Beckham is known for his strong work ethic, professionalism, and humility, all of which enhance his appeal as a role model for youth. However, although his masculine identity and working-class manliness is established through his soccer endeavors, much of his multifaceted appeal is predicated on his nonconformist and seemingly contradictory multiple off-field personas, which are outlined next.

Posh and Becks: The People's Royalty

When Beckham started dating pop starlet Victoria Adams, better known as Posh Spice from the Spice Girls, the most popular female pop group of the late 1990s, his celebrity status blossomed. Their high-profile relationship captured the public imagination and was the subject of much media fascination, which made them significant figures in popular contemporary culture. Increasingly, as befitted his newfound celebrity status, Beckham has occupied significant space on the front page and celebrity sections, as well as the sport sections of popular British newspapers. Their wedding at Luttrellstown Castle, Ireland, in 1999 garnered enormous interest and media attention, with exclusive photographs appearing in OK! magazine, including a famous one of them sitting together on golden thrones, a pose more commonly associated with royalty. This led several commentators to refer to them as the people's royalty. Known affectionately as "Posh and Becks," the young newlyweds bought a large home and country estate near London, which became known as "Beckingham Palace." Although they were famous individually, the people's royalty received exponentially more attention from the media paparazzi after they married. Piers Morgan, the former editor of the Daily Mirror, revealed to Andrew Morton, a celebrity biographer that "on a slow news day we used to lead the paper on the royals, now we go for Queen Posh and King David" (2006, p. 19). His wife, Victoria, who is known for her model good looks, fashion style and glamour, as well as her celebrity and socialite lifestyle and connections, enhanced Beckham's celebrity status and seemed to assist with his off-field interests and activities. Together, they formed a potent combination and created their own synergistic brand.

The Devoted Family Man

Posh and Becks have three children, and Beckham appears to be a doting father and a devoted husband. This wholesome family image makes him an ideal celebrity product endorser. Simon Fuller, the British music mogul famous for managing the Spice Girls and producing popular TV shows such as *American Idol*, represents the Beckhams. He claims that the Beckham brand is about aspiration and family values. Fuller is working hard to promote Beckham as an international icon of masculinity and fatherhood. Indeed, even revelations in 2004 in the *News of the World*, a popular British newspaper, that he had an extramarital affair with Rebecca Loos, his personal assistant—which he denied—did not seem to dampen his image as a devoted family man and appeared to have little lasting impact on his commercial appeal and enduring global popularity.

Dedicated Fashionista

An important part of Beckham's mystique and image as a style icon and an international model is his unashamed interest in high fashion, fashionable accessories, and his penchant for nonconformity. Beckham appears to use fashion to exude sex appeal and reveal different elements of his masculinity, and he has modeled for several high-fashion brands, such as Police sunglasses and Armani. Based on their celebrity fashion personas, Beckham and his wife, Victoria, have become lucrative endorsers of clothing and fashion lines, exercise equipment, fashion magazines, recreation and spa companies, and perfume and cosmetic products. In 2007, they were reportedly paid $13.7 million for endorsing a brand of his and hers fragrances for Coty. He is known equally for his sartorial eloquence and variety of hairstyles. For example, he wore Caribbean-style braids when he was introduced to Nelson Mandela, South Africa's first black president, and he fashioned a Mohican hairstyle before the 2002 World Cup. His unconventional appearance includes an ever-expanding number of tattoos, including a very visible winged cross on the back of his neck. Although appealing to that all-important youth demographic, his tattoos have been ridiculed in the British media, and when he plays soccer he wears long-sleeve shirts to conceal the tattoos on his arms.

Metrosexual Man

Beckham's persona is anchored in his role as a heterosexual man who excels in the world's most popular hegemonic masculine sport of soccer. However, his well-publicized interest in his appearance and grooming habits led British journalist Mark Simpson, who is credited with bringing the term *metrosexual* into the popular lexicon, to hail David Beckham as the ultimate example of a metrosexual—a heterosexual male who is in touch with his feminine side. He is known for color-coordinated fashion sense, being well groomed and manicured, and is promoted as someone who moisturizes regularly.

Gay Icon

Beckham's model good looks endear him to both sexes. Although he is clearly heterosexual, he is a popular figure in and acknowledges the gay community. At times he seems to have adopted an almost androgynous appearance through his fashion choices, which have included wearing a sarong while on holiday, as well as appearing in gay magazines dressed in a fitted black suit with his hair dyed blonde and wearing pink nail varnish. In a 2002 issue of men's magazine *GQ*, Beckham famously posed for photographs in what the magazine promoted as his most controversial shoot. He was photographed complete with facial makeup with baby oil on his uncovered chest, wearing a silk scarf and obvious nail varnish, which was reported under the headline "Camp David" in the popular British newspaper the *Daily Mirror*.

Celebrity Endorser

The multifaceted appeal of David Beckham makes him one of the most recognizable celebrities in the world. His popularity in Asia is unprecedented for a European soccer player. During the 2002 World Cup, held jointly in Japan and South Korea, he received the sort of adulation from teenage girls normally reserved for rock stars. In Thailand, a Buddhist temple has a gold-plated Beckham figure that people can worship; in Japan, the Meiji Seika chocolate factory built an almost life-size statue of him made of chocolate. His global popularity in an era of commodification has translated into him becoming the richest soccer player in the world. Although Beckham's appeal as a celebrity endorser was initially predicated on his soccer-playing ability and his credibility as a professional player, many of his portfolio of endorsements, carefully crafted by Simon Fuller, have been secured because of his multiple brand personalities—particularly his striking combination of reassuring but dissonant elements of masculinity and his style icon persona. Although Beckham is sponsored by sport apparel manufacturer Adidas and endorses their soccer shoes, his endorsements are not limited to just sport or sport-related products. His multifaceted global appeal has enabled him to transcend soccer. He has endorsed many different product lines for many different corporations. He has modeled sunglasses for Police, pitched clothing lines for Marks & Spencer, and endorsed soft drinks for Pepsi and mobile telephones for Vodafone.

The Final Score

David Beckham's decision in 2007 to play for the Los Angeles Galaxy in the MLS was a significant achievement for the league and also comes at a critical juncture in the league's development. Beckham's arrival was part of the strategic plan for league expansion and penetration in different markets. Shortly after his arrival, Don Garber, the MLS commissioner, was quoted in the *Wall Street Journal* explaining that the business rationale behind signing Beckham was to generate new revenue streams for the league.

Beckham's debut for the Galaxy against fabled English Premier Division Champions Chelsea attracted a record crowd of almost 30,000 fans. The game attracted numerous Hollywood celebrities and received unprecedented live TV coverage on ESPN, which used nineteen cameras to cover the game. One camera focused solely on Beckham, even though he spent most of the game on the bench because of an injury he acquired before he arrived in the United States. His debut set the record for TV ratings for MLS and ESPN. However overall, on the field, Beckham's first two seasons playing for the Los Angeles Galaxy were not unqualified successes. He was plagued by injuries in his first season. He joined a Galaxy team that was struggling and failed to qualify for the post-season play-offs. At the end of his first season, amid rumors that the Galaxy were going to remove him, their head coach, Frank Yallop, left the club and was replaced by Ruud Gullit. Although there were high points in Beckham's second season for the Galaxy, including scoring from seventy yards out in a game against the Kansas City Wizards, the team struggled. Midway through the season, with the team languishing in a mid-table position, the coaching instability continued when Gullit left the club by mutual consent and general manager Alexi Lalas was fired. However, Beckham's form for the Galaxy in his second season was good, and his England international career was revived by new England manager Franco Capello.

Off the field, Beckham's impact was significant for both the Galaxy and MLS. The Galaxy sold out their luxury suites. Season ticket sales and fan attendance at the clubs' home and away games increased greatly. The team signed a shirt sponsorship deal with Herbalife and the Galaxy's merchandise sales, particularly of Beckham's number 23 replica shirt, took off. Within three months of Beckham moving to the Galaxy, Tim Leiweke, CEO of Anschutz

Entertainment Group, which owns the team, declared that organization had already recouped all their investment in Beckham.

From Celebrity Endorser to Brand Beckham

David and Victoria Beckham's arrival in Hollywood generated a tremendous amount of publicity and interest from the paparazzi. Victoria was interviewed by Jay Leno on *The Tonight Show* and starred in her own one-hour NBC fly-on-the-wall documentary, aptly titled *Victoria Beckham: Coming to America*. David had his own TV show, *David Beckham's Soccer USA*, which aired on the Fox Soccer Channel and MLSnet.com. He made the front page of *Sports Illustrated* and the men's magazine *Details*. The couple was featured in a nine-page spread in the August edition of *W* magazine, which contained photographs of the couple in provocative poses in their underwear.

The early indications are that their move has given them a platform to develop their brand. Since moving to Hollywood, David has received several lucrative endorsement contracts with Giorgio Armani, GO3, and Sharpie. In 2008, Beckham's management agency also suggested that Pepsi is considering him for a spokesman's role for one of their more healthy drink brands. David opened his eponymous soccer academy, which provides approximately 15,000 boy and girls with soccer coaching at two centers, one in Greenwich, southeast London, and the other in Carson, California. He also has plans to expand the academy in other markets, such as Southeast Asia, where his brand recognition and popularity is high. As well as launching their Intimately Beckham line of his and hers fragrances with Coty, David and Victoria developed their own dVb (David and Victoria Beckham) label, with a range of sunglasses and a denim fashion collection. In 2007, the dVb brand opened its first concession in the famous Harrods department store in the West End—London's shopping district. Also, at the end of 2007, Victoria developed a line of handbags and a jewelry collection in collaboration with Samantha Thavasa, a Japanese design label. The early indications suggest that the Beckham brand has benefited greatly from the move to Hollywood. However, the question remains whether the value of the Beckham brand can continue to appreciate given that David, at age thirty-three, is coming to the end of his soccer career and although Victoria participated in the Spice Girls comeback world tour in 2007, she has publicly announced that her solo singing career is over.

Post-Game Comments

- David Beckham is soccer's first global crossover star in the new millennium.
- His appeal, initially predicated on his success on the soccer field, has blossomed through careful management, which has exploited his multifaceted appeal.
- A large part of Beckham's appeal is based on his fashion sense, his penchant for nonconformity, and his metrosexual blends of opposites.
- Some commentators question whether Beckham will be able to overcome soccer's second-class status in the United States and whether his popular appeal will endure his decline as an elite soccer player.

Web Resources

http://www.davidbeckham.com
http://www.dvbstyle.com
http://www.la.galaxy.mlsnet.com
http://www.thesun.co.uk/article/0,2002390000-2006300720,00.html
http://www.virgin.net/money/moneymakers/davidbeckham.html

Additional Resources

Aaker, D. A. (1996). *Building strong brands.* New York: Free Press.

Bell, J. (2007). Beckham gives growing MLS some star power. *New York Times,* April 4, p. C15.

Cashmore, E. (2006). *Celebrity/culture.* New York: Routledge.

Cashmore, E., & Parker, A. (2003). One David Beckham? Celebrity, masculinity, and the socerati. *Sociology of Sport Journal, 20*(3), 214–231.

Clayton, B., & Harris, J. (2004). Footballer's wives: The role of the soccer player's partner in the construction of idealized masculinity. *Soccer & Society,* 5, 316–334.

Deloitte Sports Business Group. (2006). *Annual review of football finance.* Manchester.

DVBstyle.com. (2008). Retrieved on January 28, 2008, from http://www/dvbstyle.com/news/index.html.

Giardina, M. D. (2003). "Bending it like Beckham" in the global popular: Stylish hybridity, performativity, and the politics of representation. *Journal of Sport and Social Issues, 27*(1), 65–82.

Givhan, R. (2003). Beckham gets kick out of embracing fashion. *Wall Street Journal*, July 7, p. A6.

Halpin, J. (2007). Galaxy to get Beckham in summer. AEG press release: David Beckham statement. Retrieved on January 11, 2007, from http://web.mlsnet.com/news/mls_news.jsp?ymd=20070111&content_id=81586&vkey=news_mls&fext=.jsp.

Harris, J., & Clayton, B. (2007). David Beckham and the changing (re)presentations of English identity. *International Journal of Sport Management and Marketing*, 2(3), 208–221.

Morton, A. (2000). *Posh and Becks*. London: Michael O'Mara Books.

Patrick, A. O., Weinbach, J., & Johnson, K. (2007). Will "Brand Beckham" sell in the U.S.? *Wall Street Journal*, January 12, p. B1–B2.

Rahman, M. (2004). David Beckham as a historical moment in the representation of masculinity. *Labour History Review*, 69(2), 219–233.

Rines, S. (2004). Has adverse publicity affected Beckham's sponsorship potential? *International Journal of Sports Marketing & Sponsorship*, 6(1), 22–30.

Seenan, G. (2005). David Beckham, from football saviour to the new Messiah. *The Guardian*, September 14. Retrieved on September 11, 2008, from http://www.guardian.co.uk/uk/2005/sep/14/football.gerardseenan.

SportBusiness International. (2007, July). Retrieved on August 5, 2007, from http://www.sbrnet.com/sbr/Publication_Search/Publicatoin.cfm?function=detail&Magid.

Wahl, G., 2007. The Americanization of David Beckham. *Sports Illustrated*, 107(2), 40–46.

Yu, C.-C. (2005). Athlete endorsement in the international sports industry: A case study of David Beckham. *International Journal of Sports Marketing & Sponsorship*, 6(3), 189–199.

Appendix 1 "Brand It Like Beckham": Brand Beckham's Partners

Adidas: Beckham's official supplier and partner in a £80 million lifetime deal.

Motorola: Beckham is the face of Motorola's mobile phones and Bluetooth headsets, signing a £7.5 million three-year deal in 2006.

Pepsi: Beckham acts as a spokesperson and brand ambassador for Pepsi's soccer campaigns. He reputedly earns £2 million a year in this role.

Coty: Work with the Beckhams on their worldwide fragrance brand: Intimately Beckham.

Source: http://www.davidbeckham.com

Former Endorsements Deals

1. Gillette   signed in 2004, £23 million three-year deal
2. Vodafone   £1 million a year for TV advertisements
3. Brylcreem   £1 million a year for styling his hair with their products
4. Marks & Spencer   £1 million a year for DB07 range of children's clothes
5. Police sunglasses £1 million year deal
6. Rage software   £1.5 million for starring in computer games
7. Japan   £1.6 million for advertising the Tokyo Beauty Centre

Source: *The Sun*, £20 million Becks blow. Gary Payne, 7/5/2006, http://www.thesun.co.uk/article/0,2002390000-2006300720,00.html

---

Appendix 2 Brand Beckham: Quick Stats

50,000   Number of Live! mobile phones sold in three weeks after Beckham endorsed the Vodafone brand.
                Source: http://www.virgin.net/money/moneymakers/davidbeckham.html

50 percent   The increase in Brylcreem sales after Beckham's ad campaign.
                Source: http://www.virgin.net/money/moneymakers/davidbeckham.html

90 percent   Name recognition for "Bekkamu," as Beckham is known in Japan.
                Source: *The Observer*, May 25, 2003

$41 million   *The Times* estimated value of Beckham's endorsement deals in 2006.
                Source: *The Times*, December 26, 2006

$1 million   The estimated amount Beckham earns in a week from his Galaxy contract.
                Source: *Sports Illustrated*, July 16, 2007

$100 million   The value of the biggest personal insurance policy in sporting history, taken out by David Beckham in 2006.
                Source: *The Times*, December 26, 2006

Appendix 3 David Beckham's Charitable Work

UNICEF Goodwill Ambassador with special focus on UNICEF's Sports
   for Development program
London 2012 Olympic Games Bid ambassador
Malaria No More spokesman
The David and Victoria Beckham Children's Charity

Source: http://www.davidbeckham.com

Chapter 26

Deion Sanders: The Evolution of "Prime Time"

Mark S. Nagel,
University of South Carolina

Richard M. Southall,
University of North Carolina at Chapel Hill

Discussion Questions

- Why did Deion Sanders develop his Prime Time brand?
- How did Sanders maximize his marketing opportunities?
- What could current or future professional athletes learn from Sanders' experiences?
- Are you surprised Sanders remained popular after his religious conversion? Why or why not?

The Line-Up

Deion Sanders, based on his considerable physical skills alone, likely would have left an indelible mark on both Major League Baseball (MLB) and the National Football League (NFL). However, in addition to his athletic prowess, Sanders' ability to create and mold his image expanded his notoriety beyond his athletic talents, and he became known throughout the United States simply as "Prime Time." His athletic abilities amazed fans (he once hit a MLB home run and scored an NFL touchdown in the same week), and his flair and flamboyance attracted advertising agencies hoping to maximize his ability to market products and services. When Sanders signed a free agent contract with the NFL's San Francisco 49ers, he promptly won the NFL's Defensive Player of the Year Award while helping his team to a Super Bowl Championship. The following year, he received a then-record $12.99 million signing bonus to play for the Dallas Cowboys. While contributing to the Cowboys' Super Bowl victory, Sanders became the first Super Bowl participant to catch a pass and record an interception. His popularity garnered an invitation to host *Saturday Night Live* as well as the Miss USA Pageant—rare opportunities for a professional athlete. Sanders also became the centerpiece of advertising campaigns for numerous corporations, including Nike, Pepsi, and Visa. Sanders demonstrated his athletic ability by returning to compete for additional seasons after retiring from MLB and the NFL. Sanders's Prime Time persona enabled him to have or experience nearly anything that he wanted off the field. However, after realizing that much of his personal behavior was destructive to his family and friends, he became a born-again Christian and published *Power, Money, and Sex* in 1999. Sanders wrote that he had to change much of his off-field behavior because it was literally killing his desire to live. After permanently retiring from the NFL after the 2005 season, Sanders retained immense popularity among his fans. He continues to enjoy the spotlight as he works as a broadcaster for the NFL Network, but he maintains a more private, humble existence when he is not under the watchful eye of the TV cameras.

Timeline of Events

1967
  • Deion Luwynn Sanders born on August 9 in Fort Myers, Florida.
1985–1989
  • Attends Florida State, where he plays football, baseball, and track.
1988
  • Drafted by the New York Yankees of MLB.
  • Wins Jim Thorpe Award as the nation's best collegiate defensive back.
1989
  • Drafted by the Atlanta Falcons of the NFL with the fifth selection in the draft.
  • Becomes first person to hit a MLB home run and score a NFL touchdown in the same week.
1992
  • Plays a MLB game with the Atlanta Braves and a NFL game with the Atlanta Falcons on the same day.
1994
  • Named NFL Defensive Player of the Year after leading the San Francisco 49ers to the Super Bowl.

1995

- Hosts *Saturday Night Live.*
- Released the album *Prime Time,* containing the track "Must be the Money."
- Receives a $12.99 million signing bonus from the Dallas Cowboys.

1996

- Becomes the first player to catch a pass and record an interception in Super Bowl history.

1997

- Announces first retirement from MLB after playing a season with the Cincinnati Reds.

2000

- Signs with the NFL Washington Redskins.

2001

- Retires from baseball after returning to the Cincinnati Reds for an additional season.
- Retires from the NFL and becomes a studio analyst for CBS's *The NFL Today.*

2002

- Hosts the Miss USA Pageant.

2004

- Returns to the NFL with the Baltimore Ravens.

2006

- Announces retirement from the NFL after completing second season with the Ravens.
- Becomes owner of the Austin Wranglers of the Arena Football League.
- Becomes anchor for *NFL Gameday* on the NFL Network.

2008

- *Deion & Pilar: Prime Time Love* (a reality show detailing the life of Deion Sanders and his family) becomes the most watched premiere on the Oxygen network.

Early Years

Deion Sanders was born on August 9, 1967, in Fort Myers, Florida. Throughout his early years, he demonstrated tremendous athletic skills in a variety of sports. As a high school football, baseball, and basketball star, Sanders generated attention throughout the college coaching fraternity—he was awarded all-state honors in each sport. After an intense recruiting battle, Sanders enrolled at Florida State University in 1985. While playing football for the Seminoles, he was named an All-American and won the 1988 Jim Thorpe Award as the nation's top defensive back, even though he was known to have minimal tackling skills. However, one of the reasons he did not tackle many wide receivers was his exceptional quickness and ability to neutralize them. Anyone Sanders covered rarely caught a pass. He also starred for the FSU baseball team and ran track.

Although Sanders's on-field abilities generated considerable attention, he was known by many fans more for his self-proclaimed monikers, "Neon Deion" and "Prime Time." Sanders typically exhibited his panache by high stepping on interceptions and punt returns or dancing after scoring touchdowns. During his senior year, he arrived at a home football game against Florida in a tuxedo, riding in a white limousine. Although many believed that his flamboyant behavior was his natural personality, Sanders later privately admitted that he created much of the Prime Time persona to further his career. Cornerbacks were not typically paid salaries commensurate to quarterbacks or running backs, and he hoped to increase future earnings on and off the field through his marketing strategies. Sanders noted, "How do you think defensive backs get attention? They don't pay nobody [sic] to be humble."

Professional Career Rises

Sanders's success at Florida State generated interest from professional teams in MLB and the NFL. The New York Yankees selected him to play outfield in the 1988 draft, and the Atlanta Falcons chose him with the fifth overall selection in the 1989 draft. At the NFL draft, Deion appeared wearing thousands of dollars worth of gold jewelry and an attention-getting black leather ensemble, complete with an embroidered "Prime Time." His appearance garnered instant attention as countless companies pursued his advertising services. He appeared on the cover of *Sports Illustrated*. In 1989, Sanders made an immediate impact on the field as he became the first person to hit an MLB home run and score an NFL touchdown in the same week. In 1992, Sanders played a game for the Atlanta Braves and the Atlanta Falcons on the same day. Though some perceived this act as arrogant and selfish, most were amazed that one person could have an impact on both sports in a ten-hour period. Later that year, Sanders hit .533 and stole five bases in the World Series, establishing him as a two-sport star.

In 1994, Sanders signed a free agent contract with the NFL's San Francisco 49ers. His talent helped lead the team to a Super Bowl victory, and he was named NFL Defensive Player of the Year. His numerous interceptions and high-stepping antics were popular among many NFL fans, and he established himself as one of the most marketable American athletes. After the season, Sanders signed a seven-year, $35 million contract with the Dallas Cowboys that included a then-record $12.99 million signing bonus. He agreed to sit out the baseball season and fully focused his efforts on football. During his first year with the Cowboys, he became the only player to catch a pass and make an interception in Super Bowl history as the Cowboys won their third championship in four seasons.

Sanders continued to impact American sports culture throughout the remainder of the 1990s. Though he never won another Super Bowl, he continued to play at a Pro Bowl level for the Cowboys until 2000. He played both offense and defense, a rare feat for any NFL player. He also returned to play one season of MLB with the Cincinnati Reds in 1997. Throughout these years, Sanders continued to make commercials and promote his Prime Time image as fans across the country recognized and cheered his accomplishments. His defensive impact caused other NFL teams to reevaluate their compensation priorities. Other top-flight cornerbacks began to receive salaries similar to top players at other offensive and defensive positions.

A New Beginning

Although Sanders was recognized and admired by many, his on-field success was not creating a personal feeling of happiness or inner peace. His incredible talent and dedication had enabled him to accumulate an immense personal fortune that allowed him to build his mother a house and provide his family with tremendous material comforts. However, in 1997, few realized his wife was in the process of divorcing him and after years of being Prime Time both on and off the field, he was mentally lost. At one point, Sanders intentionally drove his car off a cliff in an attempted suicide. Surprisingly, he emerged from the crash without a scratch, though he was despondent and emotionally empty. After meeting with a former teammate, he began to think about his life's purpose. He became a born-again Christian and began to renounce much of his former off-field activities and behavior. In 1999, he published *Power, Money, and Sex*, which explained to the world how the new Prime Time would lead his life. Though Sanders had changed his off-field behavior, he continued to excel on the field, being named to the Pro Bowl five times while playing for the Cowboys.

In 2000, Sanders's impact on the playing field began to wane. He signed to play one season with the NFL's Washington Redskins, and he was not the same dominant defensive player. With his skills declining, he retired from football in 2001. He also attempted a final return to MLB with the Reds in 2001, but that was largely unsuccessful. Though his athletic career appeared over, his enthusiasm for life and other opportunities increased. Sanders continued to remain in the public spotlight, hosting the 2002 Miss America Pageant and working for national TV stations as an NFL analyst.

Somewhat shockingly, Sanders's NFL career was revived in 2004 when the Baltimore Ravens convinced him to sign a contract to play cornerback in their "nickel" defense (a defensive alignment using five defensive backs). At age thirty-seven, his skills had clearly declined, but Sanders was able to contribute to the Ravens defense for two seasons. During his first season with the Ravens, he scored his ninth NFL career touchdown on an interception return, moving him into a tie for second place all-time. Sanders permanently retired from NFL competition in January 2006, culminating one of the most interesting and controversial American professional sport careers.

With his on-field career complete, Sanders continued to maintain a presence in professional sport and American society. In 2006, he became owner of the Austin Wranglers of the Arena Football League (AFL) and also began to work as analyst for the NFL Network. Though his life is much more normal than in his younger days, in 2008 the Oxygen network began airing the reality show *Deion & Pilar: Prime Time Love.* The show chronicles the lifestyle of Sanders, his wife, and five children at their home in Prosper, Texas. Sanders often talks to religious congregations and school assemblies about his life. Though he loves to discuss his career in professional sports, he attempts to warn others about destructive off-the-field activities. He remains popular with those who watched him use his incredible speed to impact two professional sports in the 1990s, and he has attracted a new generation of fans based on his time with the Ravens and by speaking about his troubled past. Although he is no longer Prime Time, Sanders is still one of the most recognizable American athletes.

The Final Score

Deion Sanders formulated an effective brand-building campaign long before he arrived in MLB and the NFL. His on-field abilities and unique self-promotion activities increased his salary and endorsement compensation and enabled him to be one of the few Americans known simply with a nickname— Prime Time. Sanders's presence in the NFL altered the salary structure as teams began to reevaluate their compensation for top-caliber cornerbacks. In addition, his actions changed sport marketing as athletes and companies began to investigate branding opportunities that could capitalize on an athlete's style as well as natural talent. Although he no longer is an active player, he is still one of the most recognized athletes in the United States—a testament to his previous and current branding initiatives. Deion Sanders continues to remain in the spotlight through his work as a NFL TV analyst and as the star of his own reality show. He also interacts with nonfans through his religious evangelism activities. He is certainly an athlete who has maximized every possible branding opportunity.

Post-Game Comments

Despite Sanders's transformation from Prime Time to good citizen, there may still remain some negative feelings regarding his previous on and off-field antics. Although he was a two-time All American and perhaps the best cornerback to play college football, he has twice been denied entrance into the College Football Hall of Fame. Some observers have noted that the hall's criteria expecting a player to prove himself "worthy as a citizen after his football career, carrying the ideals of football forward into his community" may be causing some Hall of Fame voters to reject Sanders's candidacy (Dorsey, 2008). Other skeptics wonder if Sanders may merely be trying to cash in on his new brand as a family man. Regardless of one's opinion of Sanders, there is certainly no doubt that his exploits and achievements make him one of the most discussed athletes of all time.

Resources

Dorsey, D. (2008, May 2). College Football Hall of Fame incomplete without Deion. Available at http://tallahassee.com/apps/pbcs.dll/article?AID=2008805020344.

Nguyen, Z. (2001). The faith and talent of a "Prime Time" athlete. Available at http://www.coffeeshoptimes.com/zack31.html.

Sanders, D. (1999). *Power, money, and sex*. Nashville, TN: Word Publishing.

Wilner, B. (2004, December). A flick of the switch: Just like that, "Neon" Deion Sanders is back in the NFL, trying to light up the Ravens. Availableat http://findarticles.com/p/articles/mi_m0FCL/is_4_34/ai_n6257767.

Chapter 27

Maria Sharapova:
The WTA's "It Girl"

John Vincent,
University of Alabama
John S. Hill,
University of Alabama

Internet Address: www.mariasharapova.com

The Line-Up

The world of women's tennis has changed dramatically over the past two decades as it gained in popularity and achieved some financial parity with the men's game. While past players have only the satisfaction of contributing to the build-up, current women players have begun to reap the benefits. Of these, one stands out, literally and metaphorically, head and shoulders above the rest. She is Maria Sharapova, a Russian professional tennis player who has become one of the most recognizable and highest paid female athletes in the new millennium. It all occurred breathtakingly quickly in the aftermath of winning the ladies singles title at Wimbledon in 2004.

It was a multifaceted triumph that day in 2004. Sharapova was the first Russian to reach the Wimbledon women's singles final since Olga Morozova in 1974. It was totally unexpected, since before 2004, she had never advanced past the quarterfinals in a grand slam event. Also, at the tender age of seventeen, she became the second youngest winner of women's singles in the open era after Martina Hingis of Switzerland, who won the title at sixteen years of age in 1997. Further, Sharapova was also the lowest seed (thirteenth) to win the title in the open era—impressive given Wimbledon's elitist reputation. As if that were not enough, her appearance—blond, youthful, hyperfeminine, and highly mediagenic—combined with her captivating, fearless, and passionate style of play ensured exhaustive worldwide media coverage.

Given that Sharapova was Russian, blond, and a good tennis player, it was natural that media narratives following Wimbledon compared her to her fellow Russian, Anna Kournikova. Kournikova, a former Wimbledon singles semifinalist and media, cultural, and commercial icon, had allowed her sex appeal and style to supersede her tennis game. Sharapova, however, never allowed the comparison to take root. Focusing steadfastly on her game rather than its commercial backdrop, Sharapova has never lost her focus and has consistently reached the later stages of most Grand Slam tournaments since her Wimbledon triumph. As a result, she has been a consistent presence in the Womens Tennis Association's (WTA) top five ranked players since that time. Unlike Kournikova, her star did not fade as quickly as it rose; Sharapova followed up her success at Wimbledon by winning two more Grand Slam singles titles: the U.S. Open in 2006 and the Australian Open in 2008. Her game, unlike Kournikova's, had real substance.

Sharapova's youthful appearance, blonde hair, and long legs epitomize femininity and fashion style, which contribute to a crossover appeal that has made her one of the highest paid female athletes ever. In 2005, Sharapova's WTA tour earnings were reported to be $1.9 million, placing her in the top five in tour earnings. However, *Forbes* estimated that with commercial endorsements and modeling contracts, she was the highest paid female athlete in the world, with estimated total earnings approaching $20 million in 2005. This rise to fame has been nothing short of meteoric.

Timeline of Events

1986
- Sharapova's family moves from Homel, Belarus, to Siberia, Russia, after the Chernobyl nuclear accident.

1987
- Maria Sharapova is born in Nyagan, western Siberia, Russia.

1995
- Leaving her mother Yelena behind, Yuri Sharapova brings Maria to the United States to pursue their ambition to develop Maria's tennis ability. In December 1995, Maria receives a scholarship to attend the Nick Bollettieri Tennis Academy in Bradenton, Florida.

2001
- Joins the junior tennis circuit at age fourteen, and wins twenty-five of twenty-eight matches in her first year (in 2002, wins twenty-six of twenty-nine matches).

2003

- Joins the WTA professional women's circuit and wins two titles—Quebec City and the Japan Open. Ranked number thirty-two in the world.
- Signs with IMG Models, agency for mainstream models Kate Moss and Gisele Bündchen.
- Reaches the fourth round of the championships at Wimbledon as a qualifier.

2004

- Sharapova became the youngest women's singles champion at Wimbledon in the open era since Martina Hingis.
- Ranks first in *Sports Illustrated's* top ten female athletes with a reported $23 million in earnings.

2005

- Appears with Britney Spears and Celine Dion in department stores to promote her own fragrance created by Parlux Fragrances in a $5 million deal.
- Becomes the world number one ranked player.

2006

- Sharapova defeats Justine Henin in the final to win the her second Grand Slam, the U.S. Open.

2008

- Sharapova wins the Australian Open, defeating Anna Ivanovic in the final.
- Becomes the world number one ranked player again in May after Justine Henin retires.

Sharapova's Rise to Tennis Prominence

The foregoing timeline still does not capture the drama behind Sharapova's rise to tennis stardom. Her parents moved to the Russian industrial town of Nyagan in western Siberia from Gomel in the aftermath of the Chernobyl nuclear disaster. Their only child, Maria, was born the following year on April 19, 1987. A year later, the family moved to the Black Sea resort town of Sochi. Yuri Sharapova, a construction worker, recognized and nurtured his daughter's tennis ability from a young age. Her recognition came early. In 1993, Yuri and Maria Sharapova attended tennis clinics held in Moscow during the Kremlin Cup. There, Martina Navratilova saw the young Sharapova play and informed Yuri that she had talent. However, to fulfill that talent, Navratilova noted, she must go to the United States to develop her game further. Thus in 1995, Yuri and Maria left Russia for the United States. They had to leave Maria's mother,

Yelena, behind because she could not get a visa. After much hard work, she received a scholarship to attend the mecca of tennis training, the Nick Bollettieri Tennis Academy in Bradenton, Florida, where renowned coaches such as Robert Lansdorp and Nick Bollettieri refined her game. The grueling six-hours-a-day practices, exhausting travel schedule and personal sacrifices began to pay off as the youthful Sharapova began winning tournaments. Her precocious tennis ability, combined with her feminine appearance, were recognized as a potentially potent combination when, aged eleven, she signed with sport marketing agency, IMG, where her multifaceted business interests were professionally developed and managed by the vice president of IMG Tennis, Max Eisenbud.

Brand Sharapova

Maria Sharapova's rise to prominence in women's professional tennis contains many story lines that made her appealing from a marketing perspective. Her story is frequently anchored in a "rags to riches" narrative, which epitomizes the American dream. Sharapova has been portrayed and marketed as a symbol for what individual agency, sacrifice, determination, hard work, a healthy lifestyle, and talent can achieve with professional coaching in a world-class training environment. At six feet, two inches tall, Sharapova's aggressive, all-action, fearless on-court style, including her signature grunt after each ground stroke, vividly contrasted with her feminine sex appeal and fashion style that defined her marketing appeal. This combination of athletic aggressiveness and female allure that gave her global appeal with tennis's traditional upper-middle-class demographic segment and the nontraditional sponsors that were normally attracted to the male-dominated power and performance team sports, such as football and basketball.

Sharapova's first big commercial endorsement deal came after her success at Wimbledon. Immediately after winning the women's singles title on Wimbledon's center court, she tried unsuccessfully to call her mother on a cell phone. This moment of professional rapture and her inability to share it with her mother was captured on global television. An IMG marketing executive, Alan Zucker, watching this on TV, seized the moment and called a contact at Motorola. One month later, Sharapova had her first global endorsement deal with Motorola, worth an estimated $1 million a year. This deal provided her with a mobile phone and a share of the income from downloads from HelloMoto/Maria.

By 2005, Maria Sharapova was becoming a brand, and over the next few years her brand appeal was developed in several directions, but always anchored in her unique combination of athleticism and attractiveness. Her power and athletic dimension was used by Canon as the centerpiece of their Power-Shot SD630 Digital Elph camera launch campaign in 2006. The campaign featured TV, print, Internet, and retail components that captured her power on the court with off-court moments as an entourage of tennis balls following her through the streets as she toted her PowerShot camera back to the hotel.

Sharapova's perfect physique and looks provided further marketing opportunities. Most celebrity sport stars are effective only when endorsing sport-related products and services. However, Sharapova's sex appeal and healthy lifestyle gave her appeal outside of tennis. This helped her become a promoter of PepsiCo.'s Gatorade and Tropicana brands. It also made her a natural fit to sell cosmetics and fashion accessories. In 2005, coinciding with her move to number one in women's tennis rankings, Parlux launched a Maria Sharapova fragrance that parlayed her Wimbledon success into a U.S. launch for the fragrance, followed by an international rollout into Japan and Mexico. In the same year, Colgate-Palmolive tabbed the stylistically cool Sharapova to promote Colgate-Palmolive's global deodorant, antiperspirant, and body spray brands. A company news release by Colgate-Palmolive explained their rationale for the move by stating: "Sharapova's stature as an athlete, complemented by her beauty, grace and 'active, on-the-move' lifestyle corresponds perfectly with the Lady Speed Stick brand values. She embodies everything that these brands stand for: power, protection, reliability and confidence" (Klimerman, 2005).

Her global brand status and feminine side have been used effectively by a number of international companies. Among them was Swiss luxury sports watch manufacturer TAG Heuer. She joined forces with three other brand ambassadors—NASCAR driver Jeff Gordon, actress Uma Thurman, and golfer Tiger Woods—to promote the company's midlevel watch range selling at $1,000–5,000. Her signature product, the TAG Heuer Professional Sports Watch is pink (Sharapova's favorite color) and has diamonds embedded in an elegant, slim, avant-garde design. Made of ultralight titanium and stainless steel, the product mirrors Sharapova's toughness and femininity. This product perfectly epitomized her crossover appeal, as described by Jean-Christophe Babin, TAG Heuer's president and CEO:

> Off the court, her beauty and grace have romanced the fashion world, with profiles in leading fashion magazines, and the launch of her own perfume. She is truly a phenomenon. Determined, passionate and audacious, she has shown extraordinary character in taking on the best players in professional tennis and winning. At the same time, she is graceful and extraordinarily feminine. Maria Sharapova works hard to be the best she can be, yet remains true to the joy and passion she feels for the game. Nobody in the world of sports better than Maria

embodies the fusion of sport with glamour, and therefore TAG Heuer core positioning. (TAG Heuer Press Release, 2004)

Sharapova's versatility and multisegment appeal, combined with her perceived high-profile global lifestyle, made her a natural for other luxury products. In 2006, on the back of introducing three new SUVs, Land Rover announced that Sharapova had become a brand ambassador in a multiyear deal that provided her free use of their vehicles. Her congruency with the Land Rover brand concept was explained by Mike O'Driscoll, president, Aston Martin Jaguar Land Rover North America, when he stated:

> Her drive to win on the court combined with her need for the latest technology to keep her on the road to success means this new relationship is a winning combination and a natural fit. In many ways, she reflects the same sense of adventure and extraordinary abilities that our vehicles represent. Maria's determination and inspirational success combine to make her a global icon and we are delighted that she will be associated with Land Rover. (Land Rover Press Release, 2006)

Sharapova's undoubted sex appeal is still what underpins her commercial allure. Dubbed the "Siberian siren" because of her unique sex appeal and her on-court macho grunt on ground strokes, Maria has appeared in *Vogue* and in the 2006 *Sports Illustrated* swimsuit issue, widely known for its pictures of scantily clad supermodels. In it, Sharapova posed in a six-page bikini photo shoot spread. The sport world took notice. In 2005, she had already become the most downloaded female celebrity and had been recognized by *People* magazine as among the fifty most beautiful people in the world. In 2006, *Maxim* magazine dubbed her the hottest athlete in the world for the fourth consecutive year. The laconic Sharapova has taken all of this in her stride. As she notes: "Beauty sells. I have to realize that's also part of why people want me. I understand it. It's fine. I'm not going to make myself ugly" (Kafta, 2005, p. 117).

Like other elite female tennis players such as Anna Kournikova, Serena Williams, and Venus Williams, Sharapova's interest in fashion and style has been professionally crafted and nurtured by IMG, her management agency, and her various sponsors. They have always taken care to protect as well as promote her femininity. For example, fashion for Sharapova is not just a business, it is *her* as well. As a result, she has modeled both functional and revealing outfits designed by Nike, an example of which is a *Breakfast at Tiffany's*-inspired dress, replete with sequins and futuristic neckline, that she wore at the 2006 U.S. Open (which she won). This was followed at the 2007 U.S. Open with a dress decorated with interpretations of New York's skyline.

The red dress, worn for night matches, balanced function with style. It was practical and technological, a sleek garment made of breathable wicking jersey and constructed with a no-sew technique with seams bonded by heat and silicone. It was also stylish, with more than 600 Swarovski crystals sewn into the neckline and three crystal buttons down the back.

More recently, Sharapova has also worked as a celebrity promotional model and handbag designer for luxury designer label Samantha Thavasa. The juxtaposition of Sharapova's glamorous feminine appeal and her on-court aggressive style has been the theme of several creative TV commercials from Nike and Canon. Before the 2006 U.S. Open, Sharapova was featured in a Nike TV commercial that had her walking and riding through the streets of New York to the Arthur Ashe Stadium, with "I Feel Pretty" playing in the background. The song sharply terminated as she began playing and returned a serve with her trademark grunt.

The Final Score

Only recently have elite celebrity female athletes been able to parlay athletic success and glamour appeal into sponsorships and endorsements to become brand equities worth $20 million a year. Maria Sharapova was in the right place at the right time as the new millennium sought bright, fresh personalities with unique appeals into which they could frame the "new" egalitarian status for women. Her combination of athleticism, toughness, femininity, and youthfulness, combined with her tall and slim physique, epitomized the new millennium woman as well as the highly successful tennis player. Max Valiquette, president of Toronto youth marketing firm Youthography, summarized this by stating: "Tennis is a sport that really lends itself to women being conventionally good-looking because it's all cardio and comparatively little strength training. Having a long body is really helpful in tennis, whereas in other sports you want a low center of gravity" (Lianne, 2005, p. 48).

All sports, tennis included, thrive and reward success. In women's professional tennis, most televised matches usually feature at least one top ten player. These marquee players and their endorsers are the main beneficiaries of the media exposure generated. Thus, at least in the short term, Sharapova's commercial appeal is largely predicated on her continued success on the women's professional tennis circuit. As with other athletes, endorsers want their money's worth, and Sharapova is no exception. Her endorsement contracts contain, like others, performance-related clauses that only pay out full value if she attains specific performance-related goals, such as winning a Grand Slam or rising to the number one ranking in the world.

Sharapova's father and coach, Yuri, and her managers at IMG are all aware of this. Anna Kournikova has been labeled as the most commercially successful loser of all time, but she still earns well in excess of $1 million a year. Hence, Sharapova's managers limit her sponsorship work to just three weeks a year so that it does not unduly distract her from tennis. To date, Sharapova is still on course. She won the first Grand Slam tournament of 2008, the Australian Open, and if she can continue her winning ways, her endorsement value should continue to increase. On her current earnings trajectory, this would possibly place her in a position to earn more than any other female athlete in the history of women's sports.

Even if Sharapova should falter or retire after a highly decorated tennis career, her past athletic achievements combined with her natural beauty virtually guarantee her a career in fashion and design. In this scenario, again her tennis success stands her in good stead with her brand name recognition. Happily, she wins either way over the long term.

Post-Game Comments

- Maria Sharapova has become one of the most recognizable and highest paid female athletes in the new millennium.
- Sharapova's rags to riches story marks her as a symbol for what individual agency can achieve. Her aggressive, all-action tennis game, combined with her sex appeal and fashion style also underpin her global marketing appeal.
- Sharapova's healthy, high-profile lifestyle and perfect physique provide her with opportunities to endorse a wide range of non-sport-related products, such as cosmetics and fashion accessories.
- Although Sharapova's short-term commercial appeal is predicated on continued success on the tennis court, her natural beauty, versatility, and multisegment appeal suggest that her brand can transcend her sporting success.

Resources

Anderson, D. (2005, May 23). Canon spots put focus on women. *Brandweek*, *46*(21), 22.

Kafta, P. (2005, July 4). The hot shot. *Forbes*, *176*(1), 116–121.

Klimerman, A. (2005). Colgate-Palmolive signs tennis champion Maria Sharapova to multi-year sponsorship. Colgate Company News. Retrieved from http://investor.colgate.com/print_releaseID=163970&ReleaseType=Company.

Land Rover Press Release. (2006, April 11). Land Rover pairs with Maria Shara-
    pova—Game. Set. Match. Retrieved July 18, 2008 from http://media.ford.com/
    newsroom/feature_display.cfm?release=23398.
Lianne, G. (2005). Scoring a gland slam. *McLean's, 118*(33), 46–48.
O'Loughlin, S. (2007, January 15). Focus on upscale segment pays off for TAG
    Heuer. *Brandweek,* 48(3), 6.
TAG Heuer Press Release. (2004, December 14). Sparkling tennis star Maria
    Sharapova becomes TAG Heuer new worldwide sport and glamour am-
    bassador. TAG Heuer, Marin, Switzerland.

Appendix 1 The Sharapova Appeal in Endorsement Sponsorships

Colgate-Palmolive	In 2005, Sharapova signed a multiyear endorsement deal worth approximately $2 million annually to promote Colgate-Palmolive's global deodorant, antiperspirant, and body spray brands.
Prince Sports	Lifetime endorsement deal, which includes advertising, signature product lines, junior tennis programs, global grassroots efforts, and "grow the game initiatives," reportedly worth over $25 million over ten years.
Land Rover	In April 2006, Sharapova signed a three-year deal to endorse their vehicles, worth an estimated $2 million per year.
Motorola	In addition to a fee, Sharapova received a free mobile phone, has her mobile phone bills paid, and also receives a share of the income of downloads from HelloMoto/Maria.
PepsiCo.	In January 2007, Sharapova became the first international tennis ambassador to promote healthy hydration and nutrition habits to consumers around the world when she was featured in PepsiCo.'s Gatorade and Tropicana advertising and promotions.
TAG Heuer	In December 2004, Sharapova signed an endorsement deal with the luxury Swiss sport watchmaker.
Nike	Endorses Nike apparel, footwear, and accessories.
Canon	Sharapova signed a three-year deal in 2004, worth $2 million a year, to promote both their camera and office products.

Appendix 2 Sharapova's Awards

2003   WTA Newcomer of the Year
2004   WTA Player of the Year
2005   ESPY Best Female Tennis Player
        Master of Sports of Russia
        Prix de Citron Roland Garros
2006   Named the country's best female player for the year by Russia's tennis federation
2007   ESPY Best Female Tennis Player
        ESPY Best International Athlete

Appendix 3 The Sharapova Activism File and Community Orientation

- On February 14, 2007, Sharapova became a Goodwill Ambassador for the United Nations Development Program (UNDP) and donated US$100,000 to UNDP Chernobyl-recovery projects.
- The Maria Sharapova Foundation is committed to helping at-risk children.
- Ambassador for Russia's Black Sea resort city of Sochi's bid to host the 2014 Olympic Winter Games.

Chapter 28

Tiger Woods: The First Billion-Dollar Athlete

Pamela C. Laucella,
Indiana University School of Journalism–Indianapolis

Internet Address: www.tigerwoods.com

Discussion Questions

- How has Tiger Woods's image evolved from 1996 to 2009?
- Describe the relationship between Woods and Nike?
- How has Mark Steinberg adeptly crafted Woods's image?
- How has the "Tiger effect" influenced ratings of PGA Tour events?

The Line-Up

Tiger Woods is not only the top golfer in the world with his seventy-one PGA tour victories and nearly $93 million in prize money (as of October 2009), he is also the most marketable active athlete according to *SportsBusiness Daily's* poll of sixty-five sports business and media executives. According to *Forbes,* Woods became the first billion-dollar athlete after earning a $10 million bonus for the 2009 FedEx Cup title. The magazine estimates that Woods' prize money, appearances, endorsements, and gold course design business totaled $895 million at the end of 2008. In 2009, Woods won $10.5 million in prize money and earned more than $100 million off the golf course in addition to the FedEx bonus. Woods is tied with cyclist Lance Armstrong as the most influential athlete in sports due to his ability to sell products. Woods has earned more than $750 million in endorsement deals so far in his career, including $90 million in 2008 alone. He joins Michael Jordan and Arnold Palmer as transformative global sport celebrities and marketing icons whose appeal and popularity transcend sport and time. Fifteen years ago, people wanted to "Be Like Mike" and now people want to watch Tiger and play gold like Tiger.

When the late Earl Woods called his son "the chosen one" and "the greatest," he anticipated his boy's exceptional talents and appeal. From the time Earl Woods gave his son a sawed-off golf club at age six months, Tiger was hooked. Earl Woods may have envisioned his son's place in golf history, yet initially there was skepticism and disdain.

Tiger Woods's "Hello World" announcement on August 28, 1996, officially introduced him to marketers and fans worldwide. Agents thought Woods could earn $6 million a year in deals, however, they underestimated his talent and International Management Group's (IMG) strategy. Woods won six PGA Tour events in his rookie year, including the Masters by twelve strokes. In less than a year, he signed $60 million endorsement contracts with Nike and Titleist. In 2000, Nike increased Woods's deal to more than $20 million yearly for five years. Co-founder and Chairman Phil Knight admitted there was no better way to spend the money. Woods is a top-rated athlete, world-class competitor, shrewd marketer (along with agent Mark Steinberg), and philanthropist. At thirty-two-years old, he is expected to break legendary Jack Nicklaus's eighteen major championship wins, and he is often compared to Michael Jordan when it comes to athletic skill, competitive edge, marketing prowess, and image development. Everything Tiger does has impact. From tournament broadcast ratings and newspaper and magazine sales, to skyrocketing sales of Nike golf merchandise, Q-scores and public opinion polls, Tiger's name and influence are unrivaled among current athletes.

Timeline of Events

1975
- Eldrick "Tiger" Woods is born to Earl and Kultida Woods in Cypress, CA.

1978
- Earl gives Tiger his first golf club. Tiger appears on the *Mike Douglas Show* and putts with comedian Bob Hope.

1981
- Tiger appears on *That's Incredible!* and shows off his golfing skills.

1990
- Tiger is the youngest athlete to win the U.S. Junior Amateur Championship.
- Tiger appears in the "Face in the Crowd" section of *Sports Illustrated* for the first time on September 24, 1990 (the magazine subsequently published its first profile in March 1991, when he was fifteen years old).

1992

- Tiger appears in the Nissan Open and becomes the youngest athlete to appear in a PGA Tour event. As in 1991, Tiger wins *Golf Digest* Player of the Year.

1994

- Tiger is the youngest athlete to win the U.S. Amateur Championship as a freshman at Stanford University (he won ten collegiate events there, including the NCAA title). He becomes the only golfer to win both Junior Amateur and Amateur titles. He wins three consecutive U.S. Amateur titles. He states, "I don't want to be the greatest minority golfer ever; I want to be the greatest golfer ever. I want to be the Michael Jordan of golf."

1995

- Woods plays in his first major championship, making the cuts at both the Masters and the British Open.

1996

- Woods drops out of Stanford University and becomes a golf pro. He is the first black American to earn his first PGA Tour card since Adrian Stills did in 1985. *Sports Illustrated* votes him Sportsman of the Year. He signs contacts with Nike for $40 million and $20 million with Titleist.

1997

- Woods wins four PGA Tour events and the Arnold Palmer Award as the leading money winner ($2 million). He becomes the youngest to win the Masters, as well as the first African American and Asian to do so (he considers himself multiracial). He achieves number one golf ranking—the youngest ever at twenty-one years old. He signs contract with American Express. Earl Woods publishes his first book, *Training a Tiger.*

1999

- Woods starts long-term endorsement contract with Buick. He is the PGA Player of the Year and the Associated Press Male Athlete of the Year.

2000

- Woods wins eleven tournaments: nine on the PGA Tour, one on the PGA European Tour, and the PGA Grand Slam. He joins forces with David Duval to win the World Cup team title for the United States. Woods, matching Ben Hogan's 1953 record of winning three majors in one year, joins Hogan, Gene Sarazen, Gary Player, and Jack Nicklaus in winning the Grand Slam of majors. *Sports Illustrated* names him Sportsman of the Year for the second time. The Associated Press names him Male Athlete of the Year for the third time. He is also PGA Player of the Year.

2001

- Woods wins the Masters a second time and becomes the first golfer to hold all professional major tournaments simultaneously (sometimes referred to as the "Tiger slam"). In all, he wins five times on the PGA Tour and eight times internationally. Tiger publishes *How I Play Golf: A Master Class with the World's Greatest Golfer* with the editors of *Golf Digest.*

2002

- Woods wins five times on the PGA Tour and is the tour's leading money winner for fourth consecutive year. He is the youngest golfer to win seven PGA major titles. He signs endorsement deal with TAG Heuer, the Swiss watch designer.

2003

- Woods enters sponsorship contract with Accenture.

2004

- Woods marries Elin Nordegren.

2005

- Woods wins the British Open and the Masters for the fourth time, joining Nicklaus and Palmer as the only players to win four or more.

2006

- Woods wins the British Open and PGA Championship. Father Earl dies of cancer.

2007

- Woods signs a five-year, $100 million contract with Gatorade, including the development of his own drink, Gatorade Tiger. It is speculated the deal is $100 million for five years. This is unique because it is Woods's first licensing agreement.

2008

- Woods wins four of six PGA events, including U.S. Open.
- Has season-ending knee surgery in June. Has torn anterior cruciate ligament and double stress fracture.
- Ties Arnold Palmer (62 victories) at the start of the season and concludes with 65, one victory ahead of Ben Hogan for third-place in all-time wins.

IMG, Nike, and Woods

Tiger Woods's image has been meticulously crafted. The persona has been built in large part by his agent, Mark Steinberg of IMG. Brand Tiger is an entity that has amassed great value with endorsers.

Tiger is the quintessential pitchman. As a global athlete, he is a natural tie-in to worldwide businesses. Woods has endorsed a broad array products, including prominent associations with corporate partners that include Nike, American Express, TAG Heuer, Buick, Gillette, Gatorade (a division of PesiCo.), and Electronic Arts (EA Sports). These are among the select companies that have enjoyed Woods's affiliation and attention.

Woods, like Michael Jordan, has established himself as one of the most popular athletic images of all time. A testament to his notoriety is his top two finish in the Sports Q-scores as one of the most recognizable and well-liked athletes in America. Tiger, like Jordan both have affiliations with Nike, and the associations have been monumental for success and stature.

Exhibit 28.1

In the 2008 Sports Q-scores, Michael Jordan and Tiger Woods ranked number 1 and number 2, respectively. Marketing Evaluations/TvQ sends a survey each year to 2,000 sports fans. Q-scores measure likeability and fans' dislike of athletes. After Woods, Nolan Ryan, Brett Favre, Joe Montana, John Madden, Jerry Rice, Cal Ripken Jr., Arnold Palmer, and Magic Johnson round out the top ten, showing the longevity of sports superstars.

Nike's clarity of vision is apparent in its marketing efforts. This has been exemplified through blending major ads in mainstream media outlets and major sponsorships of events. Various notable ad campaigns featuring Tiger Woods have been engrained in the cultural fabric of contemporary society. These include, "Hello World," "I Am Tiger Woods," "Hacky Sack," and more recently, "Never," which evokes pathos and emotion with its use of footage of Earl Woods and voiceovers.

Beyond the monumental campaigns, Woods is noted for being very hands-on with Nike and all his products. He meets weekly to discuss new Nike Golf products in footwear, apparel, balls, and clubs. He has helped Nike reposition the clothing line as high-end rather than mere sport apparel, and designed a new TW logo in 2001. Nike has built its reputation and stature on celebrity endorsements and recognizes the importance of affiliations with star athletes like Woods.

Sponsors gain the same focus, commitment, and confidence that Woods gives to golf. At EA Sports, he worked tirelessly with designers until the video game bearing his name had a golf swing that was realistic enough to be his own. Though this endorsement deal has ended, with Buick, Woods educated himself about the automobile manufacturer and its line, made appearances, and provided insight on his role in TV ads. He was immersed in all areas of Buick's Rendezvous SUV launch. Buick sought to attract a younger, wealthier demographic and has built online promotions around its star endorser, including 2008's Tee-Off with Tiger. In other affiliations, Woods joins tennis ace Roger Federer and soccer star Thierry Henry in Gillette's Champions series. He also contributes articles to *Golf Digest*; owns a share in NetJets; endorses TAG Heuer's first gold watch; promotes TLC Laser Eye Centers; signs autographs for Upper Deck; and helped create Gatorade Tiger by participating in sweat, hydration, and nutrition testing at the Gatorade Sports Science Institute. The latter partnership, which marks Tiger's first licensing venture, is a natural fit for a legendary workhorse.

The Injury and the "Tiger Effect"

Tiger's work ethic, physical strength, and determination were evident in his 2008 U.S. Open victory over Rocco Mediate. Afterward, Woods admitted he played injured for ten months with a torn ligament in his left knee, and had a double stress fracture in his left leg two weeks prior to winning the major tournament. This just adds to the Woods mystique, which has brought new fans and more money to the game. His 1997 Masters victory had a 14.1 Sunday TV rating, which helped the PGA secure a lucrative TV deal with CBS, NBC, and the Golf Channel. This led to a 40 percent increase in prize purses in just one year, and PGA Tour prize money has tripled since Woods became a professional in 1996.

Woods's injury evoked concern from sponsors, the tour, and its networks. The result is what has been referred to as the "Tiger effect." Woods's agent insists his sponsorships are centered on entertainment rather than golf. One agency marketer even suggested that Tiger's absence could produce more creative opportunities for brands to leverage his endorsements. For example, Nike and Accenture still had postinjury advertising shoots with Woods.

Beyond Tiger's corporate partners, the PGA Tour has more to worry about, but the American victory in the Ryder Cup will help the sport's popularity. In 2008, Tiger's effects on TV ratings were also less pronounced compared to 2007, when weekend ratings were 59 percent higher when Tiger was in the tournament. When Woods plays in a tournament, TV ratings increase by at least a third and often more. The PGA Tour started seeking ways to "Tiger-proof" events and reinforce corporate sponsorships and higher attendance rates in 2007. The FedEx Cup created a playoff system, which balanced out ratings in tournaments minus Woods. Tournaments submitted branding and marketing plans, and the tour shared information with all tournament directors to ensure profitability. Tournaments also reinforced community ties by focusing on social events.

Although sponsors and the PGA tour were concerned about his absence, Tiger's injury allowed him to devote more time to activities outside golf, including his family and philanthropic efforts. The Tiger Woods Learning Center is a $27 million education facility for underprivileged children in Anaheim, California. Woods committed to giving back, as evident in the Tiger Woods Foundation, which donated $2 million in grants to such organizations as VH1's Save the Music Foundation and the Hurricane Katrina Education Fund. Woods spent time designing Punta Brava golf course in Mexico, The Cliffs at High Carolina in North Carolina, and Al Runwaya in Dubai.

The Final Score

Sports heroes represent the good life, and spectators worship, deify, and model behavior after their favorite sports stars. Tiger Woods embodies the sports hero with his legendary golf swing, fighting spirit, strong work ethic, and shrewd marketing acumen. He is the top golfer in the world and the most marketable active athlete. Woods, Steinberg, and Nike have catapulted his global branding power. Tiger Woods's ads, the TW logo, and his apparel and equipment have established and sustained Nike Golf. Nike, American Express, TAG Heuer, Buick, Gillette, Gatorade, and EA Sports have all capitalized on Woods's mega-brand and marketability in their partnerships and business relationships. Woods is a global phenomenon and celebrity, who is the first billion-dollar athlete and will continue to make history in sport, business, and life.

Post-Game Comments

- Tiger Woods is a transcendent sport celebrity and meticulously managed marketing and mediated icon.
- Tiger Woods, IMG, and Nike have created a global dynasty rivaling Michael Jordan's magnitude.
- Agent Mark Steinberg takes a selective approach to Woods's endorsements, minimizing overexposure and maximizing impact.
- The Tiger effect is the fear that people will not watch golf or purchase Woods's products if he is injured or not playing.
- Tiger Woods has brought more fans to the game and more money to the PGA Tour and its players.

Web Resources

http://adage.com/moy2008/article?article_id=131755
http://blogs.golf.com/presstent/2008/10/tiger-says-hes.html
http://blogs.wsj.com/wealth/2008/08/13/tiger-woods-to-become-first-billion-
    aire-athlete/?mod=rss_WSJBlog
http://knowledge.wharton.upenn.edu/article.cfm?articleid=779
http://online.wsj.com/article/SB122340642160312179.html?mod=googlenews_wsj
http://sports.espn.go.com/golf/index
http://sports.espn.go.com/golf/news/story?id=3066280
http://sports.espn.go.com/golf/news/story?id=3450453
http://sports.espn.go.com/espn/page2/story?page=neel/080612
http://sportsillustrated.cnn.com/golf/pga/features/tiger/timeline/
http://www.americanwaymag.com/aw/business/feature.asp?archive_date=10/
    15/2001
http://www.forbes.com/2004/03/18/cx_ld_0318nike.html
http://www.forbes.com/2008/06/11/most-powerful-celebrities-lists-celebrities
    08-cx_mn_0611c_land.html
http://www.forbes.com/lists/2008/53/celebrities08_Tiger-Woods_WR6D.html
http://www.golf.com/golf
http://www.golfdigest.com/features/index.ssf?/features/gd200602top50.html
http://www.golfdigest.com/features/index.ssf?/features/gd200608tigeratten.html
http://www.history-timelines.org.uk/people-timelines/03-tiger-woods-time-
    line.htm
http://www.msnbc.msn.com/id/4554944/
http://www.pgatour.com/players/00/87/93/
http://www.tigerwoods.com

Additional Resources

Farrell, A. (2008, December 12). The most influential athletes. *Forbes*. Retrieved October 18, 2009, at http://www.forbes.com/2008/12/12/sports-marketing-woods-biz-sports_cx_af_1212influentialathletes.html.

Finley, R. (2008, February 17). Another record for Tiger: Off-course pay for Woods tops $100M, highest for any athlete. *McClatchy-Tribune Business News*. Retrieved from ProQuest database, October 13, 2008.

Houck, D. W. (2006). Crouching Tiger, hidden blackness: Tiger Woods and the disappearance of race. (469–484). In Arthur A. Raney & Jennings Bryant (Eds.), *Handbook of sports and media*. Mahwah, NJ: Lawrence Erlbaum.

Kellner, D. (2004). The sports spectacle, Michael Jordan, and Nike. In Patrick
    B. Miller & David K. Wiggins (Eds.), *Sport and the color line*. New York:
    Routledge. 305–325.

Lefton, T. (2006, December 4). Despite his retirement, Arnie still sells. *Sports
    Business Journal*, p. 12.

Lefton, T. (2007, June 11). Successful seasons push active NFL stars up in
    sports Q scores. *Sports Business Journal*, p. 12.

Lefton, T. (2008, July 28). Jordan, Woods maintain sports Q score popularity.
    Sports Business Journal, p. 5.

Lico, N. (2008, September 15). 100 years: General Motors marketer knows
    how to play game, from racing to teeing it up for Tiger. *Advertising Age*.
    Retrieved from EBSCO database, October 1, 2008.

Ournad, J., & Show, J. (2008, March 28). Is the "Tiger effect" on ratings shrink-
    ing? *Sports Business Journal*, p. 5.

Ozanian, M. K. (2009, September 28). The first billion-dollar athlete. *Forbes*.
    Retrieved October 18, 2009, at http://blogs.forbes.com/sportsmoneyblog/
    2009/09/the-first-billion-dollar-athlete.

Pope, S. W. (2006). "Race," family, and nation: The significance of Tiger Woods
    in American culture. In David K. Wiggins (Ed.), *Out of the shadows: A bi-
    ographical history of African American athletes*. Fayetteville: University of
    Arkansas Press. 325–351.

Rovell, D. (2008, June 19). Even injured, Tiger still sells. *Slate*. Retrieved Oc-
    tober 13, 2008, at http://www.slate.com/id/2193934.

Shain, J. (2006, August 28). Tiger's reach extends on global scale. *Miami Her-
    ald*, p. 12D.

Show, J. (2007a, March 19). Most marketable? The money's on Tiger. *Sports
    Business Journal*, p. 8.

Show, J. (2007b, April 2). Events seek ways to be "Tiger-proof." *Sports Busi-
    ness Journal*, p. 17.

Show, J. (2008, June 23). Tiger's injury challenges sponsors. *Sports Business
    Journal*, p. 5.

Yu, H. (2002). Tiger Woods at the center of history: Looking back at the twen-
    tieth century through the lenses of race, sports, and mass consumption.
    (320–353). In J. Bloom & M. Nevin Willard (Eds.), *Sports matters: Race,
    recreation, and culture*. New York: New York University Press.

Chapter 29

Bass Pro Shops:
The Great Outdoors...
Pass It On

Jason W. Lee,
University of North Florida

Eric Forsyth,
Bemidji State University

Emily Bruce,
Lender Processing Services, Inc.

Company: Bass Pro Shops
Location: Springfield, MO
Internet Address: www.basspro.com

Discussion Questions

- What immediately comes to mind when you think of Bass Pro Shops?
- What marketing strategies would you develop for Bass Pro Shops?
- Would you advise Bass Pro Shops to open a store in all fifty states? Why or why not?
- How might Bass Pro Shops expand its market beyond outdoor enthusiasts?
- What other suggestions would you make for Bass Pro Shops to promote and protect wildlife?
- What additional community outreach initiatives would you suggest Bass Pro Shops engage in?

The Line-Up

Originating out of Springfield, Missouri, Bass Pro Shops began with eight feet of retail store space aimed at providing fishing equipment for anglers. From its humble beginnings, the company has steadily grown, with stores in twenty-six states (from Florida to Massachusetts to California), as well as Canada. Today, Bass Pro Shops offers anything and everything for outdoor enthusiasts.

Bass Pro Shops encompasses many things, such as nature-themed retail stores and destinations, conservation and education initiatives, and sponsorship of outdoor events for kids and families. Bass Pro Shops just might be the most successful outdoor company in the country.

Timeline of Events

1972
- Bass Pro Shops opens as an eight-foot space dedicated to selling fishing tackle in a liquor store in Springfield, MO.

1974
- Bass Pro Shops develops and mails its first catalog, with 180 pages, for the serious fisherman.

1977
- Bass Pro Shops introduces the first fish-ready complete Bass Tracker boat package (Tracker Boats goes on to become the world's number one seller of fishing boats).

1984
- Bass Pro Shops breaks ground for its new national headquarters, Outdoor World Showroom in Springfield.

1986
- Bass Pro Shops acquires Redhead, the oldest supplier of sporting apparel in the nation.

1987
- Ethel, a seventeen-plus-pound largemouth bass, moves into Bass Pro Shops national headquarters, Outdoor World's aquarium.

1988
- Bass Pro Shop's Big Cedar Lodge opens to much fanfare on the shores of Table Rock Lake near Branson, MO.

1993
- The Bass Pro Shops Fish & Wildlife Museum in Springfield opens, showcasing wildlife and fish mounts, antique rods, reels, and more.

1995
- Bass Pro Shops Sportsman's Warehouse opens in Atlanta.

1996
- Bass Pro Shops receives the President's Award from the International Association of Fish & Wildlife Agencies.
- Web site at www.basspro.com officially goes online and quickly becomes one of the Internet's leading outdoor merchants.

1997
- Bass Pro Shops World Wide Sportsman opens in Islamorada, FL, specializing in saltwater fly-fishing.

1998
- Ft. Lauderdale, FL, store opens.

1999
- Dallas, TX; Detroit, MI; and Charlotte, NC stores open.

2000
- Wonders of Wildlife becomes a new addition in Bass Pro Shops national headquarters' showroom, containing fresh and saltwater aquariums, live animals in native habitat, interactive nature displays, virtual reality games, and more (Bass Pro Shops donated the land the museum sits on, as well as fish and wildlife mounts, and millions of dollars to support the museum. *Wonders of Wildlife* is a nonprofit organization with a board of directors that includes conservation leaders from across the nation and former Presidents Jimmy Carter and George H. W. Bush.).
- Stores open in Houston, TX; Nashville, TN; Orlando,FL; and Cincinnati, OH.

2001
- Stores in Baltimore, MD; Atlanta, GA; and St. Louis, MO open.

2002
- Store in Memphis, TN opens.

2003
- Bass Pro Shops opens in Destin, FL; Savannah, GA; Bossier, LA; Hampton, VA; and Oklahoma City, OK.

2004
- Bass Pro Shops opens first international store in Toronto, Canada. Also added stores in Auburn, NY; Las Vegas, NV; Myrtle Beach, SC; and Harrisburg, PA.

2005
- Bass Pro Shops opens stores in Columbia, MO; Broken Arrow, OK; Sevierville, TN; Clarksville, IN; Pearl, MS; Council Bluffs, IA; and Denver, CO.

2006
- Bass Pro Shops opens its distribution center in Macon, GA, as well as stores in Macon; Fort Meyers, FL; Garland, TX; San Antonio, and Branson, TX.
- Stores open in Foxborough, MA; Rancho Cucamonga, CA; Bolingbrook, IL; Portage, IN; Mesa, AZ; Olathe, KS; Pearland, TX; Prattville, AL; and Miami, FL.

2008
- Stores open in Denham Springs, LA; Independence, MO; Rossford, OH; Spanish Fort, AL; Richmond; Manteca, CA; and Leeds, AL.

2009
- Stores open in Calgary, Alberta, Canada and Altoona, IA.

The Great Outdoors ... Pass It On

Reflecting on Bass Pro Shops' mission statement, one quickly understands what the company is all about: "To be the leading merchant of outdoor recreational products inspiring people to love, enjoy, and conserve the great outdoors." In achieving its mission, Bass Pro Shops has gone far beyond selling outdoor products. The company sells nature, which has inspired people to experience the great outdoors, inevitably passing it on to others (see Figure 29.1 in image insert).

Bass Pro Shops is able to spread an affinity for the outdoors in a variety of ways. Among the ways this is accomplished is through nature-themed destinations, such as Outdoor World, Big Cedar Lodge, and Dogwood Canyon Ranch.

The Outdoor World store in Springfield (Figure 29.2) is considered to be Bass Pro Shops' "flagship store." More than 4 million people visit annually, making this "granddaddy" outdoor store one of Missouri's premier tourist attraction. Visitors marvel at the 300,000-plus square feet of retail space, the enormous Tracker Country boat showroom, elaborate architecture, wildlife museum and mounts, striking waterfalls, gigantic aquariums (see Figure 29.3) and various restaurants. Some customers have planned their honeymoons and vacations there because of the unique experience.

Big Cedar Lodge (see Figures 29.4 and 29.5) is an 850-acre resort that rest on the banks of Table Rock Lake near Branson, Missouri. Visitors can experience America's sporting traditions, including boating, skiing, trail rides, fishing, and many more outdoor activities.

Bass Pro Shops' greatest tribute to the wonders of the wild is Dogwood Canyon Nature Park (see Figures 29.6 and 29.7), a 10,000-acre wilderness dreamscape situated in the Missouri Ozarks. This sportsmen's paradise is open to the public for tram tours, biking, horseback riding, trout fishing, and more.

Conservation and Education Initiatives

Educating youth and adults, and supporting conservation and environmental corporations has created a positive image for the company. Education efforts include Bass Pro Shops Outdoor Skills Workshops, Bass Pro Shops Outdoor Women, Bass Pro Shops Outdoor Kids, and Bass Pro Shops Outdoor Families, offered free of charge in all their stores.

Sponsoring organizations dedicated to protecting wildlife gave a unique dimension to Bass Pro Shops' profile. Taking care of wildlife and nature has become a forefront of the company's efforts, leading to numerous awards and honors. A majority of their marketing efforts are provided through environmental efforts, including promoting and protecting wildlife (see Exhibit 29.1) and community outreach initiatives (see Exhibit 29.2).

Exhibit 29.1 Bass Pro Shops: Promoting and Protecting Wildlife

The following are some of the contributions Bass Pro Shops have made in its efforts to promote and protect wildlife:

2007 $10 million pledged to Wonders of Wildlife for museum renovation

2006 $5 million pledged to More Fish campaign of National Fish and Wildlife Foundation

2004 $1.1 million donated to the National Wild Turkey Federation

2004 $7 million contributed to National Fish and Wildlife Museum

2001 $10 million contributed to Wonders of Wildlife National Museum

2000 $10.4 million land donation and $2 million in cash to the IGFA World Fishing Center

1998 $500,000 cash contribution to the IGFA World Fishing Center

1997 $100,000 pledge to The Nature Conservancy for Florida Bay Watch Volunteer Program

1997 $500,000 contribution to the International Game Fish Association

1996 $100,000 contribution to the Everglades Trust

1996 $100,000 contribution to the National Wild Turkey Federation to implement a youth development program

---

Exhibit 29.2 Community Outreach Initiatives

In addition to donating money and land, Bass Pro Shops pairs with other organizations to better communities. By offering services for disabled consumers and creating awareness campaigns, Bass Pro Shops has proven to be an image-conscious company. Examples of community outreach initiatives include:

- Donated $250,000 to support the Operation USO Care Package.
- Donated venison to those in need through the Share the Harvest Program.
- Funding of a marina at the Victory Junction Gang Camp, founded by NASCAR driver Kyle Petty and his wife for children with life-threatening illnesses.
- Annual Fun and Learn Days with Wheelin' Sportsman and the National Wild Turkey Federation that offers activities and workshops for disabled outdoor aficionados.
- Project ChildSafe, which distributes free firearm safety kits.
- Natural Disaster Relief Challenge gives Bass Pro Shops customers the opportunity to donate to those affected by natural disasters, and the company matches donations made by its customers.
- Hosting MDA telethons inside some of their stores.
- Collecting Christmas trees to be used as fish habitat in area lakes.

Bass Pro Shops Products

Though fishing was the primary focus for Bass Pro Shops' products, the brains behind the company were quick to tap into the hunting and outdoor markets. After expanding to provide products for outdoor enthusiasts, the company was geared to provide ideal settings for consumers to embrace — nature-themed retail stores.

Bass Pro Shops has more than fifty retail centers. Inside their stores, consumers find a massive venue filled with high-quality items. If desired, a customer could walk into Bass Pro Shops and leave completely outfitted for a fishing or hunting trip (or both). Additionally, each of these store sites are designed and equipped uniquely to meet the needs of the regional consumer base.

Using a "one-stop" approach to outdoor activity, Bass Pro Shops makes it easy for novices and experts alike to get just what they are looking for, whether it is clothing, footwear, tools, guns, fishing poles, tackle boxes, bait products, or camping equipment. Bass Pro Shops carries well-known brands (such as

Mossy Oak, North Face, Strike King, and Browning) in addition to offering its own lines of products: RedHead, Uncle Buck, API, WorldWide Sportsman, Off Shore Angler, White River, XPS, and Johnny Morris. Furthermore, knowing that no true outdoorsman leaves out his trusted sidekick, Bass Pro Shops includes supplies for dogs.

In addition to the aforementioned enterprises, Bass Pro Shops has also partnered with other notable initiatives, including Tracker Marine Group, American Rod & Gun, and Outdoor World Incentives. Tracker Marine Group, which produces and sells more boats than any other company in the world, consists of Tracker Boats, Nitro, Grizzly, Sun Tracker, Tahoe, Fisher, Pro Craft, Mako, and SeaCraft. American Rod & Gun is a separate wholesaling entity making Bass Pro Shops-branded products available to over 7,000 independently owned retail stores worldwide. Outdoor World Incentives oversees corporate incentives programs and markets Bass Pro Shops gift cards in locations throughout the United States, Puerto Rico, the United Kingdom, Australia, and Mexico.

Exhibit 29.3 Bass Pro Shops Media Vehicles

Bass Pro Shops reaches millions of consumers through its retail stores, catalog distributions, Internet, broadcasts, radio, and newspapers.

Retail Stores: Over 100 million people visit Bass Pro Shops retail stores annually.

Catalog Distribution: Since its first catalog mailing in 1974, Bass Pro Shops has become an enterprise serving millions of outdoor enthusiasts around the globe.

Internet: More than 2 million visitors log onto basspro.com each month.

Broadcasts: Bass Pro Shops has five TV shows that air on the Outdoor Channel and other networks.

Radio: The Bass Pro Shops Outdoor World Radio Show is heard on 470 radio stations in 48 states and 179 foreign countries over the Armed Forces Radio Network.

Newspapers: Outdoor World Tips are read in 5,500 weekly newspapers across America.

Sponsorships

Bass Pro Shops is a natural partner for fishing and wildlife events, but the company has sought to have a visible presence in other venues as well. By tapping into other markets, Bass Pro Shops has stretched its reach to a broader audience. Some of the more notable sponsorship arrangements have included sponsoring NASCAR drivers such as Tony Stewart, Martin Truex Jr., and Kyle Petty (among others); headlining events such as the Bass Pro Shops MBNA 500 NASCAR race; sponsoring sweepstakes contests; and even creating its own credit card.

The company also sponsors numerous fishing tournaments, including the Bass Pro Shops Crappie Masters, which travels throughout the United States. Additionally, the company has been recognized for its work with Kansas wildlife after years of sponsoring an outdoor program for kids. Bass Pro Shops was the primary sponsor for Michael Keaton's character's race car in the Disney movie *Herbie: Fully Loaded*.

The Final Score

The popularity of outdoor activities such as hunting and fishing is widespread in North America. This popularity has certainly been evidenced by the success of Bass Pro Shops stores placed throughout North America. The company grew their entire industry when none other existed.

More than just a sport shop, Bass Pro Shops has recognized its opportunity and responsibility to protect nature. Donations and outreach programs, combined with a diverse product line, have launched Bass Pro Shops into the forefront of the outdoor market. This well-rounded company saw a need for conservation efforts and has gone to great lengths to do just that.

Bass Pro Shops has been able to market itself as a company with a true love of all things outdoors. Opening stores in various markets, promoting and protecting wildlife, pursuing community outreach initiatives, and sponsoring various events has allowed Bass Pro Shops to reach remarkable success.

Post-Game Comments

- Bass Pro Shops is the most successful hunting, fishing, and outdoor retail store in the country.
- Bass Pro Shops has become a leader in conservationist campaigns.
- Bass Pro Shops supports many outreach initiatives to better communities.
- Bass Pro Shops is recognized for its supporting efforts in outdoor programs for kids.

- Bass Pro Shops sells more than fishing and hunting equipment, it sells nature.
- The essence of Bass Pro Shops is summed in their slogan "The Great Outdoors ... Pass It On."

Web Resources

http://www.basspro.com

http://phx.corporate-ir.net/phoenix.zhtml?c=99758&p=irol-newsArticle&t=Regular&id=398562

http://vocuspr.vocus.com/vocuspr30/Temp/Sites/2632/fe902c4f2bae4ba8a1af958c8c8637db/Whole_Press_Book_1.pdf

http://www.kdwp.state.ks.us/news/kdwp_info/news/weekly_news/2_22_07/bass_pro_shops_aids_kansas_wildscape

http://www.qu.org/content/corporate_partners/bassproshops.cfm

http://www.rapala.com/bassprotrip/

Additional Resources

Garcia, Y. (2008; 2009, personal communication). Marketing Administrative Assistant, Bass Pro Shops.

Kendall, J. (2008; 2009, personal communication). Media Information Coordinator, Bass Pro Shops.

Whitely, L. (2008; 2009, personal communication). Public Relations Manager, Bass Pro Shops.

Chapter 30

The Skinny on Curves for Women

Jennifer J. Kane,
University of North Florida

Company: Curves International
Location: Waco, TX
Internet Address: www.curves.com

Discussion Questions

- What are the primary target markets for Curves for Women?
- What are the products Curves for Women offers?
- Why has Curves for Women been so successful?
- Where do you see Curves for Women in the future?

The Line-Up

The fitness industry is booming. According to the International Health, Racquet and Sportsclub Association (IHRSA), as of January 2006, there were 26,069 health, racquet, and sports clubs in the United States. There were 41.3 million health club members with total U.S. revenues reaching $15.9 billion in 2005. IHRSA also contends that the number of women who are joining health club facilities is growing. Nationally, women constitute 60 percent of the commercial health club membership. They speculate that this growth could be due to the increase in the number of women-only facilities that are opening. One such facility is Curves International. The first Curves facility opened in 1992, and in October 2006, the company celebrated its 10,000th opening. With a great deal of competition, Curves has been successful at branding its company in the industry. The concept established by the owners of this company has seemingly caught the attention of many women who seek to improve their fitness.

Timeline of Events

1992
- First Curves opened in Harlingen, TX.

1999
- Ranked the number one Best New Franchise, number fourteen Fastest Growing Franchise, number fifty-three Franchise Overall by *Entrepreneur* magazine.
- First Curves for Women opens in Canada.

2001
- First Curves for Women opens in Mexico.
- *Guinness Book of World Records* recognizes Curves for Women as the world's largest fitness center franchise.

2003
- Ranked the number one Best Fitness Franchise, number one Fastest Growing Franchise, number one Low Cost Franchise, and the number two Franchise Overall by *Entrepreneur* magazine.
- *Guinness Book of World Records* recognizes Curves for Women as the fastest-growing franchise in history.

2005
- *Club Business International* magazine ranked Curves as the world's largest club company with over 4 million members, number one in number of franchises, number one in five-year unit growth, and number one in the previous year's annual unit growth.

2006
- *Fortune* magazine ranked Curves for Women as the number one Up-and-Coming Brand.
- Curves for Women has 10,000 locations.

2007
- Curves partners with General Mills to develop food products, such as cereal and granola bars, intended to promote nutritional eating.

Curves for Women Background

Gary and Diane Heavin founded curves in 1992. Gary, who lost his mother at an early age, developed the Curves concept because of his strong belief that women needed a place to work on their fitness to improve their health and prevent disease. The concept revolves around the participation in a thirty-minute circuit that involves both strength training and cardiovascular activity. The participants move from station to station, alternating a strength developing activity with an aerobic activity. An important component of this concept is the principle that the participants would receive motivation, support, and instruction from a trainer as they moved through the circuit. Music is playing in the background, and every minute a voice interrupts the music with "change stations now." Today, with over 10,000 facilities, Curves provides over 4 million women in the world a place to improve their health and fitness.

Products

Curves for Women is a fitness circuit that involves hydraulic strength machines and alternating cardiovascular activities. It is a thirty-minute circuit that is recommended to be completed a minimum of three days a week.

In addition to the circuit, Curves offers a weight management program called Curves 6 Week Solution. This weight loss program is based on the premise that one can raise one's metabolism and be done with dieting forever. One of the ways Curves promotes the credibility of this program is by highlighting Dr. Richard B. Krieder, a scientist at Baylor University who has conducted research on the program.

In 2007, Curves International and General Mills partnered to establish a line of food products that includes cereal and granola bars. These products can be purchased in grocery stores as well as in Curves franchises across the country. These products are designed to promote sensible and nutritional eating that contributes to appropriate weight management.

Other products include dietary supplements, a magazine entitled *Diane,* and a line of clothing titled Curvaceous. All of these products are designed for women, and all contribute to the Curves marketing package. Curves has also partnered with Avon, the world's leading direct seller of beauty-related products. Some of the products Avon offers through their catalog are the Curves Heart Rate Monitor Watch, Curves Fitness Pedometer, Curves Flexibility Mat, Thermal Waist Trimmer, and Curves Free Foods on the Go.

Marketing Strategies

"The power to amaze yourself." This is the slogan used by the Curves for Women franchise operations. This slogan can be seen on the Curves Web site, on the literature that is available at Curves locations, and on the walls in the Curves facilities. In addition to the slogan, words such as *comfort, support, safe, intimate,* and *quick* are also seen in all of the aforementioned places.

Owners Gary and Diane Heavin have definitely found a niche in the fitness industry that has brought this company great success. In 2005, one out of every four fitness centers was a Curves for Women facility. What began as one man's simple idea has become a fitness phenomenon that has spread throughout the world. Anyone who has entered Curves for Women can easily see that it is truly "simple." The circuit does not take up much space, and there is no need for any additional equipment, which allows franchisees to establish a facility with few overhead costs. There are no mirrors, free weights, benches, or squat racks. No treadmills, bikes, or other fancy cardiovascular equipment. It is, as one member said, "intimate." Most do not have locker room facilities, and there are no spinning rooms, basketball courts, pools, whirlpools, or lap pools with which to contend.

An informal chat with members revealed some of the reasons they chose Curves over other fitness facilities. Comments such as "it's quick and easy to follow," "it's a great place to exercise with friends," "it's not the hard aerobic classes that are offered at other fitness centers," "the machines are not hard on your joints," and "we are treated like family" are common. Members at all locations this author visited were eager and happy to share their success and their satisfaction with their Curves membership. One particular visit revealed several women's weight loss success as well as their continued visits to Curves, even while they were going through breast cancer treatments. At this same location, several women were referred to Curves by their cardiologists.

There are some obvious ways Curves differentiates themselves from the competition. First and most obvious, it is for women exclusively. Some women just prefer to work out with other women (or probably, more important, without men). This alone does not set Curves apart from its competitors. Some of the other areas are as follows.

- It is a comfortable and accepting environment. There are no mirrors. One cannot see what one looks like at any time during one's workout.
- It is easy. There are no intimidating cardiovascular or weight machines. Many of the new, high-tech machines can be intimidating even to experienced consumers. Once a member learns how to do the machines in the circuit, they don't have to learn anything else.

- There is always a trainer available to help members. This is an area of high priority to many of the members interviewed. The relationship that exists between the trainer and the members serves to retain members and keep them coming back.
- It is quick. It only takes thirty minutes to complete the workout, and it is recommended that it be done only three times a week. This is a great selling point to busy women who struggle to fit exercise into their lives.
- It is safe. The strength training machines use a hydraulic system and the individual on the machine controls the resistance based on how hard they push or pull.

One not so obvious component of Curves for Women is their affiliation with Christianity. This is more obvious in some Curves locations than in others, there are some links that can be noticed. First, Curves makes music CDs that can be played while members are working out that contain religious music. When asked about this affiliation, one manager said that she plays those CDs at some point during each day. She did say that if a member complains, she is happy to take it off. Also, during one location's first year in business, the staff excitedly decorated the facility for Christmas and when complete, they were very proud of how it looked. The first day it was open after decorating, several Jewish members complained. The staff decided to take the most of the decorations down. The owner was a little frustrated, but decided to use angels the following year as her decorations, concluding "everyone shares a belief in angels."

The Final Score

Curves for Women locations provide a circuit-training concept that is appealing to users. Proponents of this attribute and other amenities provided at Curves locations allow for members and staff to take pride in their workout facility. In examining Curves facilities, these individuals were anxious to sing the praises of the club. When I was visiting locations, a staff member announced that I was there to learn more about the Curves for Women organization and members practically lined up to talk to me and share their stories. What was revealed to me was dozens of women who had found a place to feel comfortable working out. They had found a place where every body type was comfortable, where every fitness level was accepted, where they felt safe and cared for. It seemed as much of a social safe place as a workout facility.

It appears that Curves primarily appeals to a specific audience. Among the primary target market are, as the manager at one facility said, "most of our members are in their fifties and sixties." Furthermore, she said that she had lost three members during the past year due to old age. It was apparent that the women in these facilities were not the same type of women that you would see in other fitness centers (young and fit). When this manager was asked if there were any other common characteristics of the members, she said, "many are overweight and not comfortable in other gyms."

Another common appealing characteristic that draws various members was that the Curves workout was not "too hard." After spending time observing many members going through the workout, it was clear that one could get a good workout, but that involved a great deal of effort and motivation from the individual. The circuit could be done at a high intensity, but there needs to be a high level of self-motivation present for this to happen.

Curves for Women has found an excellent way to set themselves apart from traditional fitness facilities. Women who have been turned off by traditional gyms providing potentially intimidating machines, classes with confusing steps, and little assistance from staff thrive in this environment. Those who had previously given up on exercise and weight loss have found success in this environment with the support of others who share their same challenges. As one manager shared her own success story, she detailed how she lost 326 pounds (yes, 326 pounds) and could certainly relate to those members who were in need of losing body fat. Curves has conquered a niche in the fitness market, and women who have felt powerless in the past to get in shape or lose weight have found the power to amaze themselves.

As great as this concept is for some women, it is definitely not a place for all. As with any product, there are advantages and disadvantages depending on the consumer. This author tried a Curves for Women workout to get a first-hand feel for it. While it was interesting to experience something new, this author immediately felt like it would become repetitive and boring in time. Some individuals enjoy the traditional gym where men and women mix, the machines are plentiful, options are unlimited, the music is loud, and the steps are fancy. But that is why Jell-O comes in so many delicious flavors.

Post-Game Comments

- Curves for Women has successfully found a strong niche in the fitness industry.
- Owners Gary and Diane Heavin have done a tremendous job developing and growing the Curves franchise concepts.

- *Entrepreneur* magazine and the IHRSA have recognized Curves for Women for its accomplishments in the industry.
- Curves for Women has developed a magazine titled *Diane* that addresses issues pertaining to women. This magazine strengthens their niche in the market and provides members another tool to help with health and fitness.
- The Curvaceous clothing line is sold exclusively at Curves locations. The clothing seems to fit their clientele in that it is modest and conservative.
- Curves International has established partnerships with companies such as General Mills to produce food products designed to promote nutritional eating.
- Curves for Women is not an environment for all women. Its repetitive nature is an attraction to some, a detraction for others. In addition, women who seek variety in their workouts may become bored and unmotivated by this concept.

Web Resources

http://cms.ihrsa.org/index.cfm?fuseaction=Page.viewPage&pageId=18735&-nodeID=15

http://curves.com/about_curves/news.php

http://curvesfoods.com/StartWithCurvesFoods/default.aspx

http://www.bizjournals.com/louisville/othercities/sacramento/stories/2001/07/-23/story6.html?s=smc:3&page=1

http://www.businesswire.com/portal/site/google/?ndmViewId=news_view&newsId=20070508005243&newsLang=en

http://www.centercurves.com/index.html

http://www.curves.com/curves_right

http://www.curves.com/diane_mag

Part V

Controversies and Failure

Chapter 31

Down, but Not Out: World Wrestling Entertainment's Dance with Death

Jason W. Lee,
University of North Florida

Matthew J. Bernthal,
University of South Carolina

Company: World Wrestling Entertainment (WWE)
Location: Stanford, CT;
    with offices in Los Angeles, New York, Toronto, and London
Web Addresses: www.wwe.com, corporate.wwe.com

Discussion Questions

- What is the appeal of the WWE brand? What is unappealing about the WWE brand?
- How has the WWE maneuvered its product to be that of a "sport entertainment" product?
- What has the WWE done to diversify its product offerings and mass appeal?
- What efforts have the WWE made to have brands within the brand under the WWE moniker?
- What is the image of WWE head Vince McMahon?
- What drug-related scandals have the WWE and professional wrestling had to endure? What impact have these scandals had on the WWE brand?

The Line-Up

"Do you know how to make a small fortune in the wrestling businesses? Start with a large fortune!" This statement was made by wrestling personality and former promoter Jim Cornett. Though many aspiring entrepreneurs have found it out the hard way, it is not unprecedented to be successful in the "wrasslin'" business. Numerous regional promotions have had successful tenures, and even media mogul Ted Turner held wrestling as a component of his vast media empire. However, one individual, Vincent Kennedy McMahon, head of World Wrestling Entertainment (WWE), stands out ahead of the pack in wrestling financial prosperity.

Undeniably, the WWE brand of professional wrestling is a popular entertainment and commercial force. With its legions of followers, professional wrestling is a form of entertainment that is an obsession for its most ardent fans and an activity that is viewed as "low-brow" amusement by its detractors. For strong objectors, it is a spectacle of violence, misogyny, and degradation, or merely an entertainment that appeals to the lowest common denominator of human life and entertainment value. Though there are naysayers, supporters of WWE can note the numerous examples in which the brand has impacted popular culture. There have been prime moments such as 1985's inaugural WrestleMania emanating from Madison Square Garden to the twenty-fifth anniversary show in Houston in 2009. In addition to momentous occasions, there have been the characters associated with the WWE brand, including Hulk Hogan, "Stone Cold" Steve Austin, Dwayne "The Rock" Johnson, John Cena, and the chairman of the company himself, Vince McMahon, all well known even outside the wrestling world.

Certainly, the WWE has been able to impact contemporary culture through its integrated media efforts. Such efforts are exemplified as well-known wrestling personalities have been used to help to sell TV programming and advertisements, pay-per-view programs, DVDs, CDs, posters, T-shirts, and almost any other form of merchandise imaginable.

Though there are many commercial attributes associated with the WWE juggernaut, the group is certainly not without scandals and questionable elements. WWE has been able to flourish even in the fallout of numerous high-profile scandals, tragedies, and inappropriate happenings. One of the most disturbing "dark sides" of this form of entertainment is the extensive number of drug-related deaths that occur within the industry, including the deaths of some of its most recognized characters. This chapter examines the dilemma associated with this pseudo-sport's "culture of chemicals" and the prevalence of death, especially in the aftermath of the Chris Benoit scandal, and the subsequent relation to the marketing of the WWE.

Since the Benoit tragedy, further professional wrestling deaths have continued and WWE has been embroiled in regular scandals and alleged accusations about things that would seemingly put a chink in the armor of the company and its apparently fearless leader, Vince McMahon. With all said and done, one has to wonder where all of this will lead.

Timeline of Events

1963
- Vincent J. McMahon establishes the World Wide Wrestling Federation (WWWF).

1979
- WWWF shortens its name to the World Wrestling Federation (WWF).

1982
- Vincent K. McMahon purchases Capital Sports (wrestling) from his father, Vincent J. McMahon, and his business partners.

1984
- Birth of Hulkamania, as the "Real American Hero" Hulk Hogan appears on the WWF scene.

1985
- The inaugural WrestleMania takes place in New York City's Madison Square Garden.

1993
- *WWF Monday Night Raw* airs.

1995
- WCW begins broadcasting *Monday Nitro*, essentially beginning the "Monday night wars."

1997
- Company launches Web site, wwe.com.
- Death of Brian Pillman.

1999
- Wrestler Owen Hart dies as a result of a failed stunt associated with a theatrical ring entrance at a WWF event.
- *SmackDown!* airs.
- Parents Television Council (PTC) launches campaign against objectionable material on WWE televised programming.

2000
- WWE files suit against PTC.

2001
- WWE purchases WCW.

2002
- Settlement with World Wildlife Fund; company becomes World Wrestling Entertainment (WWE).
- WWE splits into two brands (the "brand extension") forming the RAW brand and the SmackDown brand.

2004
- Launch of the WWE 24/7 video on-demand service.

2005
- Death of Eddie Guerrero.
- *SmackDown!* becomes *Friday Night Smackdown.*

2006
- In the aftermath of Guerrero's death, WWE initiates its new "wellness policy."

2007
- Double murder and suicide by Chris Benoit.

2008
- WWE ventures into HD programming.
- Vincent McMahon gets a star on the Hollywood Walk of Fame.
- WWE issues *WWE Kids* magazine and wwekids.com.

Professional Wrestling: What Is It?

To have an understanding of WWE, it would be useful to understand the history of the company and the industry for which it is the forerunner. Professional wrestling is a popular form of entertainment, as well as a commercial force. Furthermore, it is an obsession for its most ardent fans and an activity that is viewed as "low-brow" amusement by those who view it as trash TV, "fake," or merely an entertainment that appeals to the lowest common denominator of consumers.

Professional wrestling, sporting a veneer of athleticism over scripts that read much like a "male soap opera," has surged to tremendous popularity in the United States. Viewed by some as a ritual drama or a moral play, professional wrestling is an extremely popular spectator event. The term event was used, rather than sport, as obviously professional wrestling is not true sport. Though definitions of sport vary and there is no single definition on which scholars unanimously agree, one characteristic present in the most widely accepted definitions of sport is that the outcome of the activity under consideration is uncertain.

For example, Mull, Bayless, and Jamison (2005), define sport as "playing co-operative-competitive activity in the game form" (p. 7). Vince McMahon and a preponderance of the professional wrestling industry have long acknowledged that the outcomes in professional wrestling (e.g., who wins a particular match and how, who will hold a title and for how long) are predetermined. As opposed to sport, professional wrestling is better defined as a "dramatic spectacle," which is a performance to entertain an audience (Coakley, 2004, p. 23). In the wrestling documentary *Beyond the Mat*, McMahon refers to the wrestling industry as a "movie studio." WWE has preferred that their product be viewed as "sports entertainment," but even that classification is steadily being geared more toward "entertainment" and away from a "sport" connotation. Wrestling involves elements of competition, performance, physical exertion, and institutionalization in efforts to entertain audiences through images of athletic violence.

Exhibit 31.1

"Professional wrestling is a sport that is not, in the literal sense of the word, sporting; a theoretical entertainment that is not theatre" (Mazer, 1993, p. 3).

WWE

Though it is not a pure sport per se, professional wrestling certainly involves many of the elements associated with sport. Whether it's the live crowds, the athletic combatants, the physicality, the fluid movement, or the compelling stories that are being conveyed, professional wrestling has been able to capture the imaginations and interest of its followers for over a century. In its formative stages, it began as a true athletic competition that pitted grapplers against each other in displays of strength, skill, and ability. Early wrestling matches were often long, drawn-out affairs that lacked elements that kept the paying public inclined to come back for more. Inevitably, wrestling promoters deemed that the best way to put on a good show would be to have predetermined results; ultimately, the performance would be the important thing, more so than the pure aspect of competition. These wrestling circuits (akin to if not associated with carnival circuits) provided matches in the late 1800s and early 1900s. Eventually, more structured wrestling organizations were established throughout the country. These associations, known as territories, were found throughout North America. Wrestling fans in the state of Florida had Florida Championship Wrestling; fans from Alabama and Tennessee had Southeastern

Championship Wrestling; the Carolinas had Mid-Atlantic Championship Wrestling; and so on. Furthermore, fans in the Northeast had the World Wide Wrestling Federation (WWWF) (previously known as Capital Wrestling). This entity was headed by Vincent J. McMahon, father of Vincent K. McMahon. The younger McMahon eventually bought out his father and carved a path that changed the scope of professional wrestling forever.

The concept of the territory system was fading as the 1980s progressed. Steadily, McMahon began to take over regional territories while amassing an assortment of wrestling stars that were at the foundation of his national and global expansion plans. As the late 1980s and 1990s approached, McMahon's WWF was rivaled by only one organization—Ted Turner's World Championship Wrestling (WCW). Turner, the notable media mogul, had a long history of promoting wrestling programming on his networks such as TBS and TNT. These two companies battled over wrestling supremacy well into the 1990s. Eventually, following the consolidation of Turner Broadcasting and Time Warner with AOL, Turner's role in the promotion of the WCW brand of wrestling was essentially removed, and after years of struggling with McMahon's burgeoning WWF empire, WCW and its extensive (ultimately very valuable) tape library was reportedly purchased by McMahon for the bargain price of $5 million.

With the acquisition of WCW in 2001, WWE (then still known as WWF) was faced with both opportunities and challenges. In addition to new wrestlers coming up through their own corporate development, the company had a wealth of new, extremely marketable talent available to it in the form of WCW wrestlers. On the surface this would seem like a positive for the WWE brand, but it created some initial problems: the increased number of popular wrestlers on WWE programming (*RAW* and *SmackDown!*) necessarily led to less time available to each wrestler's character and storylines/feuds. Many fans thought that this led to underdeveloped, less intriguing storylines as well as less broadcast face time for their favorite wrestlers. In other words, while the WWE had more talent available to it than ever before, the dramatic spectacle had become less of a drama and less of a spectacle in the eyes of many fans.

In response, WWE reformulated their brand to better serve the market and provide itself with increased business opportunities. In 2002, WWE turned *RAW* and *SmackDown!* into two stand-alone, distinct brands with unique talent and storylines. The company creatively worked this brand split into their storyline, with McMahon drafting thirty wrestlers for the *SmackDown!* brand, and his (storyline) rival at the time, Ric Flair, drafting thirty wrestlers for the *RAW* brand. As a result, each wrestler wrestled for one and only one brand. The brands were given their own TV program, pay-per-views, live events, and championships. On the surface, one might argue that in splitting into two distinct brands, the WWE risked cannibalism—that is, one of their brands essentially competing with the other for consumer support. However, the fairly equal division of high-profile wrestlers between both brands, combined with the better developed, more compelling storylines that resulted from fewer wrestlers competing for time on each program, resulted in fan support of both.

In addition to the *RAW* and *Smackdown* brands having their own distinct TV program, the brands also have separate touring companies, which at the time of their creation in 2002 dramatically increased the number of live events that WWE was able to produce. As a result of the brand split, WWE was able to increase the number of live events produced from 200 to 350 events in the United States and Canada alone. The brand split also created new licensing and branded merchandise opportunities, as well as additional opportunities for sponsorship/partnership offerings.

In 2006, WWE continued this branding strategy by adding yet another brand, ECW (Extreme Championship Wrestling), to their portfolio. Acquired by WWE in 2003, ECW was a wrestling organization known in part for fairly "hard-core," violent wrestling. Between 2003 and 2006, WWE kept the ECW brand alive through promotion of DVDs of past ECW action and a pay-per-view program. In June 2006, ECW became the third distinct WWE brand, with its own TV program, pay-per-views, live events, and licensed merchandise. WWE now had, according to McMahon, "a portfolio of brands for fans of all ages and interests to enjoy" and was the only major wrestling company in the market.

WWE as a Commodity

Professional wrestling has existed in some form for well over a century. Today, professional wrestling is a passion for its most ardent fans, an uncultured form of amusement, choreographed violence, a morality play, and so on. Like it or not, professional wrestling has become a prominent form of entertainment in contemporary society. The WWE is estimated as being a billion-dollar business and is now publicly traded on New York Stock Exchange.

Exhibit 31.2

The following statement from *SportsBusiness Journal*'s ten-year retrospective encapsulated WWE nicely when it stated: "In the fall of 1998, more 18 to 34-year-old males were watching pro wrestling than were watching 'Monday Night Football.' The name of the organization may have changed— World Wrestling Federation then, World Wrestling Entertainment now—but as the 74,000 fans who attended [2008's] Wrestle-Mania in Orlando would tell you, the popularity remains." (Retrieved from http://www.sportsbusinessjournal.com/index.cfm?fuseaction=article.printArticle&articleId=58742 on September 7, 2008.)

Despite being associated with numerous scandals and the attacks of detractors, the WWE and its seemingly Teflon-coated leader, Vince McMahon, were on as strong of an economic and popular footing as ever. Whether it is John Cena in national commercials for Subway and Gillette or appearing on the ABC reality series *Fast Cars and Superstars*, Triple H in the Miller Lite Man Law commercials, or many other crossover promotional endeavors, WWE has a platform that allows for broad exposure and appeal. Before John Cena or Triple H's exposures, Dwayne "The Rock" Johnson took a hiatus from his platform as wrestling's top star to be a Hollywood leading man, starring in films such as *The Game Plan, Gridiron Gang, The Mummy Returns,* and *The Scorpion King.* Individuals such as the The Rock or his adversary, "Stone Cold" Steve Austin (as Hulk Hogan and "Rowdy" Roddy Piper before them), came to be crossover media personalities. Certainly, these names are not the only ones that fit this category. However, they are vivid examples. Even the Chairman himself, Vince McMahon, has been a crossover star. He even received a star on the Hollywood Walk of Fame in 2008.

As for McMahon, he is truly a multifaceted personality. His supporters might say that he is an ingenious businessman who helped revolutionize professional wrestling (sport entertainment), pay-per-view, and much more. He is viewed as being a self-made billionaire and has promoted himself to be a popular culture star. To his detractors, McMahon is many things as well: evil TV personality, egotistical bully, a shameless promoter of filth, and even one who has ruined (or is ruining) the professional wrestling industry by removing his competition and changing professional wrestling to the "sport entertainment" model that is shown today (For a further look into WWE marketing and branding efforts refer to Chapter 32.).

Everything Has Not Been Roses

Though the WWE empire and the McMahon bank accounts have expanded, there have certainly been bumps in the road along the way. Here are samplings of issues that have arisen.

- During the early 1990s, Vince McMahon Jr. was indicted on steroid charges (he was eventually exonerated).

- The World Bodybuilding Federation (WBF) was Vince McMahon's failed venture into establishing a professional bodybuilding circuit.
- The XFL was McMahon's failed, "one and done" professional football venture.
- Battle with World Wildlife Fund over use of WWF name (as a result, the company changed from WWF to current WWE name).
- Eddie Guerrero's death and the exploitation of his name in subsequent storylines; Chris Benoit's double murder and suicide (huge media backlash that raised many questions and led to subsequent congressional investigations).

A Culture of Chemicals

In recent years, major professional wrestling associations such as the WWE have had to address areas of controversy, including violence and criminal activity (i.e., domestic violence, drug abuse). Though people admire the bulk and brawn of the battling behemoths, wrestling is categorized by numerous occupational hazards. Among these are travel conditions and scheduling demands, prevalent injury, appearance expectations (including maintaining "the look"), and leading what is often described as a rock star lifestyle. Associated with this lifestyle are numerous areas of deviance, including drug abuse. The drug abuse is categorized as heavy use of steroids and growth hormones and the abuse of painkillers, alcohol, and recreational drugs.

Wrestling with Death

The common drug abuse in professional wrestling has resulted in various arrests, suspensions, damage to reputations, widespread scandal, and even deaths—and the numbers of deaths is surprising. Perhaps the most visible problem associated with wrestling is the all-to-common occurrence of untimely deaths. Professional wrestling-related deaths have been occurring in high numbers, even claiming the lives of some of the better known wrestlers to go between the ropes in the past couple of decades. These deaths have been associated with travel, heart attack, performance, and drugs. Drug-related fatalities have included some of the most prominent names in modern wrestling history.

A study by the *Sun* stated that 105 wrestlers died from 1997 to 2007 (42 were identified as being full-time professional wrestlers and the remaining were classified as part-time). With that said, the WWE is immediate in noting that only five contracted wrestlers have died on their watch (Chris Benoit, Eddie Guerrero, Russ Haas [developmental wrestler], Own Hart [who died of stunt gone wrong associated with a theatrical ring entrance while repelling from the rafters], and Brian Pillman). Following the death of Guerrero, the WWE implemented the WWE Talent Wellness Program.

Guerrero's death garnered much attention and raised speculation about wrestling safety issues, especially in regard to drugs. This event, however, paled in comparison to the media attention that the WWE and the entire professional wrestling industry in North America received in 2007. No professional wrestling story has resonated louder than that of Chris Benoit. Benoit, a former world champion and seemingly the consummate professional wrestler, killed his wife, former wrestling valet/manager Nancy "Woman" Benoit, and their seven-year-old son, Daniel, in their suburban Atlanta home, before ultimately hanging himself in his home gym.

Oddly enough, on the Monday following deaths of the Benoit family, WWE decided to host a three-hour "tribute" on its popular *Monday Night RAW* program. The Benoit tribute show was broadcast from an empty arena in Corpus Christi, Texas (where the regularly scheduled show was to appear). Even though the local police had discovered the Benoit family dead in their home earlier during the day of the broadcast and there were many questions remaining, the show was aired on prime time television. This turned out to be serious error in judgment and a public relations nightmare. As additional results associated with the murder-suicide were made available, the WWE promptly engaged "spin control" mode. The company tried to right the wrongs stemming from their preposterous decision to go forward with the Benoit tribute. This included the removal of virtually all images and mentions of Benoit from their Web site and issuing an apology on the next broadcast program. This scenario was a PR debacle.

Exhibit 31.3

Following a tribute show to Chris Benoit on *Monday Night RAW*, CEO Vince McMahon made the following statement on Sci-Fi Network's *ECW* broadcast:

Last night on Monday Night RAW, the WWE presented a special tribute show, recognizing the career of Chris Benoit. However, now some 26 hours later, the facts of this horrific tragedy are now apparent.

Therefore, other than my comments, there will be no mention of Mr. Benoit tonight. On the contrary, tonight's show will be dedicated to everyone who has been affected by this terrible incident. This evening marks the first step of the healing process. Tonight, the WWE performers will do what they do better than anyone else in the world—entertain you.

To make matters worse for the WWE, in the aftermath of the Benoit murders, Rep. Henry Waxman, chair of the House Committee on Oversight and Government Reform, and ranking minority member Tom Davis issued a three-page letter asking the WWE to provide documentation detailing their drug-testing policy, including testing procedures and results, to the committee. Furthermore, when the Benoit autopsy results showed that he had a highly elevated testosterone level—more than ten times of that allowed under Olympics drug testing guidelines—further questions were raised. Beyond that, WWE's credibility took further blows when various news reports named numerous wrestlers, including some of the more notable superstars (i.e., Adam "Edge" Copeland) as well as deceased wrestlers Guerrero, Benoit, and Brian Adams (a wrestler who died following the Benoit incident), as having involvement with Internet prescription investigations.

The Final Score

Professional wrestling has been unapologetically "un-PC." As some would say, it has been low-class, and appeals to the more primal taste of viewers. Clearly its popularity transcends such an audience (whatever that may be). Wrestling has been wrought with problems. Whatever one may think of professional wrestling, it is a powerful economic and entertainment force. Vince McMahon and his muscle-bound corps of thespians have been able to rise up as notable pop culture icons while building a place as pay-per-view champions and TV ratings draws. In regard to commercial appeal, all one has to do is walk down the toy aisles of a Wal-Mart, Target, or Toys-R-Us and see the commercialized wares of the WWE and their superstars. Beyond the toy aisles, products may be seen in clothing, electronics, and elsewhere. The reach of the WWE is seemingly endless.

Despite all of the prosperity that the WWE has been able to reap, there are various clouds that have hung over the company, its leader, and the industry. Perhaps the most troubling scandalous areas associated with the WWE and professional wrestling as a whole is the far too common occurrence of premature deaths, particularly those tied to drugs. Throughout the past decade, WWE has been engulfed by the loss of wrestlers and former wrestlers who died within a handful of years (or less) of being employed by the WWE. As will be the case, being the industry leader bears some association and implication to larger problems facing an industry as a whole. This is certainly the case for WWE, which has had to answer questions pertaining to these early deaths (whether it is their contracted superstars or those participating in the industry for which they are the most visible brand). Whether it is fair or not, that is the way it is—and undeniably, the two most significant wrestling deaths to impact the professional wrestling industry, those of Eddie Guerrero and Chris Benoit, did fall under the WWE's watch. The Benoit tragedy opened up a hailstorm of controversy ranging from concerns about drugs, faulty drug testing, brain injuries, excessive violence, and more. It also raised various issue of corporate responsibility (or lack thereof). During the aftermath of the Benoit incident, the WWE was bombarded with scandal—including congressional inquiries. Even in the presence of these notable scandals, the WWE brand has remained strong and by far the most visible force in professional wrestling, where their mass commercial appeal has not wavered.

Post-Game Comments

- WWE is the dominant brand in the world of professional wrestling.
- WWE is a commercial and entertainment power, registering high sales of pay-per-view programs, merchandise, and high ratings on shows such as *Monday Night RAW* and *Friday Night SmackDown.*
- WWE has been wrought with scandal—particularly drug-related scandal (most notably the Benoit tragedy), but through it all has emerged more economically viable than ever.
- WWE has taken action geared at addressing drug concerns (at least cosmetically)—though these steps have been questioned and refuted.
- Despite its controversial aspects, WWE still stands strong as a highly visible and multifaceted sport-associated brand.

Web Resources

http://broadcastingcable.com/article/CA6454776.html
http://corporate.wwe.com
http://corporate.wwe.com/news/2006/2006_03_27.jsp

http://corporate.wwe.com/news/documents/TalentWellnessProgramOutline2-27-06CORPweb.pdf
http://sports.espn.go.com/espn/news/story?id=2805155
http://sports.espn.go.com/espn/news/story?id=2951586
http://sportsillustrated.cnn.com/2007/writers/chris_mannix/06/26/benoit
http://ww3.ics.adp.com/streetlink_data/dirWWE/annual/images/WWE_AR2007.pdf
http://www.bizjournals.com/atlanta/stories/2002/04/01/story1.html
http://www.wwe.com
http://wwe.corporate.com
http://www.thesun.co.uk/article/0,,2003560001-2007310067,00.html
http://www.thesun.co.uk/sol/homepage/sport/wrestling/article248338.ece

Additional Resources

Assael S., & Mooneyham, M. (2002). *Sex, lies, and headlocks: The real story of Vince McMahon and the World Wrestling Federation.* New York: Crown.

Coakley, J. (2004). *Sports in society: Issues & controversies* (8th ed.). New York: McGraw-Hill.

Muchnick, I. (2007). *Wrestling Babylon: Piledriving tales of drugs, sex, death and scandal.* Toronto: ECW Press.

Radazzo V. M. (2008). *The story of Chris Benoit and the fall of the pro wrestling industry.* Beverley Hills, CA: Phoenix Books.

Shields, B., & Sullivan, K. (2009). *WWE encyclopedia.* New York: Dorling Kindersley.

Chapter 32

Grappling with Questions: Marketing the WWE Brand to Youth

Matthew J. Bernthal,
University of South Carolina

Jason W. Lee,
University of North Florida

Company: World Wrestling Entertainment (WWE)
Location: Stanford, CT;
   with offices in Los Angeles, New York, Toronto, and London
Internet Address: www.wwe.com, www.wwekids.com,
   corporate.wwe.com

Discussion Questions

- From a child development perspective, do you believe that professional wrestling is harmful to children who watch it regularly? Why or why not?
- To what extent are professional wrestling organizations such as the WWE responsible for injuries that occur to children imitating wrestling moves? Can these organizations be blamed for these injuries to a greater degree than, for example, the NFL can be blamed for injuries to children playing football?
- Do you see any positive values that children can learn from watching professional wrestling? If yes, please describe.
- To what extent do you believe that the WWE's newest efforts to market to children (*WWE Kids* magazine, WWEKids.com) will open the company up to a new round of public criticism of marketing a potentially harmful product to children?

- From a public relations perspective, what steps could WWE take to combat the criticism that its product is harmful to children?
- Do you think professional wrestling organizations such as WWE have a private opinion on backyard wrestling that differs from their public discouragement of the practice? If so, why? If not, why not?
- Review the WWE's brand portfolio given in this chapter. Do you envision any additional business expansion opportunities for the WWE in the near future?

The Line-Up

Children are naturally drawn to professional wrestling, with the often cartoonish characters and high-flying acrobatic matches. Each week, 2.6 million children aged six to fourteen watch industry leader World Wrestling Entertainment (WWE) TV programming, which consists of RAW, SmackDown, and ECW. In addition, children purchase a large amount of WWE licensed merchandise from toymaker Jakks Pacific (to be replaced by Mattel in 2010). While children have long been drawn to WWE wrestling, the company has recently begun an even more aggressive and overt campaign aimed at targeting them. In 2008, the WWE launched *WWE Kids* magazine and developed a separate Web site, wwekids.com, just for children. While the WWE's other magazine, *WWE Magazine*, is targeted to the twelve- to twenty-four-year-old demographic, *WWE Kids* is targeted to six- to fourteen-year-old children. According to Geof Rochester, VP of marketing for WWE, "A large percentage of children in America get introduced to our brand from 6 to 10 years old. We said, 'We have a strong kids audience; let's embrace that.' We want to have a lifelong relationship with these kids" (Graser, 2008, n.p.). Shane McMahon, VP of global media for WWE, states that these efforts are part of WWE's "recommitment to provide its young audience with new, fun, age-appropriate content" (n.p.).

However, one might argue that even if the WWE were to limit *WWE Kids* and wwekids.com to age-appropriate content, the company hopes, through targeting children with these vehicles, to encourage children to tune into TV programming that many critics contend is extremely age-inappropriate and potentially harmful. However, while wwekids.com contains more age-appropriate content for children than either WWE.com or WWE TV programming, it is arguable that wwekids.com is not without content questionably suited for children. For example, a wwekids.com video clip of wrestler Chris Jericho introducing his Intercontinental Championship title belt shows him boasting,

"I'd like to introduce my first guest tonight. She's shiny, she's sexy, she's sassy, she's been around the block, but she always comes home to daddy." The sexual innuendo is clear and probably not lost on many youth who view the clip.

The WWE is a publicly traded company, and as such, is subject to government oversight. Given this fact, some have suggested that the company's new marketing efforts targeted toward children might lead to increased scrutiny from government regulators concerned about the content of entertainment marketed to children. This chapter lays out the products that comprise the WWE brand, and discusses the concerns many have about the marketing of this brand to children.

Timeline of Events

For WWE timeline, please refer to Chapter 31.

WWE Products: Expansion beyond the Ring

The WWE categorizes their product offerings in the following business segments: (1) live and televised entertainment, (2) consumer products, (3) digital media, and (4) WWE Films.

The live and televised entertainment segment encompasses ticket sales to live events, sales of merchandise at live events, TV rights fees, sales of TV advertising/sponsorships, and fees for viewing pay-per-view and video-on-demand programming (i.e., *WWE 24/7*). WWE corporate reports that the live and televised entertainment component represented a significant portion of net revenues (ranging from 65 percent to 82 percent annually since 2005). An example of this impact can be seen in the fact that venue merchandise net revenues have accounted for over $60 million since 2005.

The popularity of televised wrestling can be evidenced by the fact that professional wrestling has aired on ESPN, Fox Sports Net, NBC, the CW, USA, Spike TV, TNT, TBS, SyFy, My Network TV, and WGN America on a national scale. WWE's programming alone extends to over 100 countries worldwide. Currently, WWE produces four TV shows for a total of six hours of original domestic programming each week. The shows are *Monday Night Raw* (the USA network's top-rated program, often the top program on all ad-supported cable), *Friday Night SmackDown* (when carried on the CW network, it was the most watched program in the target demographic audience of men age eighteen to thirty-four), *ECW: Extreme Championship Wrestling* (the most popular show on the SyFy Channel), *A.M. Raw*, and *WWE Superstars* on WGN America. Furthermore, WWE began producing their programming in high definition (HD) in 2008.

In addition to the weekly programming, WWE has been one of the driving forces in the area of pay-per-view (PPV) programming. WWE has been a true pioneer in PPV as it is known today. Slightly more than once a month, WWE produces PPVs watched by both adults and children. WWE produced an all-time high of fifteen domestic PPVs in 2007 that generated net revenues of $94.3 million. The standard purchasing price for WWE PPVs is $39.95. The most popular and successful of these ventures has been the *WrestleMania* juggernaut ($54.95 in 2008) which has solidified itself as a pop culture entertainment icon.

Expanding beyond PPV, WWE unveiled a subscription video on demand (SVOD) service called *WWE 24/7*. Through this, WWE is able to offer subscribers around forty hours of content every month including classic TV shows, specials, and original programming. WWE utilizes this medium, as well as DVD, to offer programming from video libraries of other wrestling companies it has purchased (namely, WCW and ECW).

The consumer products segment includes WWE videos/DVDs, magazine publishing, and licensed merchandise (e.g., video games and toys). Whether it is T-shirts, video games, action figures, Easter baskets, jewelry, or back-to-school supplies, the WWE generates revenue from an extremely wide variety of licensed merchandise, much of which is targeted toward children. The company's success has resulted in merchandise being sold through retail chains such as Wal-Mart, K-Mart, Toys-R-Us, Target, and Best Buy, to name a few.

WWE has even ventured into the literary world, where they have actually been involved with multiple *New York Times* bestsellers (even including number one bestsellers). Through their book publishing agreement with Simon & Schuster, WWE has been able to publish literary works in genres spanning autobiographies, histories, how-to books, and fictional works. WWE is also involved in magazine publishing through their flagship publication, *WWE Magazine* (which reaped net revenues of $16.5 million in 2007), and the recent addition of *WWE Kids*.

Home video has also become a major staple of WWE's product offerings. Due in part to the aforementioned video libraries acquired from purchased competitors, the company is sitting on a wealth of wrestling footage and programming from years gone by. In 2007 alone, WWE shipped roughly 4 million DVD units, including thirty-three new home video titles, which resulted in net revenues of $53.7 million in 2007.

Beyond that, WWE also has a music division, the WWE Music Group, aimed at using various music forms as a means to extend the corporate brand.

This includes initiatives with iTunes and the promotion of artist CDs (e.g., John Cena's *You Can't See Me*) and theme music compilations.

WWE's digital media segment involves Web site advertising sales, merchandise sales from the online store, and revenue generated from WWE broadband/mobile content (mobile alerts). WWEShop is the e-commerce storefront of WWE in which fans can purchase a seemingly endless supply of branded merchandise and use regular online promotions. WWEShop saw net revenues of $18.6 million in 2007.

The WWE Films segment was established in an effort to enter the movie industry and provide yet another form of exposure for WWE superstars. To date, WWE Films has released three feature films: *See No Evil*, *The Marine*, and *The Condemned*. These films have not been met with great critical success, nor been huge blockbusters, but WWE Films is moving forward with new film projects in the works.

Through the many products under the WWE umbrella, children become attached to the WWE brand. A not far-fetched scenario might have a young male watching *Monday Night RAW*, going to bed in his bedroom adorned with posters of WWE wrestlers and Divas (the WWE term for its attractive female wrestlers), waking up and dressing in his Stone Cold Steve Austin T-shirt, and going to school to use his WWE back-to-school supplies. After school, he might head home to watch a WWE DVD or listen to a WWE music CD, followed by a trip to the movie theater to watch WWE Superstar John Cena in *The Marine*. Indeed, children are consumers of the vast majority of products offered under the WWE brand, a brand that has been built by a strong commitment to a marketing orientation.

WWE: Bringing Muscle to Marketing Orientation

To scholars of marketing, Vince McMahon and his WWE provide successful examples of a strong marketing orientation. An organization that has a marketing orientation is one that focuses on understanding the consumer and providing a product that meets consumers' needs while achieving the organization's objectives. WWE has, in part, built such a strong brand through being completely wedded to this philosophy. If there is a corporate "poster child" for giving consumers what they want, it is the WWE.

Though fans of professional wrestling are more diverse than one might expect, the WWE's primary target market is the male eighteen- to thirty-four-year-old demographic. Arguably more than any other form of live or broadcast entertainment, WWE gives them exactly what they crave: sex and violence.

From Val Venis, a wrestling character fashioned as a former porn star and Edge, the "Rated-R superstar," to the popularity of the attractive WWE Divas (several of whom have appeared in *Playboy*), the WWE clearly understands and appeals to the sexual appetites of young males. WWE Divas appear scantily clad, competing in sexuality-laced matches such as "Paddle-on-a-Pole" matches, where the winner is the first one to subdue her opponent long enough to acquire a paddle and spank her, and "Bra and Panties" matches, where the winner is the first to strip her opponent to bra and panties. Photo spreads, videos, and even items such as a Diva-worn bras are available at wwe.com. Furthermore, while WCW, WWE's fierce competitor in the 1990s, was attempting to position itself as a relatively "family-friendly" version of wrestling, the WWE fought and ultimately won the war with their rivals in part by unashamedly delivering sexually themed as well as increasingly violent content. This content included the increasing use of weapons such as steel chairs, sledgehammers, barbed wire, thumb tacks spread across the ring floor, and at one point, even the proverbial kitchen sink itself. The WWE clearly gave young males what they desired from their pro wrestling, despite many critics crying foul, particularly given the fact that children were watching in extremely large numbers.

Perhaps a deeper understanding of fan needs is evidenced by WWE's appeal to fans' feelings of nationalism. When nationalism runs strong due to geopolitical events, WWE gives them an outlet for these feelings. For example, in the 1980s, shortly after the Iranian hostage crisis and during the Cold War, the WWE used an Iranian villain named the Iron Sheik, who came to matches carrying the Iranian flag. At the height of the Cold War, they also created a Russian villain named Nikolai Volkoff, who antagonized the fans by singing the Russian national anthem before each match. At one point, the WWE even teamed the Iron Sheik with Volkoff to form a tag team called the Foreign Legion. Wrestlers such as this often feuded with wrestling characters based on the U.S. military, such as Sergeant Slaughter and Corporal Kirchner. Not coincidentally, with tensions between the United States and Russia rising again, the WWE has created a new villain, Vladimir Kozlov, to appeal to fans' desire to express their nationalism.

Being in tune with and appealing to fans' desires for sex, violence, and nationalism is only an example of WWE's strong marketing orientation. Indeed, this orientation is pervasive throughout the organization. For example, it has long been rumored that WWE floats potential storylines, feud endings, and new characters on fan Internet message boards to gauge fan reaction. In many ways, WWE strongly caters to fans' desires, and this has undoubtedly contributed to its success.

Through its commitment to understanding and catering to the desires of its primary fan base, some charge that the WWE has put a potentially harmful product into the path of children. While adult males flock to the sex and violence enthusiastically delivered by WWE programming, younger eyes are watching as well.

Marketing to Children: Criticisms and Concerns

Since the popularity of WWE began to skyrocket in the 1980s, critics have questioned its suitability for children. These critics have been vocal in their insistence that WWE programming is harmful to children in a number of ways, both physically and psychologically. By imitating professional wrestling moves, critics contend, children put themselves at harm to serious injury and even death. In addition, through regular viewing of WWE programming, critics argue that children can be harmed from a psychological development perspective. We turn to these concerns.

Developmental Consequences

Critics charge that wrestling can teach harmful "cognitive scripts." Such scripts are a form of memory structure that develops with multiple exposures to the same set of stimuli. These scripts are essentially ways of thinking that can ultimately influence behavior. Critics charge, for example, that through its characters and storylines, professional wrestling organizations such as the WWE contribute to scripts such as racial stereotypes, that being "shamed" should be responded to with aggression, that women are sexual objects that exist solely for a man's pleasure or reward, "nice guys finish last" (Messner, Dunbar, & Hunt, 2000), and cheating and verbal intimidation are effective problem-solving techniques.

As one example, critics such as the Parents Television Council (PTC) contended that the Godfather (who wrestled in the late 1990s and early 2000s) contributed to the script of seeing women as sexual objects that exist solely for a man's pleasure or reward. The Godfather played a pimp character who was escorted to the ring by a stable of women that he referred to as his "hos," claiming, "pimpin' ain't easy," and exhorting to the crowd, "all aboard the ho train." Occasionally, he would offer one of his "hos" to his opponent prior to the match. It is important to note that the Godfather was a "babyface" (i.e., a good guy who is crafted to be cheered). This character is not the only avenue to the charge that the WWE promotes women as sexual objects. Virtually every Diva on the WWE roster is extremely attractive, often appearing scantily clad on WWE programming; furthermore, a number of these Divas have appeared in pictorials and on the cover of *Playboy* magazine. As yet another example, in the early part of this decade, the WWE ran a storyline that included Eric Bischoff, then the "general manager" of *RAW* seeking to boost ratings to compete with the rival show *SmackDown* (please refer to Chapter 31 for a description of how the two WWE programs "competed" with one another). He did this by bringing two women to the ring who stripped down to bra and panties and engage in what he called "HLA" (hot lesbian action). During this event, Bischoff grew tired of the activity, and brought in his two henchmen, "Three Minute Warning," who proceed to kick and body slam the women into oblivion. Content such as this draws the wrath of critics who contend that the WWE promotes the objectification of women.

Another cognitive script that the WWE is charged with teaching is that cheating is an effective problem-solving technique, as a large percentage of matches end with one wrestler defeating the other through cheating (e.g., undetected use of a weapon, interference from a third party wrestler). Some might contend that this script is particularly powerful in that often, the babyface, with the audience's approval, cheats to defeat the "heel" (i.e., bad guy). In other words, critics contend that wrestling can teach that cheating is a valuable *and acceptable* tool.

Yet another negative cognitive script that WWE has been charged with fostering is that of stereotyping. Critics contend that WWE wrestlers are too often centered on preexisting stereotypical views and that the organization itself therefore has a hand in perpetuating these stereotypes. For example, WWE currently has a stereotypical African American tag team called Cryme Tyme. WWE's Web site promotes Cryme Tyme as a "trash-talking, car-jacking tag team duo," and offers an exclusive online video series called *Word Up*, ushered in with a theme song of *Bringin' Da Hood T U* (available on iTunes). While the WWE claims that characters such as this parody racial stereotypes with humor, critics argue that this only perpetuates such stereotypes in the minds of youth. As another example, a 2002 storyline featured a stereotypically homosexual tag team duo, Chuck and Billy. They bleached their hair blond, with one sometimes sporting a version of pigtails. They also had a personal assistant (also a wrestler) by the name of Rico, himself portrayed as a stereotypically gay character that encouraged Chuck and Billy in their relationship. This culminated in Chuck and Billy's "marriage ceremony" on *SmackDown*, where during the ceremony they were interrupted by the aforementioned Godfather who reminded them of their past heterosexual escapades with his ho train. After the Godfather exited the arena floor, Billy and Chuck indicated the homosexual angle was all a publicity stunt. During the entire run of this storyline, there were many stereotypical jokes and innuendos at which the crowd roared. Whether it is due to characters such as Chuck and Billy, Cryme Tyme, or Los Guerreros (a stereotypically portrayed duo consisting of the late Eddie Guerrero and Chavo Guerrero, whose slogan was "Lie, Cheat and Steal to Win"; further details pertaining to Eddie Guerrero are in Chapter 31), the WWE often faces criticism for the perpetuation of stereotypes.

A perception also exists that the WWE brand promotes a culture of disrespect. For example, characters in WWE programming that represent authority figures are often portrayed as either the heel or weak. Referees, for example, represent little more than impotent window dressing in most matches. Their authority is often ignored and unenforced. They consistently "miss" acts of cheating and deception by both heel and babyface wrestlers. Often, they are assaulted as part of the match story. As another example, one of the most popular wrestlers in WWE history, Stone Cold Steve Austin, was fashioned as powerful character that rebelled against authority. In Austin's case, the on-screen enemy was the "evil boss," WWE Chairman McMahon himself. Austin built his popularity by "flipping the bird" to McMahon (and others) and humiliating him in myriad creative ways, at one point holding a fake gun to McMahon's head, resulting in McMahon wetting his suit pants in the ring. On a more general level, in the course of on-screen promotions (where wrestlers are interviewed and "talk up" their feuds with other wrestlers), even the babyfaces verbally insult and demean their rivals. D-Generation X, a pair of WWE wrestlers whose name flaunts "antiestablishment," has been and is extremely popular. A D-Generation X sweatshirt is promoted online with the following: "They spit in the face of authority and offended everyone else ... Show your degenerate side with the new Anytime Anywhere Youth Sweatshirt." Furthermore, DX is associated with their crass signature catchphrase, "Suck It."

Related to this, a study conducted through Indiana University and the TV program *Inside Edition* content analyzed fifty episodes of *Monday Night RAW* between January 1998 and February 1999. Researchers found 1,658 instances of "crotch grabbing," and 157 "flippings of the finger," among other similar findings. In the past, WWE's slogan in its advertisements was "attitude." Critics contend that much of the attitude that children take away from WWE programming, if the IU study and characters such as D-Generation X and Stone Cold Steve Austin are any indication, is anything but positive.

Physical Consequences

Many children that watch professional wrestling seem naturally drawn to imitate it. In fact, what is referred to as "backyard wrestling" has become a phenomena among youth in the United States and internationally. "Backyard wrestling" is a term used to describe untrained wrestling fans (most often, young males aged twelve to twenty) getting together to perform wrestling matches/events in a nonprofessional setting. It can be thought of as "pick-up wrestling." These fans often form "backyard federations" modeled after professional wrestling companies such as the WWE, with participants imitating some variation of their favorite wrestler and engaging in feuds themed after what they see on television (e.g., feuding over women, championship titles). These federations hold events that are sometimes simple, and sometimes very elaborate, with most taking place at the home of a participant. Sometimes some form of wrestling ring is constructed, but often the matches simply take place with the outside ground as the ring. Many backyard matches are extraordinarily violent, with participants using various weapons such as fluorescent light bulbs, steel chairs, barbed wire, thumb tacks, and even cheese graters (used to literally grate an opponent's forehead). The use of weapons and risky, high-flying maneuvers (e.g., leaping onto opponents from rooftops) makes for YouTube moments, and backyard participants routinely post clips of their matches on the Internet for friends and others to see. A search for "backyard wrestling" on YouTube results in hundreds of videos of backyard action, ranging from the relatively tame to the extraordinarily violent and crass. In addition, many backyard federations have Web sites devoted to their activities. Some backyard federations have even aired regular TV shows on public access channels. As yet more evidence of the popularity of this form of imitation, backyard wrestling has fostered movie documentaries as well as video games (e.g., Xbox's *Backyard Wrestling: Don't Try This At Home*; *Backyard Wrestling 2: There Goes the Neighborhood*).

It should be noted that the WWE publicly and strongly discourages backyard wrestling, noting on its Web site that any backyard wrestling "audition" tapes that the organization receives from would-be wrestlers are returned unviewed. Certainly, part of the motivation behind this discouragement is the reduction of legal risk that is involved with the potential injury or death that could result from fan imitation of moves.

Not all imitation, of course, takes the involved form of backyard wrestling. Children also regularly imitate professional wrestling moves and actions in less elaborate forms and settings, including at school. Indeed, a survey of 370 elementary and middle-school teachers indicated that 20.9 percent of teachers observed children imitating wrestling moves involving the neck, and that their students used the words "clothesline," "chokehold," "pedigree," and "piledriver" (all common wrestling terms for moves involving the neck). Further, 8.1 percent of the surveyed teachers reported students' use of "headlocks," and 6.8 percent reported observing imitative moves that involved jumping onto another child from a raised platform (e.g., desk, jungle gym). Additionally, 42.1 percent of teachers responding to this same survey claim to have observed injury occurring as students imitated wrestling moves (Bernthal & Medway, 2005). No matter the form or setting, it has been argued that the imitation that stems from watching WWE programming and events can lead to potentially harmful physical consequences.

Over the past two decades, there have been a number of organizations that have criticized the WWE for content they claim is at best unsuitable and at worst extremely harmful to children (e.g., Parents Television Council [PTC], Common Sense Media). One of the most vocal and publicized campaigns against WWE came from the PTC. PTC states its mission is "to promote and restore responsibility and decency to the entertainment industry in answer to America's demand for positive, family-oriented television programming" (see www.parentstv.org). In the late 1990s and into 2000, PTC went on an aggressive anti-WWE publicity campaign. The organization charged that WWE was directly responsible for the deaths of four children:

- In Hudson County, Georgia, a babysitter played a wrestling video to entertain the children as she went to buy cigarettes. While she was away, a four-year-old killed a fifteen-month-old baby by stomping it to death.
- In 1999, a twelve-year-old killed his nineteen-month-old cousin with the "jackknife power bomb."
- In 1999, in a widely publicized case, twelve-year-old Lionel Tate killed his six-year-old female playmate while, it was argued in court, imitating wrestling moves.
- In Dallas, a seven-year-old boy, imitating a wrestling move known as a "clothesline," struck his three-year-old brother on the neck with a running forearm, fatally injuring him.

Further, PTC attempted to dissuade advertisers from promoting their products on WWE programming by citing what it claimed was the "fact" that WWE was responsible for these deaths and that WWE programming was altogether unsuitable for children due to its violent, sexual, and crass content. The PTC also aggressively lobbied their viewpoint to retailers selling WWE licensed merchandise, the media, and the public at large. The PTC even promoted its campaign against the WWE in its own fund-raising materials and actively promoted the number of advertisers that had withdrawn from advertising on WWE programming as a result of its campaign.

In November 2000, the WWE filed a lawsuit against the PTC, claiming defamation, among other things. After the PTC's request to dismiss was denied, the PTC settled out of court. As part of the settlement, PTC paid the WWE $3.5

million and issued a letter of apology. In this letter, PTC stated that it was incorrect in blaming the WWE for the deaths of the children and retracted its claim on the number of advertisers that had pulled support from WWE programming as a result of its campaign.

Exhibit 32.1

The following statement summarizes WWE's opinion that it is held to a double standard in being held responsible for those who imitate WWE programming content:

Vince McMahon, WWE chairman: "We push the envelope, and then we pull back. But we're not killing anyone. We're not maiming anyone. Do we slug each other with steel chairs? Yes. Do we think it should be copied? I don't advocate anyone picking up a chair and slugging anyone. I don't advocate anyone picking up an M-16 like Arnold Schwarzenegger does in his movies, either."(Source: G. Brown, http://www.infoplease.com/spot/prowrestling1.html)

The Final Score

It is not the purpose of this chapter to stake the claim that professional wrestling viewership in general, or WWE viewership in particular, contributes to child injury, death, or even the development of harmful patterns of thought (cognitive scripts). This information is presented to inform the reader that professional wrestling organizations, best exemplified by the industry superpower that is the WWE, have to constantly deal with these criticisms from the media, the public, and activists such as the PTC. Such criticism is a threat to WWE brand equity, and the organization has to creatively and continually engage in both reactive and proactive public relations to protect their brand equity from such criticisms.

The WWE is clearly aware of those critics who condemn its product's suitability for children, and outside of dramatically altering its programming to appease these critics, takes steps to protect its brand. The WWE corporate website, for example, has a Parents section where the WWE clearly labels its programming as suitable for children only with active parental guidance:

We understand how important it is for parents to take an active role in their children's free time. We encourage all parents to help their children select suitable entertainment, and to understand the differences between fantasy and real life.

All WWE television programs are rated PG in recognition of the growing appeal of our programs to all ages and as intergenerational family viewing. If parents make the decision to allow their children to watch our programming, we encourage those parents to watch with their children. We urge parents who allow younger children to watch our programming to explain that what our Superstars do on television should not be emulated or attempted in real life (corporate.wwe.com/parents/overview.jsp).

In addition, the WWE has a series of public service announcements titled "Don't Try This at Home," which feature WWE superstars emphasizing that children should never attempt to imitate wrestling moves at home or at school.

In the end, the WWE brand consistently rides the razor's edge when attempting to appeal to its two essential target markets, young adult males and children. While ratcheting up sexual and violent content to appeal to the young adult male, WWE risks the ire of the media, activists, and the broader public, who criticize it with the knowledge that children are watching as well. They question whether the WWE should encourage children to consume products infused with such base content. However, if WWE tones its brand down too much, it knows that it risks losing the rabid support of its primary target market of young men. It is a balancing act faced by few other sport and entertainment brands. With the WWE's recent efforts to target children even more aggressively and transparently, the balancing act is likely to become even more difficult, and the future success of the WWE brand depends, in part, on how well it walks this path.

Post-Game Comments

- WWE is the dominant brand in professional wrestling, due in large part to its outstanding marketing orientation. It has leveraged the brand across a wide array of consumer products, ranging from children's toys to movies to best-selling books.
- WWE's primary target market is young adult males, yet the company also actively targets children, most recently through WWEKids.com and *WWE Kids* magazine.
- Critics find that much of the material in WWE programming that is designed to appeal to the young adult male is inappropriate for child viewers. These critics charge that children can potentially learn harmful cognitive scripts through watching WWE programming.

- Among youth, backyard wrestling is a popular and potentially dangerous form of professional wrestling imitation.
- The WWE must walk a fine public relations line when delivering the sexual and violent content desired by young adult males, knowing that children are watching (and are indeed encouraged to watch by the WWE itself).

Web Resources

http://corporate.wwe.com/news/2000/2000_11_09.jsp
http://corporate.wwe.com/news/2002/2002_07_08.jsp
http://corporate.wwe.com/parents/overview.jsp (WWE site for parents)
http://ww3.ics.adp.com/streetlink_data/dirWWE/annual/images/WWE_AR2007.pdf
    (WWE 2007 Annual Report)
http://www.parentstv.org
http://www.wwe.com

Additional Resources

Ashley, F. B., Dollar, J., Wigley, B., Gillentine, J. A., & Daughtrey, C. (2000). Professional wrestling fans: Your next-door neighbors. *Sport Marketing Quarterly*, 9(3), 140–148.

Bernthal, M. J. (2003). The effects of professional wrestling viewership on children. *Sport Journal*, 6(3). Retrieved September 20, 2008, from http://www.thesportjournal.org/article/effect-professional-wrestling-viewership-children.

Bernthal, M. J., & Medway, F. J. (2005). An initial exploration into the psychological implications of adolescents' involvement with professional wrestling. *School Psychology International*, 26(2), 224–242.

Brown, G. (n.d.). Soaps between the ropes: The rebirth of professional wrestling. Retrieved September 29, 2008, from http://www.infoplease.com/spot/prowrestling1.html.

Caldwell, J. (2008). Sesame Street, Blue's Clues, and ... WWE? Retrieved September 29, 2008, from http://www.pwtorch.com.

Graser, M. (2008, March 23). Kids enter WWE ring: Wrestling company targets youth. *Variety*. Retrieved September 29, 2008, from http://www.variety.com/article/VR1117982800.html?categoryid=14&cs=1.

Herring, H. B. (1999, February 28). The pro wrestling sleazometorsleazometer. New York Times, Section 4, p. 2.

Lakshmi-Ratan, R. A., & Iyer, E. (1988). Similarity analysis of cognitive scripts. *Journal of the Academy of Marketing Science, 16*(2), 36–42.

Maguire, B., & Wozniak, J. F. (1987). Racial and ethnic stereotypes in professional wrestling. *Social Science Journal, 24*(3), 261–273.

Messner, M. A., Dunbar, M., & Hunt, D. (2000). The televised sports manhood formula. *Journal of Sport & Social Issues, 24*(4), 380–394.

Shank, M. D. (2005). *Sports marketing: A strategic perspective* (3rd ed.). Upper Saddle River, NJ: Prentice Hall.

Walsh, D. (2008). Pro wrestling: Adult entertainment marketed to kids. Media Wise. Retrieved September 11, 2008, from http://mediafamily.org/mediawise columns/wrestling_mw.shtml.

Wasmonsky, J., & Beresin, E. V. (2001). Taking professional wrestling to the mat: A look at the appeal and potential effects of professional wrestling on children. *Academic Psychiatry, 25*(2), 125–131.

World Wrestling Entertainment settles lawsuit with Parents Television Council. (2002, July 8). Corporate.wwe.com. Founder Brent Bozell Issues Apology. Retrieved October 7, 2008, from http://corporate.wwe.com/news/2002/2002_07_08.jsp.

Chapter 33

USSTC and Smokeless Tobacco Sponsorship in Sport: A Good Idea or Just Blowing Smoke?

Jason W. Lee,
University of North Florida

Company: U.S. Smokeless Tobacco Company
Location: Stamford, CT; with manufacturing facilities in
Nashville, TN, Franklin Park, IL, and Hopkinsville, KY
Internet Address: www.ussmokeless.com

Discussion Questions

- How does USSTC use sport to reach their target audiences?
- Based on the material in this chapter, is USSTC a corporately responsible company?
- How do you feel about the presence of tobacco sponsorship at sport events?
- Does it make a difference if the event is a collegiate sporting event?
- Why are sport organizations and events still willing to align themselves with controversial sponsors such as tobacco producers?
- What other sports or other entertainment activities might USSTC consider targeting?

The Line-Up

Sport sponsorship exchanges are to benefit both the sport organization and the sponsoring agencies. Corporations seek to obtain branding enhancement by increasing public awareness, enhancing or reinforcing brand image, and involving the company with the community. For sponsoring parties, the desire to obtain such benefits makes sense. Tobacco companies have had an extensive history of using sport sponsorship while seeking to reach their marketing objectives. Involvement in sport sponsorship has been sought after by these companies due to the prestige that sporting events lend to a company or brand name, as well as the wide access that events provide to reach potential consumers of their products. Corporate sponsorship is crucial to the existence and survival of sporting events at both the professional and amateur levels. There is still the potential for unease because some sponsorship arrangements may be seen as being contradictory in nature, if not completely inappropriate. Some sponsors' products may not fall in line with the goals or missions of the sport agencies and activities that are to be sponsored. Tobacco producers are among the most perplexing and controversial contemporary example of the paradoxical nature that sport sponsorship can present. For this reason, some companies prefer to have little or no involvement with tobacco producers. Other companies have built long-lasting, high-profile partnerships with such companies.

Timeline of Events

1822
- Origins of USSTC begin with the debut of Copenhagen.
- The company begins its desire to be associated with the "rugged and authentic image of the American West."

1934
- Skoal debuts.

1943
- Copenhagen begins using outdoor advertising.

1971
- TV advertisements for tobacco products are banned in the United States.

1974
- The USSTC begins awarding scholarships to college rodeo athletes.

1987
- UST Inc. is established as a holding company for the primary corporate subsidiaries, the United States Tobacco Company and International Wine & Spirits Ltd.

1993
- The Professional Bull Riders (PBR) circuit is launched.

2001
- The company changes its name from United States Tobacco Company to U.S. Smokeless Tobacco Company to more accurately reflect its product offerings.

2002
- Smokeless Tobacco Master Settlement Agreement is enacted.

2003
- The NASCAR Cup sponsorship changes its title sponsorship from the Winston Cup to the Nextel Cup.

2005
- USSTC sales of moist smokeless tobacco exceed 970 million cans for the year.
- Revel test marketed by USSTC.

2007
- UST Inc. acquires Stag's Leap Wine Cellars in California's Napa Valley.

2009
- The Altria Group acquires UST Inc.

USSTC Background

In 2009, the Altria Group acquired UST Inc., an estimated $8 billion enterprise, which served as the holding company which was comprised primarily of the U.S. Smokeless Tobacco Company (USSTC) and Ste. Michelle Wine Estates (SMWE). USSTC is the most prominent smokeless tobacco producer in the United States. Being the leading producer and marketer of moist smokeless tobacco which has annual sales of nearly 1 billion cans sold, USSTC has been able to capitalize from one of the only segments of the tobacco industry that is still experiencing increases in market share. This growth has occurred largely through concentrated efforts to reach out to (among others) the market of cigarette smokers who are seeking alternative means to get a nicotine fix.

USSTC's Smokeless Tobacco Products

USSTC takes pride in the fact that it possesses the smokeless tobacco industry's leading brands. Copenhagen and Skoal are the world's two best-known brands (each represents over $1 billion in annual retail sales). These brands, in particular, have a long history—Copenhagen dates back to 1822 and Skoal was introduced in 1934. In addition to the highly successful brands of Copenhagen and Skoal, the company's other brands include Rooster, Red Seal, and Husky. Red Seal and Husky are USSTC's mainstays in the price-value segment of the moist smokeless tobacco market. Additionally, USSTC previously test-marketed Revel Tobacco Packs, which were marketed as a unique, breakthrough product that is designed to be a discreet, smoke-free option for tobacco consumption.

The product was positioned as being an alternative to smoking, as well as an attractive substitute for "dip" or "chewing tobacco," because it requires "no need to spit." USSTC sought to accentuate the desired appeal of Revel by presenting it in a variety of refreshing, flavors including mint, wintergreen, and cinnamon, while packaging it in a container that is akin to the small tins of breath mints that can be found at the checkout aisle of any local supermarket.

USSTC and Sport Sponsorship

USSTC uses a variety of methods to spread the word of the corporate brand and their associated products. Among its primary marketing efforts, USSTC has focused on sponsorship and other promotional methods, including one-on-one marketing initiatives, direct mail, ongoing product innovation, and various other traditional means of advertising to build awareness. USSTC has made concentrated efforts to be a visible entity in sport endeavors such as fishing, hunting, motor sports, and rodeo/bull riding. In this approach, motorsports and rodeo/bull riding have received the lion's share of USSTC sponsorship interest.

USSTC and Motorsports

USSTC has proudly sponsored numerous motorsports events. The company considers having a strong presence in motorsports to be of great importance because they believe that such involvement appeals to those who embrace an adventurous lifestyle. This company first ventured into sponsorship of motorsports in 1981 when it began its association with NASCAR through its sponsorship of the Skoal Bandit Grand National Race Car. Among the contemporary motorsports endeavors that USSTC have sponsored have been the Skoal Racing funny car that competes on the National Hot Rod Association circuit, sponsorship of the EA Sports Supercross Series, and has included the traveling tours of the Skoal Racing Tour and the USSTC Motorsports Experience Tour, which have served mobile marketing units featuring memorabilia, artifacts, and a variety of simulated activities and competitions.

USSTC and Rodeo/Bull Riding

Essentially, since the inception of the company in 1822, USSTC has sought association with activities reflecting the rugged image of the American West. Affiliations with rodeo and bull riding programs have provided an open path to that means. The company has had a major presence in both the Professional Rodeo Cowboys Association (PRCA) and the Professional Bull Riders (PBR) circuits (see Exhibit 33.1). The reach of these entities are widespread. For example, the PBR's traveling circuit includes approximately thirty major events that take place in venues ranging from traditional rodeo hotbeds such as Odessa, Texas, and Billings, Montana, to nontraditional sites like the Staples Center in Los Angeles and the Ice Palace in Tampa.

Exhibit 33.1 Examples of Sponsorship Initiative Provided by USSTC in Rodeo and Bull Riding

- Copenhagen Cup Series Standings
- Copenhagen Cup Finale
- Copenhagen Bull Riding Team
- Copenhagen Bull Riding Challenge Tour
- USSTC Scoreboard
- USSTC Pro Rodeo Championship Awards Program
- USSTC Bull Riders Master Pro Series
- USSTC Bull Riders Master Pro Finals
- USSTC Bull Riders Master 90-Point Club
- USSTC Western Legends Tour
- USSTC Challenger Tour

Additionally, among the other forms of rodeo and bull riding sponsorship, USSTC has sponsored cowboys such as Trevor Brazile—PRCA world-champion all-around cowboy in 2004, 2006, and 2007—and 2005 and 2007 PBR world champion Justin McBride.

NIRA

In addition to rodeo involvement with PRCA and PBR, USSTC is perhaps the most significant corporate partner of collegiate rodeo, standing out beyond other established brands such as Wrangler, Dodge Rodeo, and Redwing Shoes.

The National Intercollegiate Rodeo Association (NIRA) serves as the governing body of intercollegiate rodeo. With a student membership of more than 3,500 participants from over 130 colleges and universities, the NIRA hosts over 100 collegiate rodeo competitions annually. In addition to establishing and maintaining standards for collegiate rodeo competition, the NIRA is also instrumental in the promotion of collegiate rodeo on a national level, seeking to promote rodeo as a standard collegiate sport, while promoting an appreciation, understanding, and interest of rodeo and Western culture.

Concern Regarding Smokeless Tobacco Sponsorship

Tobacco sponsorship has sparked concern and even legislative initiatives in the United States and throughout the world, including countries such as Australia, Canada, France, New Zealand, Norway, and Sweden. Apprehension over tobacco sponsorship stems from a few chief concerns: the link between tobacco and disease, the ability to penetrate the youth market, and subverting bans on advertising.

The Link between Tobacco and Disease

Sport is generally thought to promote ideals such as health, fitness, and success. The dangers associated with tobacco use have been widely covered, and opinions of government health officials, health activists, and sport organizers toward tobacco sponsorship of sporting events have been widely discussed and debated. Opponents of tobacco sponsorship allude to the hypocritical nature of linking the health of sport with the detrimental aspects of tobacco use. Furthermore, smokeless tobacco companies have readily promoted their products as a safe alternative to smoking. This, however, is a myth that is far too often accepted as fact.

The Ability Penetrate the Youth Market

According to a government report in 2003, there were an estimated 7.7 million Americans twelve years and older who reported the use of smokeless tobacco products. A figure such as this causes alarm, especially when it is taken into account that sponsorship is tied to demographics and that sport often attracts youth. The exposure of young people to smokeless tobacco advertising campaigns will be virtually inescapable.

The Ability to Subvert Advertising Restrictions

TV advertisements for tobacco products have been banned since 1971 in the United States. Restrictions like these set the groundwork for tobacco companies to look for new ways to spread their message. Sponsorship was naturally viewed as a means to reach target audiences while essentially escaping the push to prohibit forms of tobacco advertisement.

USSTC and Corporate Responsibility

Though there is great concern over the presence of tobacco companies such as the USSTC having a strong presence in sport environments, USSTC proclaims itself as a socially responsible company. It does this by proudly stating that it is the only smokeless tobacco manufacturer to sign the Smokeless Tobacco Master Settlement Agreement (STMSA).

Under this agreement, USSTC agreed to pay $100 million over a ten-year period to the American Legacy Foundation, an organization that funds public programs aimed at reducing youth tobacco use and substance abuse support programs aimed at reducing youth access to tobacco products and youth substance abuse.

In addition to this involvement, the USSTC was subjected to marketing restrictions, including banning the distribution of nontobacco merchandise products such as shirts, hats, and jackets; restricting the distribution of free samples of smokeless tobacco (i.e., the tear-out cards that were in publications such as *Sports Illustrated*); guidelines for the removal of outdoor advertising, billboards, and other forms of signage; and agreement to not sponsor concerts and events in which adolescents are a considerable percentage of the intended audience or events in which any of the paid participants or contestants are young people.

In addition to these significant limitations regarding sponsorship by tobacco companies by the STMSA, there are other limitations on tobacco brand-name sponsorships, including limiting to a single brand-name sponsorship in any twelve-month period, corporate name sponsorships, prohibition on sponsoring teams and leagues (specifically such events as football, baseball, soccer, or hockey league), and naming rights prohibition. Regarding the sponsorship of sport, the door has not been closed, but there is certainly less room for these companies to maneuver through than in the past.

Conclusion

The presence of companies such as the USSTC in sport will continue to spark great debate. Sport marketers should to be mindful of the potential for problems and concerns when organizations choose to align themselves with potentially contradictory or inflammatory corporate partners. For some, the

USSTC is an important company providing products that offer great pleasure. Others see the USSTC as a plague on society.

One thing is certain—as a company, the USSTC will not be going anywhere anytime soon. Therefore, the question remains—how long will it be a factor in the world of sport, and what will be the ramifications of its presence?

The Final Score

Companies commonly use sponsorship of sport activities to help reach marketing objectives. Such benefits have clearly been sought by leading companies in the tobacco industry. With legal restrictions placed on methods of advertisement that tobacco companies can use, companies have sought for ways to send their corporate messages out to the masses. USSTC is one such company that is leading the charge.

Especially in the past two decades, there has been a noticeable backlash toward tobacco sponsorship in sport. However, it would be unfair to think that there are not those who encourage and value the tobacco industry's financial involvement in sport. Proponents of tobacco sponsorship in sport contend that the loss of sponsorship dollars would result in elevated ticket prices, decreased revenue potential, and even reduction in prize monies. On the other hand, such arguments are contended by the standpoint that such sponsorship arrangements could be replaced with sponsorship from other products and industries.

Through its promotional literature, USSTC steadily refers to its moral obligation to be a "socially responsible" company. Their corporate philosophy of giving revolves around various areas of corporate interest, though the focus is centered on three principal areas: education, community enrichment, and preserving American traditions. Though connections with such entities can produce positive corporate benefits, the association of such activities with a company who produces tobacco products is questionable at best. If a corporation is to buy into a true corporate social responsibility model, they are obligated to be mindful of the needs of all stakeholders. The level of responsibility extends beyond that of just worrying about financial considerations, including gains. There is a need to consider legal, philanthropic, and ethical concerns.

Such areas are important to consider, even though it is easy for critics to dismiss any notions of a tobacco producer being truly responsible. Considering ethical shortcomings and controversy should always be paramount to a company who wishes to be social responsible. Clearly, the affiliation with sport events such as collegiate rodeo poses some potential concerns. For one thing, a significant number of those attending collegiate rodeo events are going to be underage for tobacco products, including the participants themselves (competitors from a state such as Alabama need to be nineteen years of age to legally purchase tobacco products). Additionally, consider the reach toward younger children. Rodeo events on the collegiate level attract children of all ages. These may be family members of participants or rodeo followers in general. This is not even taking into account the high visibility of tobacco imagery projected on a TV screen during a professional rodeo event, such as those sanctioned by PBR or PRCA.

Additionally, USSTC proudly touts their willingness to conform to guidelines established by the STMSA. Their entrance into the agreement was not motivated entirely for purely benevolent motives. USSTC and other tobacco producers were under extreme social, legal, and legislative pressure to modify their presence in areas such as corporate advertisement and promotion. With impending class action suits and governmental initiatives looming, USSTC needed to comply with such initiatives.

Understandably, USSTC will continue to market their products to target audiences. Seeking to align themselves with consumers and potential consumers who are attracted to the lifestyle interests and values of those who wish to be aligned with their product, USSTC needs to look at the whole picture. In today's world, the NCAA would never proudly align itself with a tobacco producer. Contrarily, the NCAA restricts the use of such products. Obviously, the NCAA and the NIRA are very different in structure and mission, but there is a common thread. Each of these bodies is responsible for the governance of collegiate athletics. A clear example of the paradoxical nature of such associations is found in one NIRA-related program, the RAWHIDE program. RAWHIDE is positioned as a program that seeks to encourage collegiate rodeo participants to make positive choices regarding drug and alcohol use. Such illogical connotations alone should be reasonable justification for the argument against the appropriateness of tobacco sponsorship on such a level. For numerous reasons, arguments can continue to be made for further restrictions or abolishment on any level.

Post-Game Comments

- Potentially controversial sponsorship arrangements need to be thoroughly evaluated by sport organizations. Just because companies may be willing to part with significant amounts of money does not mean that it is a practical or proper thing to do.
- Organizations need to be mindful of their goals and missions. Potentially controversial sponsors may seek an association with sport in efforts to legitimate the corporate offerings or gain acceptance by certain audiences.

This should be avoided if the sport provider's primary functions are in conflict with associations involving such products and/or producers.

- Sport, by nature, is generally viewed as being healthy in nature. The affiliation with known unhealthy products could send a definite mixed message to audiences—especially children.
- The desire to be associated with images such as the "rugged West" and "American traditions" has led the USSTC to primarily target activities such as rodeo and motorsports.

Web Resources

http://www.altria.com/about_altria/1_6_1_altriastory.asp
http://www.collegerodeo.com/foundation.asp#Rawhide
http://www.collegerodeo.com/Sponsors/sponsors.asp
http://www.prorodeo.com
http://www.pbrnow.com/competition/ct
http://www.ussmokeless.com/en/cms/Company/About_USSTC/default.aspx
http://www.ussmokeless.com/en/cms/Home/default.aspx
http://www.ussmokeless.com/en/cms/Products/Marketing_Approach/default. aspx
http://www.ussmokeless.com/en/cms/Products/Products_Brands/default.aspx
http://www.ussmokeless.com/en/cms/Responsibility/Smokeless_Tobacco_ Settlement_Agreement/default.aspx

(These are Web references that were used at one time, but are not longer active.)
http://www.ustobacco.com/corp_giving/community_enrichment/index.asp
http://www.ustobacco.com/corp_giving/philosophy.asp
http://www.ustobacco.com/corp_giving/education/index.asp
http://www.ustobacco.com/corp_giving/preserve/index.asp
http://www.ustinc.com/corp_res/partner.asp
http://www.ustinc.com/smokeless/farmer
http://www.ustinc.com/smokeless/motorsports
http://www.ustinc.com/smokeless/profile.asp
http://www.ustinc.com/smokeless/rodeo
http://www.ustinc.com/smokeless/revel

Additional Resources

Muellner, A. (2000, July 10). No bull: Pro rodeo events standing tall in the saddle. *SportsBusiness Journal*. Retrieved on August 7, 2002, from http://sportsbusinessjournal.com.

Turco, D. M. (1999). The state of tobacco sponsorship in sport. *Sport Marketing Quarterly, 8*(1), 35–38.

Chapter 34

The WUSA: Why Did Women's Professional Soccer Fail in the United States?

Richard M. Southall,
University of North Carolina at Chapel Hill

Mark S. Nagel,
University of South Carolina

Organization: Women's United Soccer Association

Discussion Questions

- Identify several mistakes made by WUSA ownership and league management.
- In your opinion, could a national women's professional soccer league succeed in the United States? Why or why not?
- What specific activities should future investors implement if they attempt to reconstitute the WUSA?

The Line-Up

Founded in 2001, the Women's United Soccer Association (WUSA) began its existence basking in the reflected glory of the extensive media coverage of the 1999 Women's World Cup. After Brandi Chastain's penalty kick—and famous jersey removal—clinched a U.S. victory over China in the finals, it appeared women's soccer was on the verge of becoming a viable American consumption sport. The WUSA was quickly seen as the world's premier women's professional soccer league, and the best players from around the world signed up to participate. Unfortunately, fan interest from the 1999 World Cup was not sustained as the WUSA evolved from a novelty item to one of many sport-entertainment options. First year attendance averaged 8,104 a game, decreased to 6,957 in 2002, and again to 6,667 during the 2003 season. Unable to generate sufficient media or sponsorship revenues to cover three-year losses estimated at $100 million, the league folded after the 2003 championship game. Despite initial promise, the WUSA was unable to sufficiently develop its brand in the highly competitive U.S. consumer sport landscape. Unfortunately, the leagues' founders and administrators too often made poor management and marketing decisions, which doomed the league to failure. Although discussions concerning a revival of the league have occurred, any potential investors should learn from the WUSA's mistakes before proceeding.

Timeline of Events

1972
- The United States passes Title IX of the Educational Amendments Act, establishing that no person in the United States shall, on the basis of sex, be excluded from participation in, be denied the benefits of, or be subjected to discrimination under any education program or activity receiving federal financial assistance. Sport programs at all educational levels slowly begin to expand opportunities for women.

1990
- The U.S. team qualifies for its first Men's World Cup in forty years.

1991
- The United States defeats Norway to win the first Women's World Cup.

1994
- The United States hosts the Men's World Cup.

1995
- Norway defeats Germany to win the Women's World Cup finals. The United States finishes in third place.

1996
- Major League Soccer (MLS) is founded in the United States.

1999
- The United States defeats China in the World Cup finals after Brandi Chastain scores the winning penalty kick. The championship game attracts 90,000 people to the Rose Bowl in Pasadena and generates an 11.4 Nielsen TV rating in the United States.

2001
- The WUSA is founded with eight teams across the United States. First-year average attendance is 8,104, with especially large crowds for opening day matches and games involving Mia Hamm's team, Washington Freedom.

2002
- The WUSA completes its second season with average attendance of 6,957 per game, a decrease of 14.2 percent from 2001.

2003
- After average attendance decreased 4.2 percent to 6,667, the WUSA folds in September.
- Germany wins the Women's World Cup, with the United States finishing in a disappointing third place.

2008
- Women's Professional Soccer League (WPS) formally launched their Web site www.womensprosoccer.com and announced plans to begin play in 2009.

Establishing Professional Soccer in the United States

Soccer has long been a popular participation sport in the United States. However, despite the rapidly increasing numbers of participants, soccer has not enjoyed widespread commercial success as an American consumption sport. In 1996, Major League Soccer (MLS) was founded. While the MLS experienced limited initial success, its failsafe asset was that its early investors were Phillip Anschutz and Lamar Hunt, two of the wealthiest people in America, who also happened to love soccer. In addition to vast financial resources, MLS owners and administrators established a plan for slow growth, with a firm hold on extravagant expenses and a realistic understanding that the American sport and entertainment market was crowded. Despite numerous years of financial losses, after ten years MLS investors began to see dividends as attendance stabilized, numerous soccer-specific facilities were opened, and certain individual franchises began to turn a yearly profit.

The steady, though limited, growth plan implemented by MLS was not imitated by the Women's United Soccer Association (WUSA). Although the excitement of the 1999 Women's World Cup provided an excellent backdrop from which to launch, WUSA owners and administrators mistook the strong Women's World Cup attendance figures (over 660,000 for the entire event) as a devoted interest to consistently consume women's professional games twice a week for an entire season. Specifically, the league's founders committed critical errors by not (1) accurately predicting the decreased level of fan interest and devotion to a yearly league, (2) properly assessing ownership's financial resources and long-term commitment to soccer, (3) adequately controlling expenses, (4) developing a sound long-term marketing strategy, and (5) understanding the sponsorship hierarchy that exists in the U.S. entertainment environment. These errors made it impossible for the WUSA to develop a successful brand identity in the sport-entertainment marketplace and eventually led to its failure after only three seasons.

WUSA Errors Lead to Failure

Although 90,185 fans attended the 1999 Women's World Cup Finals in Pasadena's Rose Bowl, the WUSA founders—Jim Robbins (Cox Communications), Amos Hostetter (Pilot House Associates, LLC), Amy Banse (Comcast Corporation), Mel Huey (Time Warner Cable), Jerome Ramsey (Time Warner Cable), and John Hendricks—incorrectly believed the passion for women's soccer displayed throughout the summer of 1999 would translate into consistent consumption of WUSA games throughout a twenty-one-game season. Since the WUSA was positioned as the premier women's soccer league, it secured almost every top American player, including stars Mia Hamm, Julie Foudy, Joy Fawcett, Brandi Chastain, and Kristine Lilly. However, the personalities and synergy that had marked the U.S. women's national team was no longer present in the new WUSA format. Prominent U.S. players were no longer teammates but were placed on different franchises throughout the league. Fans that had followed the exploits of the national team showed some initial interest in the WUSA, but that interest did not translate into consistent attendance or large crowds.

The league's first-year average attendance (2001) was only 8,104 per game. Average game attendance declined 14.2 percent in 2002 (6,957) and 4.2 percent in 2003 (6,667). The decline in the attendance figures also reflected the diminishing reflected glory effect from the 1999 Women's World Cup and the end of a first-year novelty element, reflected in first-game attendance figures, such as the Washington Freedom's debut crowd of 34,000 and the Atlanta Beat's 2001 home opener of more than 20,000 fans. These single-game attendance figures inflated these franchises' inaugural 2001 average attendance figures by approximately 17 percent and 19 percent, respectively. In addition, most teams experienced considerably larger crowds for games involving the Washington Freedom, Mia Hamm's team. Too often, the "Mia Hamm effect" disguised minuscule attendance figures that continued to decline each season. The WUSA was not able to develop a consistent following for each of its eight franchises, with market research indicating the majority of fans attended only one game per season, and many fans used free tickets rather than purchasing them from the teams.

Many successful leagues—such as the NBA and NFL—have emerged from humble beginnings to eventually develop into present-day powerful brands. Long-time NBA and NFL owners have repeatedly noted their leagues began as regional leagues, with bare-bones budgets and limited travel. Initially, WUSA investors projected limited expenses for the first years of operation (see Exhibits 34.1 and 34.2). However, rather than follow a conservative financial model, the WUSA spent extravagantly—with its league offices located in New York City and teams spread from coast to coast across the United States. Although the league spent money as if it was an established sports league, fan attendance and ancillary revenues could not support the WUSA's spending habits. The league moved offices to Atlanta and implemented other cost-containment actions after the first year of operation, but expenses continued to greatly exceed revenues. By the end of the third year the league had lost over $100 million—nearly $85 million more than was originally projected! These losses greatly exceeded the investors' ability to sustain the league, forcing the league to cease operations after its third season.

Exhibit 34.1 WUSA 2001 Projected League Expenses

Projected Expense	Amount ($)
Projected Player Costs	
Salaries	6,460,000
Benefits	1,292,000
Total Projected Player Costs	7,752,000
Projected League Office Expenses	
Sales & Marketing	
Advertising	2,000,000
Corporate Sales	175,000
Consumer Products	150,000
Sponsor Services	400,000
Public Relations	200,000
Total Sales & Marketing	2,925,000
Administrative	
General Expenses	3,710,100
Player Administration	400,000
Insurance	200,000
Total Administrative	4,310,100
Total Projected League Office Expenses	7,235,100

Exhibit 34.2 WUSA Projected League Budget 2000–2003

	2000	2001	2002	2003
Revenue	$0	$13,222,900	$14,306,689	$15,733,226
Expenses	$3,022,537	$17,648,781	$18,165,629	$19,297,010
Net Income (Loss)	($3,022,537)	($4,425,881)	($3,858,940)	($3,563,784)

Source: ???

In addition to not having sufficient financial resources to sustain a national league, the WUSA also committed errors in building and marketing its brand. Television is a critical component of any sport leagues success. Although the WUSA had planned to sell their TV rights, lack of interest from broadcasters resulted in the league purchasing weekly time on TNT. First-year TNT ratings of WUSA games averaged 0.4, equaling roughly 425,000 households. Prior to the 2002 season, unhappy with its initial TV deal, the league announced a new deal with PAX TV, a less recognized media outlet. During the 2002 and 2003 seasons, WUSA games were broadcast during the 4–6 p.m. Saturday time slot. Recognizing that PAX did not have the national recognition of TNT, WUSA President Lynn Morgan still expressed satisfaction with the WUSA's decision to switch to PAX as a broadcast partner by stating, "Our continuation on PAX is also a very positive step. We have a season under our belt where we have had the opportunity to educate our fans on where they can find PAX in their local markets." However, contrary to league claims, few fans found WUSA games on PAX during the 2002 and 2003 seasons. In fact, WUSA game broadcasts averaged a 0.1 rating, equating to approximately 100,000 households nationwide, making WUSA telecasts one of the least watched broadcasts.

Perhaps the WUSA's greatest error involved its brand positioning in the minds of consumers and sponsors. After the league's formation and throughout its first year of operation, the league attempted to create an identity as a major sports league. However, lack of attendance and media coverage clearly established the WUSA as not nearly as popular as MLS, let alone the NBA or NFL. Realizing this, the WUSA belatedly attempted to position its brand as a "cause" rather than as a bona fide sports league. Fans and sponsors were encouraged to support the league as a philanthropic venture designed to support the advancement of women. Lynn Morgan stated, "I think there was a hope on our part that as a show of support for what we were hoping to achieve, sponsors would understand they would be paying in the early years a premium to be affiliated with the league. For us to get the high level we were asking for, there certainly needed to be more of an emotional play on the sponsor side." The problem with using such a philanthropically based tactic is that cause-related nonprofit charitable organizations are better positioned to leverage such emotional appeals to sponsors and consumers. Certainly, youth soccer leagues, high school, and college programs, can make stronger emotional pleas for financial support of women's soccer to sponsors than a professional league. Few corporations ignore pleas for general support through donations by established nonprofit organizations such as the March of Dimes, Salvation Army, or Red Cross. However, since the WUSA was established as a for-profit venture, it was difficult to convince consumers and sponsors to "support the cause" when the owners of the WUSA would likely be perceived as the primary financial beneficiaries from any cause-related support.

The Final Score

By 1999, women's soccer, personified by Brandi Chastain's "golden goal," was on the cover of numerous news magazines in the United States. Despite this springboard, the WUSA's failed business model and inability to position its brand to gain support in a crowded marketplace doomed it to failure. The WUSA's founders, flush from the World Cup victory, seemed unwilling to settle for anything less than the big time. This meant big-time office rent and big-time coast-to-coast travel costs. The league wanted to be treated the same as the other major sport leagues and seemingly attempted to spend its way into sport fans' consciousness, resulting in losses exceeding $100 million after only three seasons. When the league switched its marketing focus in an attempt to be known primarily as a "cause," it found that potential consumers and sponsors did not look favorably on for-profit entities taking this approach. The WUSA was therefore unable to attract fans or business partners since its product was not perceived as valuable and it was unable to solicit philanthropic support because it had investors looking to generate a profit. The league might have succeeded if it had entered the crowded sports entertainment marketplace with a conservative and sustainable long-term strategy. Rather than attempting to fight in a highly competitive national marketplace, the WUSA could have started as a regionally-based league. As ticket sales and media attention increased, the league could have gradually expanded its influence throughout the United States. Leagues such as the NBA and NFL took decades to develop their brands, but the WUSA owners were unwilling and unable to take this approach. As a result, the league quickly found itself financially insolvent and the United States found itself without a women's professional soccer league.

Post-Game Comments

- Mia Hamm, Julie Foudy, Joy Fawcett, Brandi Chastain, and Kristine Lilly led the United States to soccer gold medals at the 2004 Olympic Games. Each of the five women's soccer pioneers has since retired from international competition.
- Women's Soccer Initiative, a not-for-profit entity dedicated to the relaunch of women's professional soccer in the United States, was established in 2004.
- On January 17, 2008, the Women's Professional Soccer League (WPS) formally launched their Web site—www.womensprosoccer.com—and began playing games in 2009.

Web Resources

http://soccernet.espn.go.com/wwc/headlinenews?id=277467
http://www.usatoday.com/sports/soccer/wusa/2003-09-15-wusa-folds_x.htm

Additional Resources

Southall, R. M., Nagel, M. S., & LeGrande, D. (2005). Build it and they will come? The Women's United Soccer Association: A collision of exchange theory and strategic philanthropy. *Sport Marketing Quarterly, 14*(2), 158–167.

About the Authors

Matthew J. Bernthal is an Associate Professor in the Department of Sport and Entertainment Management at the University of South Carolina. He serves as Director of Graduate Studies for the department. His research interests lie in the areas of consumer behavior and marketing ethics in sport and entertainment. His work is published in outlets such as the *Journal of Consumer Research, Sport Marketing Quarterly, Journal of Sport Behavior,* and *Journal of Non-Profit and Public Sector Marketing.* He teaches undergraduate and graduate classes in sport and entertainment marketing, integrated marketing communications in sport and entertainment, ethics in sport and entertainment management, and marketing research.

Dr. Matthew T. Brown has been at the University of South Carolina since 2005 where he teaches and researches in the areas of sport business and finance. His research has lead to publications in journals such as the *Journal of Sport Management, Sport Marketing Quarterly, Entertainment and Sport Law Journal, International Journal of Sport Finance,* and *Sport Management Review.* In addition, Dr. Brown has made more than 40 national and international research presentations.

Emily Bruce is a graduate from the University of North Florida. Upon graduation, she received the Outstanding Journalism Student Leadership Award from the Department of Communication. She is currently employed by Lender Processing Services, Inc., where she received the company's Maverick of the Month Award in 2007.

Galen Clavio is an Assistant Professor of Sport Management at Indiana University. Dr. Clavio's research focuses on sport communication and new media, including online communities, video game branding efforts, and convergence. He has been published in numerous scholarly journals, including the *International Journal of Sport Management* and the *International Journal of Sport Marketing and Sponsorship.*

Coyte G. Cooper, Ph.D., is an Assistant Professor of Sport Administration at the University of North Carolina at Chapel Hill. He received his Doctorate in Sport Management from Indiana University. While he has taught a variety of Sport Management courses, his area of teaching specialization focuses on the business aspect of sport (e.g., Sport Economics/Finance, Sport Marketing). With an emphasis on issues in college athletics, Dr. Cooper has a directed line of research focusing on the challenges facing nonrevenue sport teams. In particular, he is currently working closely with the National Wrestling Coaches Association, developing research to help enhance the sustainability of college wrestling programs.

Dan Drane is Assistant Director of the School of Human Performance and Recreation (HPR) and Associate Professor of Sport Management at the University of Southern Mississippi. Dr. Drane has extensive experience in the sport industry and academia and was recently named Distinguished Researcher of the Year for the USM's College of Health. He was also selected to train, manage, and supervise volunteers for the 2008 Olympic Games in Beijing, China. Dr. Drane is an accomplished researcher and writer with articles published in many sport management journals.

Dr. Andrea N. Eagleman is a member of the faculty in the Department of Kinesiology at Indiana University, where she teaches undergraduate and graduate courses in the sport management and sport communication programs and serves as both the Director of the Sport Marketing & Management undergraduate program and the Coordinator of Associate Instructors. Her main research interests focus on the portrayal of athletes in the mass media and the differences in media portrayals of race, nationality, and gender. She has presented her research at numerous national and international conferences, and has published her research in journals such as the *International Journal of Sport Communication, International Journal of Sport Management,* and *Journal of Contemporary Athletics.*

Eric Forsyth is a Professor at Bemidji State University. He received his doctorate in sport administration from the University of New Mexico, with a minor in marketing management. At Bemidji State University he teaches undergraduate and graduate courses in sport marketing, sport finance and economics, sport business management, socio-culture and ethical issues, and thesis proposal seminar. To date, Dr. Forsyth has written numerous articles on the topic of interscholastic sport sponsorships, has presented over 40 conference presentations, has served as president of the Minnesota AAHPERD Association, and serves as a panel member for the NASPE/NIAAA graduate interscholastic athletic administration curriculum standards.

Dr. John S. Hill is Miller Professor of International Business at the University of Alabama, Tuscaloosa, Alabama. He has published over 40 articles in the international business field and has authored three textbooks in the area. Dr. Hill's publications have appeared in scholarly journals including *Harvard Business Review, Journal of International Business Studies, Long Range Planning, Journal of International Marketing,* and *International Marketing Review.*

Jennifer J. Kane is an Associate Professor and Program Director of Sport Management at the University of North Florida. Dr. Kane's research interests are in professional preparation of sport management, sport marketing, and fitness education. Dr. Kane's most recent scholarly work has been focused on the development of community partners for community-based learning opportunities within sport management and related fields. She teaches courses in the Administration of Sport, Introduction to Sport Management, and Resource Development for Nonprofit Organizations in which she incorporates community-based learning opportunities for her students.

Patrick Kraft is the Senior Assistant Athletic Director for Marketing at Indiana University. He received his Ph.D. in Sport Management from Indiana University. Dr. Kraft previously served as a Clinical Professor of Sport Management in the School of Business Administration at Loyola University Chicago. He has been published in *Sport Marketing Quarterly*, the *International Journal of Sport Management,* and the *International Journal of Sport Marketing and Sponsorship.*

Pamela C. Laucella, Ph.D., is an assistant professor of sports journalism at Indiana University School of Journalism–Indianapolis. She is also Director of Sports Journalism Graduate Studies and Coordinator of Sports Journalism Sequence. She obtained a Ph.D. in journalism and mass communication from the University of North Carolina at Chapel Hill, and her research investigates sociocultural-historical aspects of sport communication.

Jason W. Lee is an assistant professor of sport management at the University of North Florida, in Jacksonville. Dr. Lee has served as editor of the academic journal, *Sport Management and Related Topics (SMART) Journal* and was lead editor for the text *Sport and Criminal Behavior* (2009). Dr. Lee maintains an active research agenda in the areas of sport branding, sport symbolism, and the use of film as an educational tool.

Greg Letter is an assistant professor and director of the undergraduate and graduate sport management programs at Adelphi University. His current research agenda is primarily focused toward marketing, specifically endorsements and sponsorships as well as information technology (IT) in sport management. Dr. Letter also consults the United States Youth Soccer Association for the past three years on the focus of achieving youth sport leagues marketing objectives through the use of information technology. Dr Letter holds a PhD in Administration and Teaching with a concentration in Sport Administration and a Master's of Science in Sport Administration from the University of Southern Mississippi as well as a Bachelor of Science in Health and Physical Education Teaching from Temple University.

Kimberly S. Miloch, Ph.D., is an Associate Professor and the Coordinator of the Sport Management Program at Texas Woman's University. She received a Ph.D. from Florida State University and has previously taught at Indiana University and Northern Illinois University. Her research interests include sport consumer satisfaction and loyalty, sport public relations and media management, and sport brand management. Before entering academia, Miloch was the public relations and game operations director for a minor league hockey team. She also worked in communications and marketing for the United States Tennis Association, Texas Section.

Mark S. Nagle is an associate professor in Sport and Entertainment Management Department at the University of South Carolina. He has published numerous research articles investigating sport finance, sport law, and college athletics. He has also served as treasurer for the North American Society for Sport Management and the Sport and Recreation Law Association.

Dr. Fritz G. Polite is a clinical professor of Sport Management, at the University of Tennessee. He is the Director and founder of the Institute for Leadership, Ethics & Diversity (I-LEAD). He is also the Director for community outreach and global engagement in The College of Education, Health and Human Sciences. Polite earned his Ph.D. in Sport Management from Florida State University. He has a wide array of professional experience spanning across the sport industry and his primary research focus is in the area of socio-cultural aspects of sport, including leadership, hiring practices, race, gender and diversity. His secondary line of research is in the area of brand and vertical extension. He has presented and published extensively internationally and has been published in numerous journals and has appeared on ESPN Outside the Lines, ESPN National Radio, and USA Today News.

Brian Rothschild is an Assistant Dean in the School of Business at Adelphi University since 2003. He holds an endowed chair at the Turnaround Management Association. He has extensive experience in higher education and technology, having served as director of Internet strategies at Fordham University and having taught as an adjunct professor at Dowling College, John Jay College, and Iona College. Assistant Dean Rothschild was also manager of business development at Itochu Technology, where he led a higher education marketing team for the world's leading reseller of Sun Microsystems. He holds an M.B.A. and B.A. in economics from Iona College and an M.S. in education from Fordham University.

Raymond G. Schneider, Ph.D., is an Associate Professor of Sport Management at Bowling Green State University. He is the co-author (with Paul Pedersen, Ph.D.) of *Bobby Bowden: Win by Win*. He has also published numerous manuscripts in journals such as the *Journal of Sport Management, Sport Marketing Quarterly*, and the *International Journal of Sport Management*.

Dr. Richard M. Southall is presently an assistant professor of Sport Administration and Coordinator of the Graduate Sport Administration Program at the University of North Carolina at Chapel Hill. He is also Director of UNC's College Sport Research Institute (CSRI).

John Vincent, Ph.D., (Florida State, 2000) is an Associate Professor in the Kinesiology Department at the University of Alabama. He is the coordinator of the graduate sport management program and teaches sport management, sport sociology, and sport marketing classes. His main research focus is on how newspaper narratives portray elite athletes competing in major international sporting events, particularly in relation to their gender, race, and national identity. He has published over 30 articles in scholarly, refereed journals.

Steven N. Waller is an Assistant Professor in the Department of Kinesiology, Recreation, & Sport Studies at the University of Tennessee–Knoxville. Dr. Waller holds terminal degrees from Michigan State University and United Theological Seminary. His research interest include religious beliefs as a constraint to sport and leisure behavior, capacity building and sustainability strategies for sport and recreation nonprofit organizations, and sport and recreation as catalysts for community and economic development. He teaches graduate levels courses in research methods, organizational behavior, management strategies, and fiscal policy.